T0319734

Knowledge Management and Innovation in Networks

Knowledge Management and Innovation in Networks

Edited by

Ard-Pieter de Man

VU University, Amsterdam and Atos Consulting, The Netherlands

Edward Elgar

Cheltenham, UK • Northampton, MA, USA

Published by
Edward Elgar Publishing Limited
The Lypiatts
15 Lansdown Road
Cheltenham
Glos GL50 2JA
UK

Edward Elgar Publishing, Inc.
William Pratt House
9 Dewey Court
Northampton
Massachusetts 01060
USA

A catalogue record for this book
is available from the British Library

Library of Congress Cataloguing in Publication Data

Knowledge management and innovation in networks / edited by Ard-Pieter de Man.
p. cm.
Includes bibliographical references and index.
1. Knowledge management. 2. Business networks. 3. Knowledge management—Case studies. 4. Business networks—Case studies. I. Man, Adrianus Pieter de, 1967-
HD30.2.K636843 2008
658.4′038—dc22

2008023874

ISBN 978 1 84720 230 7

Printed and bound in Great Britain by MPG Books Ltd, Bodmin, Cornwall

Contents

Figures

Tables

Contributors

Hans Berends is Assistant Professor in Organization Science and Marketing at Eindhoven University of Technology. He completed a Ph.D. on knowledge sharing in industrial research. His current research interests include knowledge management within and between organizations and the design of learning and innovation processes.

Ard-Pieter de Man is Professor of Management Studies at the VU University, Amsterdam and Principal Consultant at Atos Consulting, The Netherlands. Both his research and consulting work are directed at firm strategy, alliances, networks and innovation. He is the author of ten books on these topics and over 30 articles. His consulting clients include companies and public sector organizations in Europe and the USA.

Pim Eling started studying Industrial Engineering and Management Science at the Eindhoven University of Technology after he obtained a Bachelors degree in Electrical Engineering. He is interested in purchasing within the high-tech industry and is currently employed as initial buyer. His Masters thesis concerns supply relationships in the network of ASML.

Tim Graczewski is Vice President–Strategic Alliances at Intuit. He has considerable experience in alliance management, having held positions in this area for a number of years.

Irene Lammers holds a Ph.D. in Economics from the VU University, Amsterdam. Her thesis is based on ethnographic research into the rise and fall of knowledge management within a large multinational firm. She is currently an Assistant Professor at the VU University, where she teaches courses on innovation management. Her research focuses on knowledge, creativity and organizational learning, with a special interest in the cultural industry.

Elco van Burg is a Ph.D. candidate in entrepreneurship and innovation at Eindhoven University of Technology, The Netherlands. He holds BSc and MSc degrees in Industrial Engineering and Management Science from this university. His research is directed at academic entrepreneurship and network collaboration.

Erik van Raaij is Assistant Professor of Purchasing and Supply Management at RSM Erasmus University (Rotterdam, The Netherlands).

His primary research interests are business-to-business relationships, new technologies in marketing and purchasing, and market orientation. His research has been published in academic and practitioner journals, including the *Journal of Business Research*, *European Journal of Marketing*, *Industrial Marketing Management*, *Journal of Purchasing and Supply Management* and *Holland Management Review*.

Arjan van Weele holds the NEVI Chair in Purchasing and Supply Management at Eindhoven University of Technology, Faculty of Industrial Engineering. His research interests are related to sourcing strategy, procurement governance and building effective supply chain collaboration. He is the author of several major textbooks in the field and many publications in both academic and professional journals. From 2002 to 2006 his course on Strategic Sourcing received the first prize for the best Masters course as awarded by faculty students.

Preface

Networks, knowledge and innovation are the triumvirate of modern business. Innovation is the basis for competitive advantage. It requires the build-up of and access to knowledge. Networks are able to deliver that knowledge. Hence, just as the divisional form was the organizational structure of the industrial economy, networks are the organizational structure of the knowledge economy. This in short appears to be the reasoning behind most recent thinking on management. But if this is true, how can companies ensure knowledge flows through networks in such a way that it benefits their competitive strength? This question formed the point of departure for this book.

Research in this area is abundant. Dozens of papers have been and continue to be published in the academic journals. However, if a manager were to read these papers in order to find an answer to the question concerning how he should manage knowledge flows in networks, he would not find many answers there. The literature has mainly focused on interesting, but abstract theory. Few case studies exist that shed light on knowledge management in networks from a managerial perspective. One paper, co-authored by Dyer and Nobeoka, was an exception and that paper was an important source of inspiration for this project. The authors' approach involved an in-depth case study, showing what mechanisms Toyota's management used to get knowledge flowing in the supplier network of this Japanese car manufacturer.

To replicate and extend Dyer and Nobeoka's findings, a research team was assembled, consisting of researchers with a variety of backgrounds. The team included experts in knowledge management, supply chain management and network management. This diversity was necessary to tackle the complexity of the themes of innovation, knowledge and networks. The members of the research team were: Hans Berends, Elco van Burg, Pim Eling, Tim Graczewski, Irene Lammers, Erik van Raaij, Arjan van Weele and I. Masters students Ingrid van der Burg, René Heunen and Jan Spruijt provided invaluable assistance in organizing the vast amount of data collected from the many interviews.

As a group we went through the normal academic routine of defining our propositions and frameworks, finding suitable cases to study, gathering the material and interpreting it. This book represents the final stage of academic research: writing it down. Altogether the project lasted over two years. It is tempting to look at the research team as a network on its own and to apply the concepts we use in this book to ourselves. I quote Arjan van Weele, who wrote to me about the process we went through:

> During the many exchanges that we had, group learning evolved as did group identity. As a result our small research network did not suffer too much from motivation problems. Neither were we confronted with problems related to free riding as the group kept a tight, though unspoken social and professional control of the contributions of each team member. As the team members started to get to know each other better and the direction the team would go became clearer, knowledge transfer became more structured and efficient. Moreover, as the project moved along each team member became more interested in the results of the others. Although initially many boundaries existed due to the different research backgrounds of the individuals involved and the different disciplines that they represented, these were overcome through constant dialogue and frequent interaction.

No matter how active the research team was, the project would not have succeeded without the help of many others. During the research process we obtained support from a large number of people. First of all I would like to thank the dozens of persons we have interviewed (sometimes more than once) and who have read through our case descriptions. I am grateful so many persons were willing to participate and invest their time in this project. Second I would like to thank Transforum for the financial support for the project. This was instrumental in getting the project of the ground. Through Transforum we also got access to the pig-breeding case. Finally we sent our manuscript to two experts on knowledge networks: Geert Duysters of UNU-MERIT in Maastricht and Marleen Huysman at the VU University, Amsterdam. They read through the manuscript and provided us with numerous ideas to improve it. Thanks to both of them for taking the time to do this. Their insights helped to bring more focus to our work. Naturally any remaining errors are the exclusive responsibility of the research team.

The book has a straightforward structure. The first three chapters are dedicated to theory. Chapter 1 describes the model behind the book. Chapters 2 and 3 respectively deal with networks and knowledge management. Chapters 4 to 8 are devoted to cases of innovative knowledge-sharing networks. Chapter 9 draws conclusions across these cases. The final chapter contains lessons for managers.

Ard-Pieter de Man

1. Knowledge and innovation in networks: a conceptual framework

Ard-Pieter de Man, Hans Berends, Irene Lammers, Erik van Raaij and Arjan van Weele

Increasingly, innovation no longer takes place within individual firms, but within networks of organizations. An important requirement for such network-based innovations to come to fruition is that knowledge flows across organizational boundaries. Yet, it is not self-evident or easy to create and sustain knowledge flows within and across companies. This chapter presents a framework for studying knowledge management in alliance networks. This framework is used in subsequent chapters to analyse five case studies of knowledge sharing and innovation in networks. This chapter starts with a brief review of existing literature on alliance networks and knowledge management, leading to a conceptual model for studying knowledge management in networks. This conceptual model incorporates knowledge-sharing problems, solutions to those problems, and the contingent effects of network and knowledge type. The chapter concludes with a short introduction to the five case studies.

KNOWLEDGE AND INNOVATION MANAGEMENT IN NETWORKS

How was METRO, one of the world's largest supermarket chains, able to create an innovative, ground-breaking future store with over 50 widely different partners? How are small family-owned companies in the Dutch cut-flower industry able to remain at the forefront of innovation and practically corner the world market? Why was Glare, a new material, finally used by Airbus after a long and arduous development process? The answer lies in the dynamics of the networks that collaborated on these innovations. In each case numerous partners were involved in creating something new. Getting those partners to collaborate and to exchange the necessary knowledge required a major effort. Innovation is difficult inside a company. It is even harder in a bilateral alliance. It seems nearly impossible in an alliance network with several partners.

Studies into bilateral alliances have shown the difficulties of knowledge management in an inter-company context. They have also identified the conditions and micro-level mechanisms companies employ to bring about effective knowledge management. As to conditions stimulating knowledge exchange, effective knowledge transfer is easier when both firms already have a knowledge base in place which enables them to absorb knowledge from another company; in other words, when they have absorptive capacity (Cohen and Levinthal, 1990; Lane and Lubatkin, 1998; Lane et al., 2001; Mowery et al., 1996). Cultural homogeneity of alliance partners makes knowledge transfer less difficult as well (Parkhe, 1991; Lyles and Salk, 1996). In relation to micro-level management processes supporting knowledge management, Inkpen (1998) and Inkpen and Dinur (1998) show that rotation of personnel plays an important role in transferring knowledge from one organization to the next. Training and managerial support by parents of a joint venture have a similar effect (Lyles and Salk, 1996). Furthermore, and in particular for the transfer of tacit knowledge, tie strength, trust and shared values play a stimulating role (Dhanaraj et al., 2004).

At network level, few studies on micro-level processes exist. Many theoretical and empirical studies on networks assume knowledge and information flow between firms. Usually, these studies infer that knowledge sharing and transfer have taken place from an increase in patenting activity by the firms involved (Duysters and Lemmens, 2003; Rowley et al., 2000). The micro-level mechanisms that underpin such knowledge exchange are not studied. The question as to how knowledge flows from one firm to another and whether companies consciously manage knowledge flows in networks is relevant as knowledge does not flow automatically between companies. How do companies manage knowledge in networks? How do they ensure the right knowledge flows to the right network partner? What is left to chance and which knowledge is consciously transferred?

Empirical research in the area of knowledge management in networks has mainly been limited to the role of IT support in networks (Carlsson, 2003; Olin et al., 1999; van Baalen et al., 2005). Related literature on virtual collaboration (e.g. Markus et al., 2000) and communities of practice focuses mainly on online settings of collaboration between individuals, not organizations, and is less applicable to non-Internet forms of collaboration. No one has come closer to defining an overarching framework to study knowledge management in networks than Dyer and Nobeoka (2000). Their detailed analysis of knowledge sharing in Toyota's supply network centres on problems specific to knowledge management in networks and their solutions (see Table 1.1). Their framework is based on the idea that networks

Table 1.1 Knowledge management problems in the Toyota network and their solutions

Problem	Solution concept	Micro-level mechanism in the Toyota network
Motivate to share knowledge	Show clear value	Subsidize early stages of collaboration
	Create network identity so suppliers identify with network success	Supplier association Consulting teams Voluntary learning teams Interfirm employee transfer
	Make rules for knowledge protection and value appropriation	Proprietary knowledge about the production process does not exist Supplier can appropriate 100% of the value in the short run, but will share with Toyota over time
Prevent free-riding	Sanctions	Toyota is major client of partners
	Agreement to share knowledge	Knowledge sharing mentioned in written agreements
Efficient knowledge transfer in multi-partner setting, lower search cost	Multiple processes, strong ties, close structural holes	Different types of meetings, teams, associations enable transfer of both tacit and explicit knowledge. Firms can choose the most efficient route for knowledge transfer Knowledge sharing does not rely on Toyota's facilitation

Source: Compiled by de Man (2004) based on Dyer and Nobeoka (2000).

face three specific challenges regarding knowledge management. The first challenge is motivating the partners to share knowledge. This problem has also been identified by other authors on knowledge management and bilateral collaboration. The extra complication for interorganizational networks is that in networks the pay-offs for contributing to networks may be indirect and unclear. Partners need a long-term perspective to see the real value of collaboration materialize. The problem of motivation can be solved by showing clear value to participants, by creating a network identity which leads companies to take a longer-term view on collaboration and by implementing correct rules of ownership and value appropriation.

The second challenge to knowledge management in networks is to prevent and correct free-riding behaviour in the network. The larger the group of partners, the easier it becomes for companies to profit from the network without making a comparable contribution. Toyota solves the free-riding problem by explicitly agreeing companies are to share knowledge with the network and by the fact that Toyota as a client can unilaterally impose sanctions on a free-riding partner by ending the supply relationship.

The third challenge is to realize efficient knowledge transfer in a multi-partner setting. When substantial numbers of partners are involved in a network, it may take a long time before knowledge required by one of the partners actually reaches that partner. Lowering the search costs connected with finding the right company and person in a network is a problem that must be solved in order for a viable knowledge-sharing network to exist. Toyota's solution to this problem is to create as many opportunities as possible for people to meet each other. By creating strong ties (Granovetter, 1973; Brass et al., 1998) between companies and multiple processes for people to meet (events, meetings and associations), network density is increased and structural holes are closed.

Dyer and Nobeoka's (2000) framework highlights the micro-level mechanisms one successful company has implemented to stimulate knowledge sharing. The efforts and investments required to attain a smooth flow of knowledge are substantial. A large number of people are involved and a variety of mechanisms are in place to ensure that knowledge from one partner in a network ends up with the right network partner in a timely and efficient way. Clearly knowledge does not automatically flow through a network.

In addition to the challenges identified by Dyer and Nobeoka (2000), the literature has pointed towards another problem of specific relevance to managing knowledge in networks. The problem of crossing boundaries between companies that have diverse knowledge bases is particularly challenging in networks. Carlile (2002), for instance, recognizes syntactic, semantic and pragmatic boundaries between knowledge-sharing partners in a network. Orlikowski (2002) has identified boundaries created by time, geography, culture and technology. In networks containing a large number of organizations from many different backgrounds, many boundaries need to be crossed. The literature has pointed to two possible solutions to this problem. First, building absorptive capacity (Cohen and Levinthal, 1990) in companies may help to reduce the problem. When companies have overlapping knowledge bases, boundary-crossing becomes much less onerous. Second, dedicated knowledge transfer personnel may be employed who are capable of transferring knowledge between dissimilar partners (Schuurmans, 1999). We have added the challenge of crossing boundaries as a fourth problem in network knowledge management.

Figure 1.1 summarizes the four challenges for knowledge management in networks. Obviously these problems may impact each other. Low

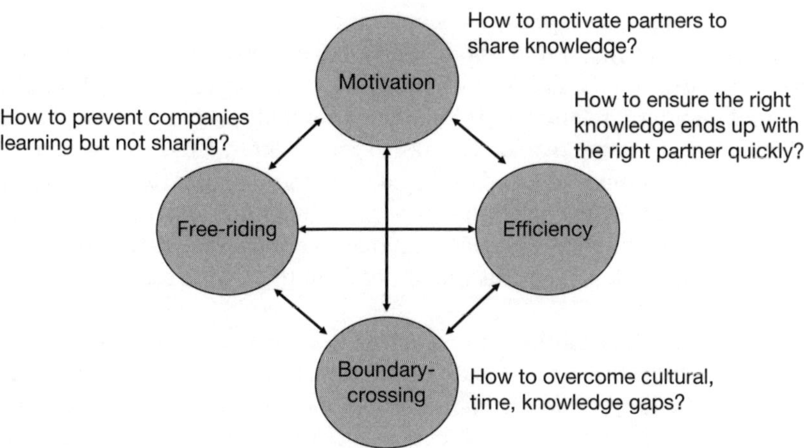
How to motivate partners to share knowledge?
Motivation
How to prevent companies learning but not sharing?
How to ensure the right knowledge ends up with the right partner quickly?
Free-riding
Efficiency
Boundary-crossing
How to overcome cultural, time, knowledge gaps?

Figure 1.1 Four problems in network knowledge management

motivation to share knowledge may enhance free-riding; the more boundaries between firms, the lower the efficiency of knowledge sharing is likely to be; efficient knowledge sharing may increase the motivation of companies to share knowledge themselves, etc.

CONTINGENCIES

The problems mentioned in Figure 1.1 and the solutions to the problems presented in Table 1.1 may not be universally applicable. So far, the only relatively strong test of the validity of three of the four problems and their solutions has been the Toyota case (Dyer and Nobeoka, 2000). A first question therefore is whether the four problems can be found across different types of networks and whether some problems are more prevalent in some networks and less relevant in others (Inkpen and Tsang, 2005).

Second, solutions to the problems may be more effective in some circumstances than in others. Indeed, the solutions identified are mainly based on the Toyota case. Whether there are other solutions is as yet unknown. Extending the list of solution concepts is relevant for both theory and practice. For theory, a list of solution concepts will enable large-scale research to take place, making it easier to test the effectiveness of solutions in various circumstances. For practice, an overview of solution concepts will give managers a broader tool-kit to choose from when building knowledge-sharing networks, instead of the limited set proposed by Dyer and Nobeoka (2000).

Two contingencies appear to be relevant: network type and knowledge type (de Man et al., 2001; de Man, 2004). Regarding network type, Toyota has a vertical supplier network with a strong core player, with local suppliers and long-term relationships extending over multiple innovations. These characteristics may enable Toyota to guide knowledge management strongly: the suppliers depend on Toyota and they are in proximity to each other, enabling regular meetings. It is relevant to find out whether other networks have different knowledge management characteristics. In particular we may look at elements that differ from the Toyota case, such as:

- Single versus multiple innovations. Do companies collaborate on one individual project or does their collaboration involve various projects over a longer time frame? This distinction may affect knowledge management tools and processes because in continuous networks creating multiple innovations, it may be valuable (and possible) to invest in other, more costly, mechanisms than in 'one off' networks (for example, expensive IT systems; creating a network culture). Also, in networks with multiple innovations, the 'shadow of the future' (Axelrod, 1984) may reduce the scope for free-riding when compared to networks focusing on individual projects (Ariño et al., 2001).
- Decentralized versus central. A network with a strong central partner may make more use of hierarchical coordination mechanisms than a decentralized network. Powerful central companies may also force dependent firms to share knowledge. Also, a network without a central partner may have more difficulty in bringing about the interventions required to start up and sustain the transfer, integration and development of knowledge. Literature on strategic centres (Lorenzoni and Baden-Fuller, 1995) and network orchestrators (de Man, 2004; Hagel et al., 2002) has shown the importance of central players in a network. On the other hand, examples of successful non-centralized networks exist as well. The Italian tile manufacturing industry is a case in point (Best, 1990; Porter, 1990). Small family-owned firms collaborate and compete in the tile industry in Italy, but they have been able to maintain their position vis-à-vis large firms in the same industry.
- Dispersed versus localized. Local networks may have some advantages over dispersed networks. Not only are cultural differences in localized networks smaller, they also make it possible to have frequent face-to-face contact which enhances knowledge sharing. Some successful dispersed networks have come into being on the Internet, notably around open source software (Markus et al., 2000). Online collaboration by individual enthusiasts focusing on an explicit task like software development is however quite different from real-life

collaboration by companies that focus on different types of innovation. The extent to which dispersed networks may effectively share knowledge and the conditions that are required for it to take place are as yet unclear.

A second relevant contingency is the type of knowledge that is to be shared. Not all types of knowledge flow in the same way. The most important distinction regarding the nature of knowledge is the perceived coreness of the knowledge (de Man et al., 2001). Companies may be willing to collaborate and share knowledge when this knowledge is non-core, but may be more reticent about sharing knowledge that is perceived to be at the core of their competitive advantage. The coreness of knowledge can be determined by studying the extent to which companies fear the loss or spillover of knowledge and by looking at the duration of the competitive advantage they expect to gain from certain knowledge.

Another distinction that is made regularly when studying knowledge is the distinction between tacit and explicit knowledge (Nonaka and Takeuchi, 1995). Explicit knowledge can be communicated easily, either verbally or in writing. Tacit knowledge however is implicit, difficult to communicate and partly intuitive. This distinction can be found in practice, but it is often hard to study these types of knowledge separately because both tend to occur simultaneously. We may expect however that the exchange of tacit knowledge requires different management mechanisms than the exchange of explicit knowledge. Tacit knowledge may require close interaction between people and demands collaboration over a longer time period. Explicit knowledge may be shared via documents, websites and seminars.

Based on the discussion so far, Table 1.2 presents the key research question and sub-questions underlying this book.

Table 1.2 Research questions

Key research question

- How can knowledge management in networks be organized in such a way that it contributes to successful collaborative innovation?

Sub-questions

- What are the problems of knowledge management in innovative networks?
- Which solution concepts are used by organizations to overcome these problems?
- How do contingencies like network type and knowledge type affect knowledge management in innovative networks?

CONCEPTUAL MODEL

Taking the previous discussion into account, a conceptual model to study knowledge management in networks can be proposed (see Figure 1.2). The conceptual model relates knowledge sharing and innovation to four specific knowledge-sharing problems, solution concepts to tackle those problems, and two contingent factors: network type and knowledge type. The four problems are, as discussed earlier: motivation, free-riding, efficiency and boundary-crossing. These problems may be alleviated by the implementation of solution concepts. Solution concepts are management tools, mechanisms and processes that companies may implement in networks in order to get knowledge sharing going. The term 'knowledge sharing' is used in a broad sense here, and includes all knowledge processes that enable two or more organizations to access, transfer, integrate or develop knowledge together. The model points to seven themes that are relevant.

The first theme is the relation between knowledge sharing and innovation (1). The innovation success of a network of organizations is positively affected by the success of knowledge sharing between network partners. In other words, interorganizational knowledge sharing is conducive to network-based innovation.

Second, the success of knowledge sharing may be negatively affected by the existence of knowledge-sharing problems, such as lack of motivation to share, free-riding behaviour, obstacles to efficient knowledge sharing, and difficulties in crossing boundaries between network partners (2). In other words, these four problems hinder successful knowledge sharing.

Third, the occurrence of knowledge-sharing problems is negatively affected by the utilization of solution concepts (3). In other words, the solution concepts alleviate knowledge-sharing problems. One of the key objectives of this research project is to identify such solution concepts from the case studies.

Next, the occurrence of knowledge-sharing problems is affected (positively or negatively) by network type (4) and knowledge type (5). In other words, some problems will be particularly salient in certain types of networks and in cases where certain types of knowledge are to be shared.

The sixth and seventh themes in relation to knowledge sharing in innovation networks relate to the question of whether different solution concepts are used in different network types (6) and whether different solution concepts are used to cope with the challenges posed by different knowledge types (7).

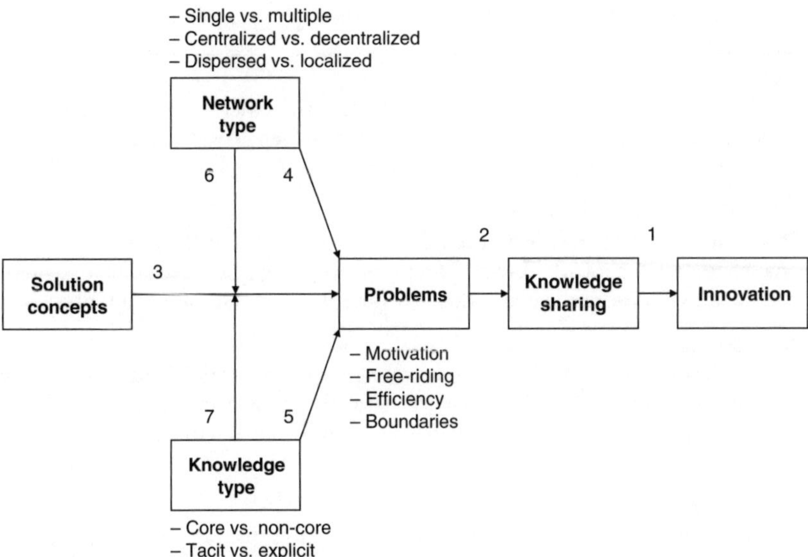

Figure 1.2 Conceptual model

SELECTED CASES

To explore and elaborate the framework depicted in Figure 1.2, five case studies were conducted. The case study is a suitable method whenever there is little control over behavioural events, when there is a focus on contemporary events and when the research question is of the 'how' type (Yin, 2003). In addition, case studies are particularly suitable when theory is being developed as opposed to tested (Eisenhardt, 1989). The topic of knowledge management in networks fits the criteria for case studies: it cannot be controlled in a laboratory-like setting, it takes place in contemporary networks, it focuses on 'how' questions and theory development. As using multiple case studies allows for the development of a rich theoretical framework (Ellram, 1996) and makes it possible to study more of the contingent factors described in our conceptual framework, a multiple case design has been chosen.

Case selection was guided by the notion of theoretical sampling, that is, sampling on the basis of either expecting similar results or expecting contrasting results for predictable reasons (Yin, 2003). In order to increase our understanding about the circumstances that simplify or complicate knowledge management, it was our intent to maximize the variation in the network characteristics discussed above. By selecting cases from different

Table 1.3 Description of the five case studies

ASML The supplier network of the leading manufacturer of wafer steppers for the semiconductor industry is extensive. It faces the challenge of dealing with rapid innovation on the frontier of nanotechnology.
METRO's Future Store Initiative This network of 50 companies developed the supermarket of the future. Challenges in the network were bridging knowledge gaps between companies and meeting a tight deadline, while realizing a variety of innovations simultaneously.
Pig-breeding Pig breeders in The Netherlands have created one of the world's leading networks in the breeding of pigs. Challenges in the network are collecting and disseminating knowledge across hundreds of companies and managing international knowledge flows.
Horticulture A dynamic network of small- and medium-sized enterprises that are world leaders in the growing of plants and flowers has emerged in The Netherlands. Challenges are keeping pace with the speed of innovation and sharing knowledge among hundreds of companies.
Glare Glare is a new aircraft material, developed by an international network of players from academia, industry and government. Key challenges in the Glare case included managing a dispersed network, keeping faith in the innovation and ensuring progress was made.

industries, each with unique characteristics, contrasting results are expected. As both core and non-core knowledge and tacit and explicit knowledge tend to be shared simultaneously, knowledge characteristics have not been chosen as a criterion for case selection. The five cases studied are briefly described in Table 1.3. The network characteristics for each of the case studies are shown in Table 1.4.

Table 1.5 shows which data collection methods were used for the case studies. The primary source of data was the interview. All the case studies rely on semi-structured interviews, conducted with representatives of the multiple partners in the network, to avoid getting a one-sided view of the networks. Sometimes, key informants were interviewed more than once. Data triangulation was attained by using other data sources as well. Company documents, such as internal reports, presentations and annual reports, provided more detailed information in each specific case. External documents were mainly used to get a better understanding of a sector or to

Table 1.4 Characteristics of the networks

Network characteristic	ASML	METRO's Future Store Initiative	Pig-breeding	Horticulture	Glare
Single/ multiple	Multiple	Single	Multiple	Multiple	Single
Central/ decentralized	Central	Central	Lightly centralized	Decentral	Decentral
Localized/ dispersed	Localized	Localized/ dispersed	Localized	Localized	Dispersed

Table 1.5 Methods of data collection used in the cases

	Persons interviewed	Company documents	External documents	Site visit(s)	Workshop
ASML	27	x	x	x	
METRO FSI	21	x		x	
Pig-breeding	10	x	x	x	x
Horticulture	9		x	x	
Glare	17	x	x	x	

compare a network with competing networks. They include sector reports, press releases, academic articles and books. Site visits were made to observe business processes, including the innovation process, in practice. In one of the cases, the pig-breeding case, a workshop was held with members of the network to test and validate the findings. In all the case studies, the case descriptions were checked by the respondents. Generally, these checks resulted only in minor changes to the case description.

In qualitative research, it is important that case descriptions transcend the perspective of the researcher, and its corollary, the perspective of the informants (Stewart, 1998). Interviewing multiple partners and data triangulation are two strategies that were used to achieve these aims. In addition, the heterogeneity of the research group was used to reduce subjectivity in the case studies. All the case studies, except for the pig-breeding case, were executed by a team of up to four researchers. Researchers from different backgrounds, levels of seniority and experience were purposefully combined in these case study teams. As soon as a case description was produced, the text was read by the other researchers. This improves objectivity and enriches the analysis.

In terms of data analysis, we need to make a distinction between within-case analysis and across-case analysis. The results of the within-case analyses are presented at the end of each chapter in Chapters 4 to 8. The conceptual model as depicted in Figure 1.2 guided the within-case analysis. While the team members for each specific case executed the analysis, the case descriptions were also discussed within the larger team of researchers. The within-case analyses mainly focused on the success of the innovation and the role of knowledge sharing in that success, any knowledge-sharing problems that occurred, and the incidence and effectiveness of solution concepts to alleviate knowledge-sharing problems.

Cross-case analysis is presented in Chapter 9. This cross-case analysis studies how network type and knowledge type influence the occurrence of knowledge-sharing problems. In addition it analyses the use of the solution concepts in different networks and knowledge types. It also summarizes across cases which solution concepts were used and which knowledge-sharing problems they addressed. Most members of the research team participated in this cross-case analysis.

SUMMARY

In this chapter a conceptual framework for studying knowledge management in networks was defined. Four key problems for network knowledge management were identified: motivation, free-riding, efficiency, and crossing boundaries. These key problems may be alleviated through the application of solution concepts. Depending on the network type and the knowledge type, solution concepts may be more or less effective in solving particular problems. Five case studies from a diverse range of industries were selected to study the existence of problems, the application of solutions, and the impact of problems and solutions on knowledge sharing in networks.

REFERENCES

Ariño, A., J. de la Torre and P. Smith Ring (2001), 'Relational quality: managing trust in corporate alliances', *California Management Review*, **44** (1), 109–31.

Axelrod, R. (1984), *The Evolution of Cooperation*, New York: Basic Books.

Best, M.H. (1990), *The New Competition: Institutions of Industrial Restructuring*, Cambridge: Polity Press.

Brass, D.J., K.D. Butterfield and B.C. Skaggs (1998), 'Relationships and unethical behavior: a social network perspective', *Academy of Management Review*, **23** (1), 14–31.

Carlile, P.R. (2002), 'A pragmatic view of knowledge and boundaries: boundary objects in new product development', *Organization Science*, **13** (4), 442–55.

Carlsson, S.A. (2003), 'Knowledge managing and knowledge management systems in inter-organizational networks', *Knowledge and Process Management*, **10** (3), 194–206.

Cohen, W.M. and D.A. Levinthal (1990), 'Absorptive capacity: a new perspective on learning and innovation', *Administrative Science Quarterly*, **35**, 128–52.

de Man, A.P. (2004), *The Network Economy: Strategy, Structure and Management*, Cheltenham, UK and Northampton, MA: Edward Elgar.

de Man, A.P., P. Koene and O. Rietkerken (2001), 'Managementtechnieken voor interorganisatorische kennisoverdracht', *Holland Management Review*, **80**, November/December, 57–65.

Dhanaraj, C., M.A. Lyles, H.K. Steensma and L. Tihanyi (2004), 'Managing tacit and explicit knowledge in IJVs: the role of relational embeddedness and the impact on performance', *Journal of International Business*, **35** (5), 428–42.

Duysters, G.M. and C.E.A.V. Lemmens (2003), 'Cohesive subgroup formation: enabling and enforcing factors in strategic technology alliance networks', *International Studies on Management and Organisation*, **33** (2), 49–68.

Dyer, J.H. and K. Nobeoka (2000), 'Creating and managing a high-performance knowledge-sharing network: the Toyota case', *Strategic Management Journal*, **21**, 345–67.

Eisenhardt, K.M. (1989), 'Building theories from case study research', *Academy of Management Journal*, **14** (4), 532–50.

Ellram, L.M. (1996), 'The use of the case study method in logistics research', *Journal of Business Logistics*, **17** (2), 93–138.

Granovetter, M. (1973), 'The strength of weak ties', *American Journal of Sociology*, **78** (6), 1360–80.

Hagel, J., J.S. Brown and S. Durchslag (2002), 'Orchestrating loosely coupled business processes: the secret to successful collaboration', White Paper, www.johnhagel.com

Inkpen, A. (1998), 'Learning, knowledge acquisition, and strategic alliances', *European Management Journal*, **16** (2), 223–9.

Inkpen, A.C. and A. Dinur (1998), 'Knowledge management processes and international joint ventures', *Organizations Science*, **9** (4), 454–68.

Inkpen, A.C. and E.W.K. Tsang (2005), 'Social capital, networks, and knowledge transfer', *Academy of Management Review*, **30** (1), 146–65.

Lane, P.J. and M. Lubatkin (1998), 'Relative absorptive capacity and interorganizational learning', *Strategic Management Journal*, **19**, 461–77.

Lane, P.J., J.E. Salk and M.A. Lyles (2001), 'Absorptive capacity, learning and performance in international joint ventures', *Strategic Management Journal*, **22**, 1139–61.

Lorenzoni, G. and C. Baden-Fuller (1995), 'Creating a strategic center to manage a web of partners', *California Management Review*, **37** (3), 146–63.

Lyles, M.A. and J.E. Salk (1996), 'Knowledge acquisition from foreign parents in international joint ventures: an empirical examination in the Hungarian context', *Journal of International Business Studies*, **27** (5), 877–903.

Markus, M.L., B. Manville and C.E. Agres (2000), 'What makes virtual organization work?', *Sloan Management Review*, Fall, 13–26.

Mowery, D.C., J.E. Oxley and B.S. Silverman (1996), 'Strategic alliances and interfirm knowledge transfer', *Strategic Management Journal*, **17**, 77–91.

Nonaka, I. and H. Takeuchi (1995), *The Knowledge Creating Company*, Oxford: Oxford University Press.

Olin, J.G., N.P. Greis and J.D. Kasarda (1999), 'Knowledge management across multi-tier enterprises: the promise of intelligent software in the auto industry', *European Management Journal*, **17** (4), 335–47.

Orlikowski, W.J. (2002), 'Knowing in practice: enacting a collective capability in distributed organizing', *Organization Science*, **13** (3), 249–73.

Parkhe, A. (1991), 'Interfirm diversity: organizational learning and longevity in global strategic alliances', *Journal of International Business Studies*, **22**, 579–601.

Porter, M.E. (1990), *The Competitive Advantage of Nations*, London: Macmillan Press.

Rowley, T., D. Behrens and D. Krackhardt (2000), 'Redundant governance structures: an analysis of structural and relational embeddedness in the steel and semiconductor industries', *Strategic Management Journal*, **21**, 369–86.

Schuurmans, P. (1999), 'Strategic sourcing: the network structure of ASM Lithography', in H. van der Zee (ed.), *Business Transformation in a Networked World*, Amsterdam: Addison-Wesley, pp. 148–58.

Stewart, A. (1998), *The Ethnographer's Method*, Qualitative Research Methods, volume 46, Thousand, Oaks, CA: Sage.

van Baalen, P., J. Bloemhof-Ruwaard and E. van Heck (2005), 'Knowledge sharing in an emerging network of practice: the role of a knowledge portal', *European Management Journal*, **23** (3), 300–14.

Yin, R.K. (2003), *Case Study Research: Design and Methods*, third edition, London: Sage.

2. Networks as the organization form of the knowledge economy

Ard-Pieter de Man

This chapter provides a general background to the relationship between networks and knowledge. It argues that networks are the organization form of the knowledge economy for two reasons. First, competition in knowledge forces companies to focus on increasingly narrow areas of knowledge in which they are able to maintain a competitive edge. This simultaneously increases the need to collaborate with other companies in other knowledge areas in order to deliver a complete product or service to customers. Knowledge access links are sufficient to achieve this. This leads to modular networks. Second, learning from other companies has become a necessity to upgrade existing competencies. This requires more intense forms of collaboration with other companies to achieve knowledge exchange. Learning may lead to either social capital or structural hole types of networks.

TOWARDS A NETWORK ECONOMY

An increasing number of innovations are not developed inside one company, but require collaboration between companies. More and more, collaboration leads to an economy in which networking becomes the most characteristic feature of business organization. Intensive supply relationships, joint ventures, outsourcing, minority holdings and contractual alliances have become so common that many companies have become interconnected, either directly or via partners. This phenomenon is called a network. Networks exist when companies are directly or indirectly related through one or more collaborative agreements between them.

The trend towards networks can be found back at industry level. An example is the flat screen industry. Figure 2.1 shows the collaborative agreements announced between companies in this industry in the years 2000–2001. In only two years, 75 per cent of the companies in this

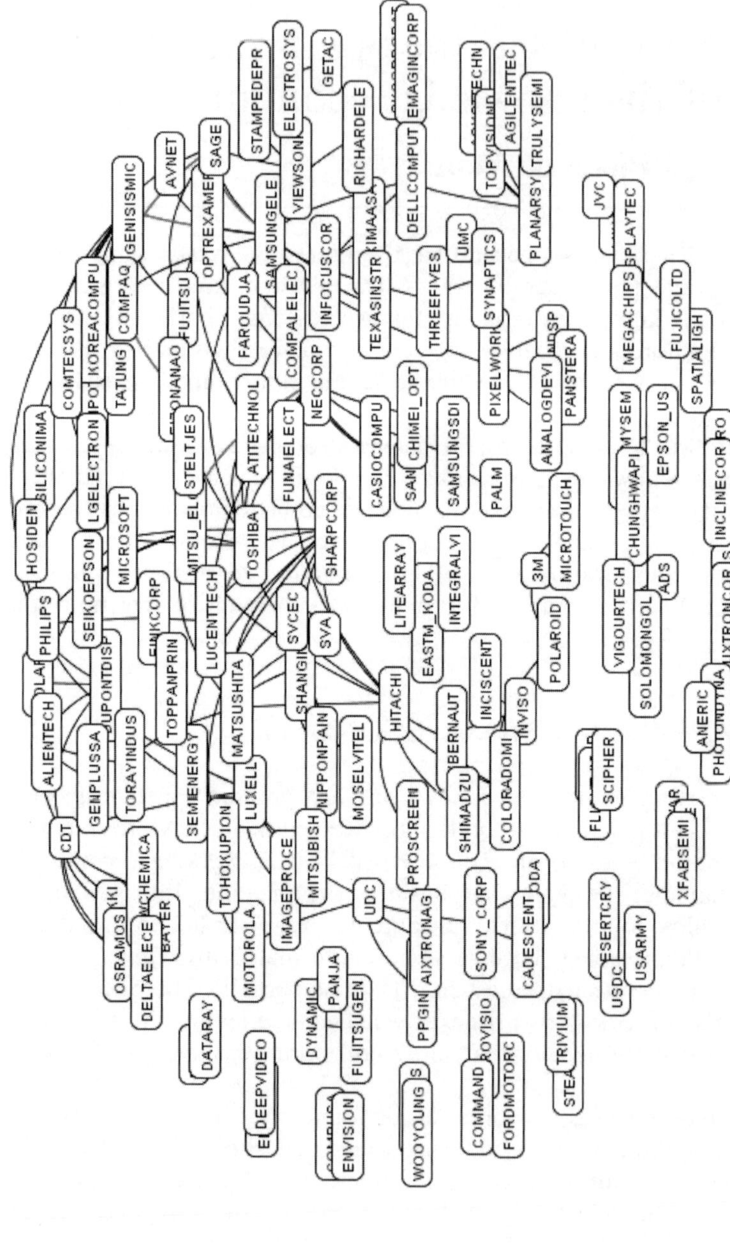

Figure 2.1 Network in the flat screen industry 2000–2001

industry have become directly or indirectly related to each other. This trend not only occurs at industry level. Increasing collaboration means that companies are part of their own company network as well. Companies like IBM, Philips, Nokia, Microsoft and SAP are all embedded in vast networks of inter-company relationships. Similarly, from the viewpoint of regions, local networks have emerged that are highly competitive. Silicon Valley in the USA (IT), Emilia-Romagna in Italy (tiles), Westland in The Netherlands (flowers and plants) and the German Ruhr area (industry) are well-known examples of regional networks of companies.

There are five driving forces behind the network economy (de Man, 2004):

- Liberalization and internationalization. A significant proportion of partnering activity is carried out across borders. Liberalization has made it possible to access knowledge, resources and markets in other countries by teaming up with partners in those countries. Markets, knowledge and sources of supply in foreign countries can now be accessed more reliably than ever before.
- Increasing competition. Firms must continue to seek the most productive ways of using their resources. This will lead them to specialize in those competencies in which they are top performers. This kind of specialization automatically entails a need for new partnerships. Specialization in core competencies is intensified by strong competition (Prahalad and Hamel, 1990) and the pressure to create shareholder value. Next to enhancing specialization, competition also makes companies look for partnerships in order to form a countervailing power against their competitors.
- The development of new management techniques and organizational innovations makes it possible to govern hybrid relationships like networks. With the development of new management tools, some notable successes have been achieved in the partnering arena (Draulans et al., 2003). If new management tools and approaches continue to be devised and applied, partnering success rates will continue to improve. Networking then becomes an even more viable alternative to mergers and acquisitions (M&A).
- Changes in demand. The general level of wealth in modern economies generates a demand for solutions and individualized products. This type of demand acts as a significant driving force behind partnering activities, because few firms are able to respond to it on their own (Jones et al., 1997). In business-to-business situations, integrated solutions may be the way forward. Companies do

not wish to buy their computers, servers, routers, software and implementation separately. They want them to be combined and seamlessly integrated. This demand for integrated solutions lies behind many networks in the IT industry, but is found in other industries as well.

- The rapid pace of technological progress. An important driving force for networking is the fact that technology (especially in the fields of IT and biotechnology) is advancing so rapidly that it is impossible for firms operating alone to stay in the technology race. Instead, firms need to develop a portfolio of alliances to protect themselves against the risk of missing out on a new technology. Another aspect of technology leading to alliance networks is convergence. The combination of different technologies from different fields may lead to interesting new technologies. Bioinformatics is such a technology, as is multimedia. As the competences for converged products tend not to be present in one organization, collaboration is required.

These and other drivers behind the world economy have made the world an increasingly global marketplace. Friedman (2005) shows how today components for computer LCD-screens are produced in China and Vietnam, final products are assembled in Singapore and then shipped to Europe where they are merged with PCs through fourth-party logistics providers, who deliver the final products through electronic catalogues that are managed by the large PC distributors, directly to the final consumer. Workflow software, outsourcing, offshoring and supply chain orchestration have lead to a situation where entire value chains are managed effectively, connecting a large number of global partners. Internet and common IT platforms have provided new solutions and business models to partners in the supply chain, enabling them to collaborate closely and to manage their supply operations effectively.

The need to meet the requirements of the business environment demands collaboration. This collaboration tends to centre on knowledge. Whether it is technological or market knowledge, knowledge accessing or knowledge transfer, the knowledge component in networks is usually easy to observe. Even when networks revolve around the production of tangible goods, knowledge has become a key factor in network success as shown by the Toyota case (Dyer and Nobeoka, 2000). Other networks do not have a tangible component at all. Nowadays R&D networks, focusing on the development of knowledge, do not directly lead to products. In short, the role of knowledge in networks is an important one and has increased in importance over time.

SPECIALIZATION AS A DRIVER FOR NETWORKS

The first reason why networks are more important in the knowledge economy is in fact not new: specialization. Adam Smith already pointed to the power of specialization in his *Wealth of Nations* (Smith, 1776). By specializing in a certain field of production, productivity can be raised. For knowledge, a similar argument applies. The knowledge-based view of the firm states that firms are more efficient in creating, storing and sharing knowledge than markets (Conner and Prahalad, 1996; Grant, 1996; Nonaka, 1991; Spender, 1996). The reason behind this lies in some specific characteristics of knowledge. First of all, most knowledge has a tacit dimension, making it difficult to transfer knowledge without the close interaction of individuals. Second, knowledge is partly contextual: it is easier to transfer knowledge between individuals operating in a similar context. For example, colleagues are more credible than outside sources; information systems are similar within a firm and modes of communication in a firm are more diverse (Almeida et al., 2002). Third, much knowledge is embedded in routines or capabilities. It cannot always be isolated from organizational processes and procedures. Finally, in organizations it is easier to get the right knowledge at the right place at the right time. An important mechanism to achieve this is building personal networks. The more people are connected, the likelier it is that knowledge gets to the right place fast (Coleman, 1990). Hence, to transfer knowledge, close interaction between individuals in a similar organization is more effective than using market relationships or even intermediate forms like alliances.

There is empirical confirmation for this theory. Both Almeida et al. (2002) and Gomes-Casseres et al. (2006) study patent citations and show that companies tend to cite patents owned by themselves more often than patents owned by other companies. This indicates that knowledge flows more easily within companies than across firm boundaries. Companies involved in an alliance also tend to cite each other's patents more often than those of companies that did not collaborate, but the effect is smaller than the within-company effect. In short, knowledge transfer works best inside a company, next best in an alliance, and a market relationship is less suited to knowledge exchange.

However, the knowledge-based view argues that this only holds in related areas of knowledge. Specialization in a certain area of knowledge improves a company's innovative capability (Prahalad and Hamel, 1990). Such specialization leads to dependency on other firms. When companies specialize in certain areas of knowledge because it is easier to build up knowledge inside one firm, they need to collaborate with other companies to get access to complementary knowledge.

If this is true, why then have networks not been around much longer? The reason is that until the 1980s knowledge was much less important for attaining competitive advantage than economies of scale and scope. The changes in the economy mentioned earlier have forced companies to focus on more specific areas in which to build up knowledge. No company is able to perform at a world-class level in all areas. By investing in a broad set of competences, companies run the risk of being outcompeted by specialized players with higher quality competences in a specific area. For that reason, companies need to focus on their core competencies (Prahalad and Hamel, 1990). By building up world-class knowledge in a few areas, they are able to compete effectively.

This trend automatically leads to networks. Because of specialization companies no longer have all the capabilities in place to serve a market. For example, a company that has completely specialized in making computer chips may be very effective in that, but it is not able to deliver a complete laptop. It needs to connect to other companies and complementary assets (Teece, 1987) to make its product useful. Networks emerge because they enable companies to deliver jointly a complete product or service by connecting the core competences of the network members.

The concept of the modular organization (Hoettker, 2006; Sanchez and Mahoney, 1996) is developed in the literature to describe this phenomenon. In modular networks, a variety of companies each deliver a standard component to be integrated in a larger product or service. Members of these networks do not aim to learn from each other. Instead, they only want access to their partners' competencies, without building up a similar competency themselves (Grant and Baden-Fuller, 2004). Ideally, the companies only need to agree on the interfaces between the components of the products they deliver.

Often one of the partners in a modular network is responsible for tying the network together. The literature finds that this integrator role comes with some extra costs. It requires the integrator to have a certain level of knowledge to be able to check all the partners' performance and technology and to be able to act as problem solver in the last resort (Brusoni, 2005). Only this will enable them to select the partners with the superior capabilities (Hoettker, 2006). Keeping such knowledge in-house raises the costs of a modular network in comparison to producing everything inside one company. Capabilities need to be maintained in the integrator and in the supplier. This extra cost is a drawback of modularization and may therefore limit the growth of modular networks. In addition, integrators have the function 'to guarantee the overall consistency of the product and to orchestrate the network of companies involved' (Brusoni and Prencipe, 2001). Coordinating the network requires further investment in people, in knowledge about

Table 2.1 Examples of modular networks

Q-search: a network of companies in human resource management with specialist companies providing administrative, legal, training services.
ASML: a producer of wafer steppers using a network of dozens of suppliers, each responsible for a product module.
Talentgroup: a network of companies providing construction, maintenance, exploitation, finance and installation services for new schools.
Charles Schwab: a financial services retailer which set up a network of partners providing different services like investment advice and investment research.
Health care: treatment of chronic diseases requires a network of, among others, specialist surgeons, a general practitioner, revalidation centres.
AirPlus: a travel management company that has partners providing services to business travellers and their companies, like airlines, hotel chains, travel agents, software companies.

collaboration and in network coordination, all of which further add to the cost of the integrator. A further disadvantage of the integrator role is that it is seen as the company responsible for the network. Failure of a supplier will therefore be interpreted as failure of the integrator. Damage to a carefully built brand may be caused by a partner making mistakes.

The advantage of the integrator role is that an integrator has access to the best and the most information. The status that an integrator usually has also attracts the best partners. The best partners will offer to collaborate with a high quality integrator, thereby making the best knowledge available to that integrator. Successful modular networks have a competitive advantage because they combine top specialist knowledge. It is not necessary for the relationships to be long term, because the benefits of modular collaboration may be reaped by a loose form of partnering. Integration between partners in the modular network is low, making it easy to sever ties and set up new ties with new partners. Table 2.1 lists some examples of modular networks.

In short, new market conditions force companies to focus on building up knowledge in increasingly specialized areas, while forgoing investment in other areas. Complementary knowledge is accessed by means of setting up relationships with other companies, resulting in modular networks.

LEARNING AS A DRIVER FOR NETWORKS

Internal knowledge build-up and knowledge transfer is easier than external acquisition of knowledge, but it also has its drawbacks. Even with extreme specialization companies may not have all the knowledge they require in-house. Learning from other companies may be necessary to further develop core competences (Hamel, 1991; Khanna et al., 1998). In addition, the phenomenon of groupthink limits learning: when companies become too internally oriented they may miss out on new knowledge developed outside the firm boundaries (Leonard-Barton, 1992). The patent citations studied by Gomes-Casseres et al. (2006) indicate knowledge flows well within a company, but they may also indicate myopia. Employees mainly learn from each other, but pay less attention to what happens outside the company.

Therefore companies also need to learn from other companies in order to maintain their knowledge lead. Next to internal learning, external learning is the second driver behind networking in a knowledge economy. On a network level, two theories have emerged focusing on this issue: social capital theory and the structural holes theory. The core of the debate between these two theories is that the structural holes school (Burt, 1992) maintains that the benefits accruing to companies having alliances with companies that are themselves not connected via an alliance are high. Companies should therefore avoid membership of alliance groups in which everybody shares knowledge with each other. The social capital approach (Coleman, 1990) states that in order to profit from knowledge and information transfer, trusting, long-term relations need to be built and that these relations can only come into being in relatively tight-knit groups, in which everybody collaborates with everybody else.

This debate is set out in more detail in Table 2.2. Both theories highlight the importance of networks for gathering new knowledge and information. However, their prescriptions for the best way for a focal firm to position itself in a network differ substantially. According to the social capital view, companies should set up tightly knit groups of companies, all connected to each other. The alliances between the companies may be 'redundant': the more alliances between companies in the group, the better. Rent accrues to membership in the group, with the actual allocation of rents to individual members determined by rules set in the network and/or bargaining power (Kogut, 2000). The structural holes approach believes in the efficacy of non-redundant ties and bridge positions. According to this theory, rent accrues to the firm bridging the 'structural hole' between unconnected companies, because it has access to a variety of information sources (Kogut, 2000).

Within the social capital approach, the importance of trust and commitment is emphasized. The more intense relationships are, the more knowledge and information is shared and the easier it becomes to transfer knowledge. This benefits the entire group of companies. The structural holes approach points to the drawback of this strategy: once you know

Table 2.2 The social capital view compared with the structural holes view

	Social capital	Structural holes
Competitive advantage best realized via	Redundancy in networks: firm A and firm B have the same partners and there is an alliance between A and B	Taking a bridge position between two sub-networks which have no ties between them (information brokerage: when X and Y have no relationship between them and A sets up alliances with X and with Y, then A is able to profit from combining the knowledge of two different partners)
Because these social-cognitive dimensions apply	Trust, commitment and long-term relationships are required before knowledge can be meaningfully exchanged or built up between companies	Companies need to be exposed to diverse stimuli in order to develop new knowledge
Pitfall of the approach	Groupthink, not seeing what goes on in the outside world	Companies may not want to exchange knowledge for fear of being exploited or for fear of knowledge spillover

Source: Adapted from de Man, 2004.

everybody in your group, no new insights may be generated. It advocates that companies should be exposed to diverse types of knowledge (Nooteboom, 1999). They are unlikely to find that in a closely-knit group of long-standing relationships. Instead, partners from other networks may contribute more new insights.

The pitfalls of each approach are clear. Social capital may lead to groupthink, an internal focus, conservatism and the exclusion of new ideas. A structural holes approach, on the other hand, may be interpreted as opportunistic. Companies working with a company pursuing a structural hole strategy may not be willing to share knowledge and information to the extent that they would in a group in which social capital is built up.

There has been some large-scale empirical research into the effectiveness of the two strategies (e.g. Gulati, 1999; McEvily and Zaheer, 1999; Powell et al., 1996; Rowley et al., 2000; Uzzi, 1997; Walker et al., 1997). These studies show that the optimal number of alliances, the optimal network location of a firm and the optimal density of alliance networks depend on specific circumstances. For example, having many alliances in combination with dense networks (with all partners connected to each other) does not raise innovativeness (Rowley et al., 2000). Another conclusion emanating from this research is that different industries require different strategies. The structural holes theory works well in microelectronics (de Man and Duysters, 2003) and in biotechnology (Powell et al., 1996). Both are turbulent industries with many new, emerging technologies. Another study comparing microelectronics with the steel industry indicated that a social capital approach was more beneficial in the steel industry, whereas structural holes appeared to be more effective in microelectronics (Rowley et al., 2000). In order to reap scale economies and increase efficiency, companies need to work more closely together in the steel industry. As the steel industry does not face turbulent technological change, companies do not need to hedge their bets via structural hole positions.

Empirical studies carried out conclude that different positions are optimal in different industries. An important distinction is between high-tech and fast-changing industries on the one hand, and low-tech and stable industries on the other. In high-tech industries, spreading the risk over a number of technologies appears to be a sensible network strategy.

THREE TYPES OF NETWORKS

The previous sections have shown that there are three types of networks, when the lens of knowledge is applied. Two are aimed at learning: social capital and structural holes networks. In a social capital network, all partners are connected; in a structural hole network, one company connects two otherwise unconnected sub-networks. Modular networks are aimed at getting access to complementary knowledge (see Figure 2.2). The three are ideal types and will rarely occur in practice in a pure form. In that sense, the three types can also be used as different lenses to study networks and to find out to what extent a network meets either one of the ideal types. Studying this may help to unravel complex knowledge flows in networks. It forces companies and researchers to look at the optimal division of knowledge in a network and the optimal learning strategy.

Each network type has its own distinct characteristic. Table 2.3 compares the three types on a number of points. In social networks, the partners have a low degree of specialization: their competences overlap. In modular networks on the other hand, partners are more specialized. They have a low degree of overlap in their knowledge; ideally, only interfaces between products need to be specified and partners do not need to know much about each other's specific knowledge base. Structural holes networks lie between

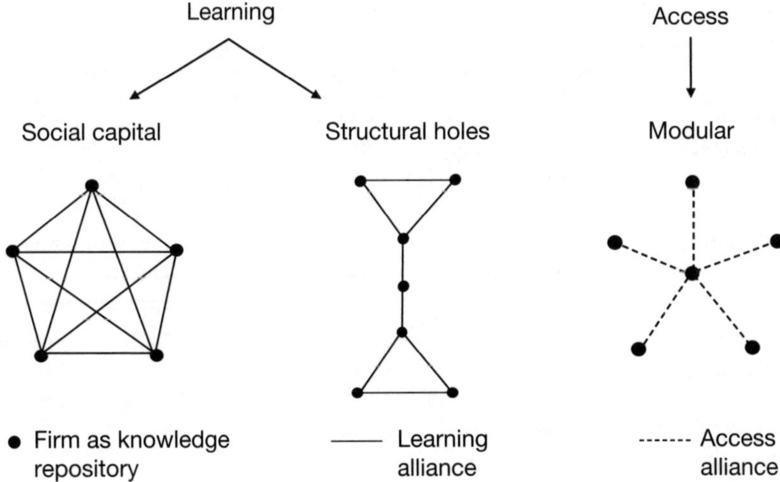

Figure 2.2 Three basic types of knowledge networks

these two extremes: they are used either to learn a new technology or to 'scan' a technology to see if it is sufficiently valuable to bring into the firm. These differences also translate into different aims for collaboration. Social capital networks aim to learn from partners; modular networks are not aimed at learning, but combine current capabilities (Hoettker, 2006).

In keeping with this, the type of knowledge exchanged in social capital and structural holes networks tends to be core or close to the core of the knowledge of the partners. In modular networks, no core knowledge is exchanged. What is core knowledge for one partner is non-core for the other. It is the combination of two different types of core knowledge that counts. In social capital networks, non-core knowledge is exchanged as well. Partners in social capital networks may also help each other with managerial issues, for example quality management or project management.

In social capital networks, the value of previous relationships is high: experience with a partner, knowledge and trust built up with the partner are valuable because they increase knowledge exchange and make the collaboration more efficient. Changing a relationship would involve switching costs. In modular networks, the relationship between partners is more akin to a supplier relationship. Switching costs are much lower because only interfaces need to be specified and no extensive knowledge exchange between partners is required for the relationship to become effective.

Modular networks can only exist when products or services are modular (the reverse is not true: not all modular products are produced in modular networks). When product modularization is not possible,

Table 2.3 Three types of networks compared

	Social capital	Structural holes	Modular
Partners' competencies	Non-specialized; high degree of knowledge overlap between partners	Specialized; intermediate degree of knowledge overlap	Specialized; low degree of knowledge overlap
Collaborate for	Learning; develop new capabilities	Learning; develop new capabilities	Access; combine current capabilities
Knowledge involved	Core and non-core (e.g. help partners improve quality)	Core knowledge is exchanged	Different types of core knowledge are combined
Value of previous relationships	High	Low	Low
Product characteristic	Systemic: components or production processes are inseparable	Systemic	Modular: discrete components
Communication	Highly interactive; continuous; multilateral; substantial investment	Highly interactive; continuous; bilateral; medium investment	Low interaction; incidental; bilateral; low investment
Central player	Non-existent	Aims to learn to get a competitive advantage	Aims to integrate modules

modular networks cannot exist. When components of a product or service are intimately connected or when production processes require tight integration, it is not possible to implement a modular network.

As a result of these differences, communication in networks differs as well. In social networks, there is continuous interaction between all the partners in a network. A substantial investment is made in communication across all partners in the network, as is shown by Dyer and Nobeoka (2000) in the case of Toyota. In a structural holes network, communication is not multilateral but bilateral. A company in a structural holes network may have numerous partners to communicate with bilaterally, but it will not make an effort to have its partners communicate with each other as well. The investment required to get this communication off the ground is therefore more limited than in social capital networks. Modular networks have low interaction among partners. In contrast to the other two types of network, communication in modular networks is incidental rather than continuous. As knowledge transfer is not required, it is not necessary to have regular, close interaction. Bilateral communication suffices as well. The central company only needs to enter into agreements with individual partners on the specification of the interfaces. As a consequence, the cost of communication in modular networks is low.

The role of the central player in the three network types differs as well. Even though in social capital networks some companies may do more of the network management than other companies, in general a central player is absent. In a structural holes network, the central player's objective is to learn as much as possible to get a competitive advantage. In this case, the central player has to seek out new partners based on the unique knowledge capabilities each partner possesses and it needs to manage its network in such a way that its partners do not enter into alliances among themselves. The role of the central player in a modular network is that of integrator, as discussed earlier.

These three network forms are the pure forms of network in a knowledge economy. In reality, there are many grey areas. Even in social capital networks there will be specialization, alongside overlap in knowledge, while in modular networks there will always be more communication required than about the interfaces and production planning. Modular networks learn, while social capital networks modularize and there will be few networks that fit the pure network types.

WHEN TO APPLY WHICH NETWORK TYPE?

Based on Table 2.3, it is possible to predict when each of the models is applicable. A modular network can only exist when modularization of knowledge and products is possible. It also presupposes that each partner's knowledge is best-in-class and that partners exist that have competencies that precisely fit the module. This last idea in particular may not be valid: the knowledge boundaries of companies are probably more idiosyncratic.

Social capital networks on the other hand require history in the relationship. Building trust and intimate relationships requires interaction over a longer term. As a consequence, social capital networks cannot be set up overnight. Modular networks and structural holes networks can be set up faster, because they do not require much history between the partners.

A structural holes approach is also more relevant when there is a strong appropriation regime: the more benefits can be appropriated by one firm from certain knowledge, the more they will want to try to be the sole owner of it. The pharmaceutical industry is a case in point: a patented drug is well-protected and very valuable. The willingness to share the knowledge with others will be low in that case. Weak appropriation regimes will be more conducive to social capital networks.

The nature of competition is also relevant for the choice of network. When competition is group-based (Gomes-Casseres, 1994), a social capital approach may ensure that knowledge gets shared inside an alliance group, thus strengthening the group in its competition with other groups. When competition is company to company, sharing of knowledge may not benefit the individual firm. In that case, structural holes networks are more likely.

Finally, in a situation where the benefits of learning are high, companies will opt for a social capital or a structural holes network. When the benefits of learning are limited, modularization may be the first choice. In choosing the optimal network form, companies therefore need to have a clear view on the importance of learning.

DYNAMICS IN THE MODELS

An additional question is whether the models may evolve into each other. In a setting where knowledge is still explorative (March, 1991) and where consequently the boundaries of knowledge areas are still fuzzy and shifting, it will be impossible to create a modular network. Modularity presupposes the existence of relatively clearly identifiable knowledge areas. Modular networks may therefore not occur early in a knowledge lifecycle. The opposite may not be true: social capital networks may still occur late in a lifecycle because exploitative learning may still be relevant and require close interaction, even at the end of a lifecycle.

For structural holes networks, the same holds as for social capital networks. Structural holes may be more relevant early in the knowledge lifecycle than later, because the competitive advantage to be had from owning a specific piece of knowledge is much smaller later in the lifecycle than early on. Later in the lifecycle, learning will be more incremental and hence it is unlikely that a piece of knowledge by itself will be decisive in getting ahead of competitors. In addition, early in the knowledge lifecycle, betting on different parts of knowledge is more important. In that situation, it is still unclear which parts of knowledge are really valuable. When knowledge moves into exploitative learning, the value of different elements of knowledge is much easier to assess. Spreading risk via structural holes is therefore less necessary.

It may not be easy for companies to move from one type of network to the next. Moving from social capital to structural holes or modular networks will involve a breach of trust in the relationships with partners. Where close interaction and a group feeling existed, these are now replaced by arm's length collaboration on a bilateral basis. Whether partners are willing to accept this change is a big question. It will also require companies to work differently with existing partners, and existing routines may be hard to break.

Moving in the other direction from modular and structural holes networks towards social capital is also difficult. It takes much time to build up the trusting and deep relationships that are necessary in a social capital network. Changing the routine of not sharing knowledge between partners in the network to an attitude of sharing with everyone will also require a major effort. For these reasons, transitions from one type of network to another will take a long time.

SUMMARY

Networks are the organization form of the knowledge economy for two reasons. The first reason is that improving, accumulating and exchanging knowledge is better done by companies specializing in a specific knowledge area. As a consequence of specialization, knowledge access relationships emerge to give firms access to complementary knowledge. In the extreme, this leads to perfectly modular networks.

Second, networks are important in a knowledge economy because knowledge flows between companies help improve company capabilities through learning. This learning may take place via structural holes or via social capital. In the former, a company sets up a network of bilateral relationships with partners that remain unconnected, ensuring that the focal company learns the most. In the latter, all partners learn from each other.

This chapter has stressed the general relevance of the issue of knowledge management in networks. It shows for what knowledge-related purposes networks are relevant. It does not show whether knowledge in networks can be managed and if so how. This specific element is the focus of the remainder of this book. The operational processes of knowledge management, the tools, functions, barriers and best practices to get knowledge flowing in networks will be investigated. The next chapter focuses on this issue by looking at solution concepts (tools, processes, functions, mechanisms that help to overcome barriers to knowledge exchange) identified in the literature so far.

REFERENCES

Almeida, P., J. Song and R.M. Grant (2002), 'Are firms superior to alliances and markets? An empirical test of cross-border knowledge building', *Organization Science*, **13** (2), 147–61.

Brusoni, S. (2005), 'The limits to specialization: problem solving and coordination in "modular networks" ', *Organization Studies*, **26** (12), 1885–907.

Brusoni, S. and A. Prencipe (2001), 'Unpacking the black box of modularity: technologies, products and organizations', *Industrial and Corporate Change*, **10** (1), 179–205.

Burt, R.S. (1992), 'The social structure of competition', in N. Nohria and R. Eccles (eds), *Networks and Organizations*, Boston, MA: Harvard Business School Press, pp. 57–91.

Coleman, J. (1990), *Foundations of Social Theory*, Cambridge MA: Harvard University Press.

Conner, K. and C.K. Prahalad (1996), 'A resource-based theory of the firm: knowledge versus opportunism', *Organization Science*, **7**, 477-501.

de Man, A.P. (2004), *The Network Economy: Strategy, Structure and Management*, Cheltenham, UK and Northampton, MA: Edward Elgar.

de Man, A.P. and G.M. Duysters (2003), 'De positie van Nederlandse bedrijven in innovatienetwerken', EZ onderzoeksreeks, Ministry of Economic Affairs, The Netherlands.

Draulans, J., A.P. de Man and H.W. Volberda (2003), 'Building alliance capability: management techniques for superior alliance performance', *Long Range Planning*, **36** (2), 151–66.

Dyer, J.H. and K. Nobeoka (2000), 'Creating and managing a high-performance knowledge-sharing network: the Toyota case', *Strategic Management Journal*, **21**, 345–67.

Friedman, J.L. (2005), *The World is Flat*, London: Penguin Books.

Gomes-Casseres, B. (1994), 'Group versus group: how alliance networks compete', *Harvard Business Review*, July–August, 62–74.

Gomes-Casseres, B., J. Hagedoorn and A.B. Jaffe (2006), 'Do alliances promote knowledge flows?', *Journal of Financial Economics*, **80**, 5–33.

Grant, R.M. (1996), 'Toward a knowledge-based theory of the firm', *Strategic Management Journal*, **17**, Winter special issue, 109–22.

Grant, R.M. and C. Baden-Fuller (2004), 'A knowledge accessing theory of strategic alliances', *Journal of Management Studies*, **41** (1), 61–84.

Gulati, R. (1999), 'Network location and learning: the influence of network resources and firm capabilities on alliance formation', *Strategic Management Journal*, **20**, 397–420.

Hamel, G. (1991), 'Competition for competence and inter-partner learning within international strategic alliances', *Strategic Management Journal*, **12**, 83–103.

Hoettker, G. (2006), 'Do modular products lead to modular organizations?', *Strategic Management Journal*, **27**, 501–18.

Jones, C., W.S. Hesterly and S.P. Borgatti (1997), 'A general theory of network governance: exchange conditions and social mechanisms', *Academy of Management Review*, **22** (4), 911–45.

Khanna, T., R. Gulati and N. Nohria (1998), 'The dynamics of learning alliances: competition, cooperation and relative scope', *Strategic Management Journal*, **19**(3) 193–210.

Kogut, B. (2000), 'The network as knowledge: generative rules and the emergence of structure', *Strategic Management Journal*, **21**, 405–25.
Leonard-Barton, D. (1992), 'Core capabilities and core rigidities: a paradox in managing new product development', *Strategic Management Journal*, **13**, 111–25.
McEvily, B. and A. Zaheer (1999), 'Bridging ties: a source of firm heterogeneity in competitive capabilities', *Strategic Management Journal*, **20**, 1133–56.
March, J.G. (1991), 'Exploration and exploitation in organizational learning', *Organization Science*, **2** (1), 71–87.
Nonaka, I. (1991), 'The knowledge creating company', *Harvard Business Review*, **69**, 96–104.
Nooteboom, B. (1999), 'Innovation and inter-firm linkages: new implications for policy', *Research Policy*, **28**, 793–805.
Powell, W.W., K.W. Koput and L. Smith-Doerr (1996), 'Interorganizational collaboration and the locus of control of innovation: networks of learning in biotechnology', *Administrative Science Quarterly*, **41** (1), 116–45.
Prahalad, C.K. and G. Hamel (1990), 'The core competence of the corporation', *Harvard Business Review*, May–June, 79–91.
Rowley, T., D. Behrens and D. Krackhardt (2000), 'Redundant governance structures: an analysis of structural and relational embeddedness in the steel and semiconductor industries', *Strategic Management Journal*, **21**, 369–86.
Sanchez, R. and J.T. Mahoney (1996), 'Modularity, flexibility, and knowledge management in product and organisation design', *Strategic Management Journal*, **17**, Winter, 63–76.
Smith, A. (1776), *An Inquiry into the Nature and Causes of the Wealth of Nations*, 1981 edition, Indianapolis: LibertyClassics.
Spender, J.C. (1996), 'Making knowledge the basis of a dynamic theory of the firm', *Strategic Management Journal*, **17** (2), 45–62.
Teece, D.J. (1987), 'Profiting from technological innovation: implications for integration, collaboration, licensing and public policy', in D.J. Teece (ed.), *The Competitive Challenge*, Cambridge, MA, Ballinger Publishing Company.
Uzzi, B. (1997), 'Social structure and competition in interfirm networks: the paradox of embeddedness', *Administrative Science Quarterly*, **42**, 35–67.
Walker, G., B. Kogut and W. Shan (1997), 'Social capital, structural holes and the formation of an industry network', *Organization Science*, **8** (2), 109–25.

3. Organizing knowledge sharing in networks: the theory

Elco van Burg, Hans Berends and Erik van Raaij

INTRODUCTION

Over the past decade, knowledge has become a central concept in the field of organization studies. Knowledge helps companies to outperform competitors (Winter, 1987). Knowledge can be compared with an accurate map. Having a map of the territory in which we want to travel gives us the coordinates of the places we want to go to and routes to get there. The map enables efficient travelling and avoids moving around by trial and error. Thus, knowledge about technology, customers, competitors and ways of organizing helps organizations to act efficiently and effectively.

It is widely claimed that the importance of knowledge in our economies and societies is increasing (Nonaka and Takeuchi, 1995; Drucker, 1993). More and more people in developed countries perform knowledge-intensive work and knowledge is becoming more and more quickly outdated. Technologies, for example, develop at an increasing speed. This means that organizations can differentiate themselves from competitors through their knowledge and capabilities. It is especially the tacit component of capabilities that makes them a source of competitive advantage (Winter, 1987; Berman et al., 2002). Tacit knowledge is the knowledge that we use unconsciously when we take conscious actions or apply explicit knowledge (Polanyi, 1958). Tacit knowledge is difficult to transfer, observe or sell. Capabilities built on tacit knowledge are therefore hard to replicate by others. Competitive advantage based on collective and tacit capabilities has a higher chance of being sustainable.

The recognition of the importance of knowledge and knowledge processes in organizations has spurred interest in knowledge management. Organizations stimulate internal knowledge sharing, so that knowledge can be re-used, re-combined and leveraged. Another challenge for organizations is to increase their stock of knowledge in order to increase efficiency, to develop new technologies or to adapt to the environment. This is the more important when environments change, existing knowledge becomes outdated and competitive advantages erode.

Knowledge management can be oriented at exploitation and exploration (March, 1991). Exploration consists of 'the pursuit of new knowledge, of things that might come to be known'. It is the process leading to the development of new competences. Exploitation, in contrast, consists of 'the use and development of things already known' (Levinthal and March, 1993: 105). Exploitation helps to improve existing competences. Both exploration and exploitation involve learning, but the object of learning differs with respect to its familiarity. Because exploitation is concerned with learning how to do the same things better, feedback on exploitation is characterized by certainty, speed, proximity and clarity. Returns from exploration are systematically less certain, more remote in time and more distant from the locus of action. As a result, the knowledge management challenges associated with exploration and exploitation differ. While the emphasis on these basic processes may change over time, the viability of organizations depends on their capability to do both (March, 1991).

Organizations have often focused on developing new knowledge internally. However, more and more it is realized that the outside world is an important source of new knowledge as well (Chesbrough, 2003). By building strategic partnerships and networks the knowledge of different organizations can be combined in order to create complex innovations. In modular networks, organizations combine each other's knowledge base while keeping their own specializations. Yet, often organizations do more than just accessing knowledge of other parties. They actually share their knowledge and learn from each other. This chapter focuses on the facilitation of this knowledge-sharing process in interorganizational networks.

As Dyer and Nobeoka (2000) explain, knowledge sharing between companies in a network faces several potential problems. Sharing knowledge is often not in the interest of a company, which creates a potential motivation problem. Free-riding is another threat to knowledge sharing in interorganizational networks. A network partner may be inclined to reap the benefits from acquiring knowledge without intending to contribute to others. A third potential problem lies in the efficiency of knowledge sharing in a multi-partner network, as knowledge may be hard to find and transfer. Finally, it has been argued that boundaries between cultures, groups and languages may complicate learning processes between organizations. In order to overcome these barriers, management needs to support interorganizational knowledge sharing by appropriate means.

Dyer and Nobeoka (2000) also identified three mechanisms used to solve the knowledge-sharing dilemmas in Toyota's process innovation network. These mechanisms are network identity, network rules for knowledge protection and value appropriation, and multiple knowledge-sharing processes. In the Toyota network, these mechanisms are effectuated by solutions like a supplier association, network-level consulting teams, voluntary learning teams, interfirm employee transfers and rules. Other authors have presented similar insights (e.g. Gittel and Weiss, 2004; Inkpen and Tsang, 2005) and have added other mechanisms, like trust (e.g. Liebeskind et al., 1996; Newell and Swan, 2000; Ring, 1999), commitment (e.g. Knight and Pye, 2005; Swan and Scarbrough, 2005), absorptive capacity (e.g. Brown and Duguid, 2001; Powell et al., 1996) and relationships (e.g., Lorenzoni and Lipparini, 1999; Hardy et al., 2003).

This chapter seeks to integrate existing research on the management of knowledge in networks in a comprehensive model, by means of an extensive literature review. We follow Denyer and Tranfield's (2005) design-oriented approach, to synthesize both theoretical research and more managerial studies. In addition to exploring management instruments as means to facilitate knowledge sharing in networks, we also focus on contextual factors influencing their effectiveness. These contextual factors have not been systematically investigated (Brown and Duguid, 2001). In this literature review, the network and knowledge characteristics as defined in Chapter 1 are taken into account as contextual factors.

RESEARCH MODEL AND APPROACH

In this review we adopt a 'design-oriented perspective'. This emerging perspective aims to reconnect organization theory to the practice of organization design (van Aken, 2004; Romme, 2003; Romme and Endenburg, 2006). The aim of design-oriented research is to provide practitioners with validated prescriptive knowledge, to be used for the design of solutions for managerial and organizational problems.

Prescriptive design knowledge is codified in design rules (also called technological rules). These rules are comprised of four components: a context, a solution concept, a mechanism triggered by the solution concept and an intended outcome (Denyer and Tranfield, 2005). The general layout of such a rule is: to achieve outcome A, in context C, use solution concept B (van Aken, 2004; Romme and Endenburg, 2006). Solution concepts are the core of such a design rule. Solution concepts are generic principles or systems which managers can implement or realize to influence organizational processes (Denyer and Tranfield, 2005). They form the practical or instrumental basis for design work in organizations (Romme and Endenburg, 2006).

In our guiding framework, presented in Chapter 1, all elements of the design-oriented approach could be recognized. In the end, interorganizational collaboration is a means to increase the innovative capacities of organizations. We focus particularly on knowledge sharing in networks, which is an important enabler of the innovation process. Knowledge sharing is taken as the intended outcome of solution concepts and mechanisms. The context factors that are taken into consideration are the nature of knowledge and type of network.

Paper Collection

The publications incorporated in this literature review were collected in a semi-structured manner, through a combination of keyword search and the snowball method. The ABI/Inform database was searched using combinations of the following keywords: 'knowledge network', 'innovation network', 'knowledge', 'interfirm', 'interorganizational', 'learning', 'alliance', 'network', 'partners' and 'collaboration'. Furthermore, the articles that were identified were scanned for references to other relevant articles. In total, 45 publications were identified and included in this review.

Analysis

Following the design-oriented approach to literature reviews as advocated by Denyer and Tranfield (2005), we analysed the collected literature for solution concepts and contextual elements which explain the outcome: knowledge sharing in an interorganizational network. Solution concepts were defined above as the means that managers have to influence organizational processes. So, the 'mechanisms', 'tools' and so on that managers can employ to influence organizational processes, are interpreted as solution concepts. We also identified 'mechanisms', 'instruments' and so on that are less tangible and are sometimes the consequence of solution concepts, like 'trust' and 'network identity'. In our literature review, we distinguished these from the more tangible, first-order solution concepts. By distinguishing between these two categories of solution concepts we were to some extent able to deal with the problem that examined solutions act on different abstraction levels and at different places in the causal chain. For example, 'trust' and 'selection systems' may both enable collaboration, but they are quite distinct types of concepts, as Grandori and Soda (1995) noted.

The review was complicated by the fact that a lot of different terms are used in the literature. In a way comparable to grounded theory building, we developed a standard set of codes, and coded articles for the different elements of the framework. We captured part of this coding exercise in the Appendix, which increases the traceability of the findings presented.

TANGIBLE SOLUTION CONCEPTS FOSTERING KNOWLEDGE SHARING

In this section, we discuss eight solution concepts that were identified within the literature. In this discussion, we note when these solution concepts are related to less tangible solution concepts discussed in the next section. In the Appendix, we present an overview of the literature that supports the findings presented below.

Personnel Transfer

The first solution concept for stimulating knowledge sharing is the transfer of personnel among organizations. These transfers may consist of relatively short stays of individuals at partner organizations, but also of more permanent employment at the partner's organization. Transferring personnel from one partner to another may stimulate knowledge sharing in two ways. First, personnel transfer creates opportunities for knowledge sharing. By transferring individuals from one part of the network to another, particular technological knowledge can be dispersed. People are also able to build new relationships, therewith increasing the efficiency of knowledge transfer (Inkpen and Tsang, 2005). Furthermore, personnel transfer generates a greater dispersion of knowledge about available competences, systems and technology (Dyer and Nobeoka, 2000), thus improving the efficiency of searching knowledge (Inkpen and Dinur, 1998). Finally, employees learn to understand multiple perspectives, thus improving the sharing of tacit knowledge.

Personnel transfer also stimulates knowledge sharing by fostering the creation of network identity. By transferring personnel, the unit of analysis for job rotation is not the individual firm, but the network (Dyer and Nobeoka, 2000). People who are transferred to other companies come to see members of other organizations as colleagues as well and their colleagues within their home organization will also be tempted to do so.

Printed and Electronic Media

Sharing documents and using information systems are common ways to exchange information and are applicable within interorganizational networks. Because these channels usually provide little context, it is hard to share knowledge that is difficult to codify. But using information systems and documents for the transfer of codified knowledge improves the efficiency. Regarding information systems, empirical research among 22 supply chain networks shows that integrative mechanisms (EDI, integrated business systems, IT integration) are an important means to support learning (Spekman et al., 2002; Gittel and Weiss, 2004). On the other hand, a lack of information systems can decrease the efficiency of knowledge sharing (Newell and Swan, 2000).

Knowledge Brokers

Efficient knowledge sharing in a network can be enhanced by knowledge brokers who are able to span the boundaries of different organizations, groups or practices and are able to integrate and combine the knowledge of different partners (Grant and Baden-Fuller, 2004). Three types of brokers can be distinguished: network platforms, (consultancy) groups, and individuals. First, Soekijad and Andriessen (2003) describe network platforms that fulfil the brokering role. These network platforms bring different partners in the network into contact with each other and are sometimes able to bridge boundaries. Second, consulting groups could bridge the boundaries between the network partners, by having access to different communities, transferring knowledge from one social community to the other and translating the knowledge if necessary (Swan and Scarbrough, 2005). Third, individuals can fulfil the brokering role. For example, certain companies have appointed cultural ambassadors: people who act as interpreter between individuals from various industries who cooperate in the network (Duysters et al., 1999).

Direct Communications

Direct communications in a network context come in different forms: (co-located) team working, social events, conferences, site visits and frequent discussion sessions. Especially co-location of teams is a means that enables deep interactions and increases the efficiency of knowledge sharing because of the opportunity for frequent communication and interaction.

Frequent direct communication in an interorganizational network enables and improves knowledge sharing in three ways: by providing knowledge-sharing opportunities, by creating network identity and by constituting trust. First, direct communications are an important means of dispersing knowledge because they provide knowledge-sharing opportunities. When people are meeting each other (face to face) they are able to communicate and thus to share knowledge (e.g. Dyer and Nobeoka, 2000; Spekman et al., 2002). Second, network identity is created by network-level meetings. Frequent face-to-face meetings create a social community (Dyer and Nobeoka, 2000; Orlikowski, 2002) and help to develop relationships (Hansen, 1999; Soekijad and Andriessen, 2003). These processes create a shared purpose among partners and help them to believe that they are part of a larger collective. Third, frequent direct communications can create trust. Trust is process-based in the sense that firms test each other's integrity in small exchanges and then decide to move to more open-ended deals with substantial risk (Inkpen and Tsang, 2005). This process of testing each other also happens at the individual level, thus enabling behaviour-based trust (Newell and Swan, 2000; Orlikowski, 2002).

Goal Alignment

Goal alignment is the process by which partners bring into line their perspectives, by taking decisions, thus generating shared goals, constituting commitment and trust. If decision-making is balanced, partners tend to be more committed towards the goal of cooperation (Muthusamy and White, 2005). Having unequal influence on decisions and agreements may result in the development of a sense of injustice and this could end in loss of commitment (Larsson et al., 1998; Muthusamy and White, 2005). Regarding trust, Ring (1999) argues that joint decision-making develops trust through negotiation and transaction between individuals and organizations. In the case of the university network that Newell and Swan (2000) examined, however, it is demonstrated that formal power and control mechanisms impede the development of trust if not accompanied by informal mechanisms like communication and relationships.

A second aspect of goal alignment is the establishment of shared goals and norms. Shared goals and norms are a source of trust as they define what appropriate and what inappropriate behaviour is. This gives some assurance to members of the network that if they share knowledge with somebody, someone else will be willing to do the same for them in the future (Reagans and McEvily, 2003). Furthermore, network partners' shared perceptions about their interaction stimulate absorptive capacity, which is the ability to recognize, assimilate and apply new knowledge by means of prior related knowledge (Cohen and Levinthal, 1990). Goal alignment creates a bonding mechanism that helps to integrate knowledge through the mutual understanding and exchange of ideas and resources (Inkpen and Tsang, 2005; Knight and Pye, 2004, 2005).

Interpersonal Relationships

Another important way to increase knowledge sharing is the development of interpersonal ties between members of different network organizations. Interpersonal relationships enable and improve knowledge sharing through a number of effects: by providing opportunities for knowledge sharing, by engendering trust and commitment, and by generating absorptive capacity. First, relationships provide a channel for knowledge sharing. Knowledge is not a resource that can be transferred as a commodity from one organization to another. It needs social and personal interaction, especially for the transfer of tacit knowledge and the creation of new knowledge (Berends, 2003; Hamel, 1991; Hardy et al., 2003; Kale et al., 2000; Powell et al., 1996; Reagans and McEvily, 2003). By having deep interpersonal contact both codified and non-codified knowledge can be shared. Second, relationships enhance trust. People who interact with each other frequently form strong relationships or even friendships. Both interpersonal and interfirm relationships form the basis for the development of trust. Based on the behaviour of firms and individuals, partners develop a sense of their trustworthiness and reputation (Inkpen and Tsang, 2005; Muthusamy and White, 2005; Newell and Swan, 2000; Ring, 1999; Ring and van de Ven, 1994; Soekijad and Andriessen, 2003). The third effect of relationships is commitment. Through ongoing interactions and exchanges in relationships, negotiation of purposes and goals takes place, thus developing commitment that exists in psychological contracts (Ring and van de Ven, 1994). This relationship-based commitment motivates knowledge sharing, thus enabling the transfer of tacit knowledge (Reagans and McEvily, 2003). Finally, absorptive capacity may be developed by relationships and communities. These communities mediate between individuals in large formal and informal structures. Within a community meanings can be created and shared, developing common understanding and associated knowledge (Brown and Duguid, 2001; Swan and Scarbrough, 2005).

Rules and Agreements

Agreements and rules at dyadic and network levels create trust and commitment. When network members are also each other's competitors, trust may be difficult to establish. Clear rules can reduce distrust between network partners (Inkpen and Tsang, 2005; Ring, 1999). Such agreements need to be unambiguous and beneficial for both parties in order to engender trust (Newell and Swan, 2000). Too many regulations, however, can be a symptom of mistrust (Soekijad and Andriessen, 2003). Furthermore, by making agreements, contracts and rules, the mutual benefits and efforts of the relationships are defined, thus providing a basis for commitment to deliver according to the details of the contract (Newell and Swan, 2000; Ring, 1999, Spekman et al., 2002; Steensma and Corley, 2000). These formalized agreements are not the commitment itself, but these agreements form the basis for the development of commitment, constituted by demonstrating the formal reciprocal attitude (Muthusamy and White, 2005). One special type of rules has to be mentioned here, namely rewarding rules. Several authors have found evidence that rewarding rules can help to create commitment (Dyer and Nobeoka, 2000; Larsson et al., 1998; Mody, 1993; Orlikowski, 2002; Spekman et al., 2002).

Partner Selection

In the formation of a network (or reformation of a network) careful partner selection can yield trust and stimulates absorptive capacity. Trust can be constituted in two ways: first, partners can be chosen that are trustworthy (Muthusamy and White, 2005; Powell et al., 1996; Soekijad and Andriessen, 2003). Second, if a partner is selected that is comparable as a peer, mutual respect with regard to the competency of the person or organization can be established, thus enabling competence-based trust (Newell and Swan, 2000; Soekijad and Andriessen, 2003). Furthermore, the selection of partners who are engaged in comparable practices stimulates mutual absorptive capacity. A shared practice provides a work context within which a shared perspective can be constructed. Within such a context, complementary knowledge can be shared and new knowledge can be created (Brown and Duguid, 2001). Similar organizational routines (complex patterns of coordination), similar professions, common models, tools and methodology enable organizations' members to work closely together, and to cross organizational boundaries (Carlile, 2004; Grant and Baden-Fuller, 2004; Inkpen and Dinur, 1998; Knight and Pye, 2004; Podolny and Page, 1998; Orlikowski, 2002).

LESS TANGIBLE SOLUTION CONCEPTS FOSTERING KNOWLEDGE SHARING

We identified three less tangible solution concepts in the literature: absorptive capacity, trust and commitment, and network identity. Each of these solution concepts in some way enables knowledge sharing in a network. In the foregoing section, we already noted that these solution concepts are sometimes constituted by other solution concepts, or have a mediating effect for other solution concepts. We will discuss them below.

Absorptive Capacity

To share knowledge among partners, these partners should be able to absorb it. Absorptive capacity is a prerequisite for effective knowledge sharing in interorganizational networks. This concept is based on the idea that people usually learn new ideas by associating these ideas with what they already know. Therefore, people may more easily absorb knowledge from areas in which they already have some knowledge. An implication is that the ability to absorb knowledge from a network partner is contingent on the stock of related knowledge (Cohen and Levinthal, 1990; Podolny and Page, 1998). Thus, partners require both common knowledge to be able to absorb knowledge and complementary knowledge to provide learning opportunities (Powell et al., 1996).

Trust and Commitment

Trust results in stability of relationships and confidence in the interaction of network partners. Confidence and stability are important conditions for ongoing interactions and deep exchanges (Newell and Swan, 2000; Podolny and Page, 1998; Ring, 1999). Trust is a substitute for formal control mechanisms as it constitutes implicit norms and sanctions (Newell and Swan, 2000; Podolny and Page, 1998), and makes firms more willing to invest resources in learning and knowledge sharing. In a situation with sufficient trust, partners are not afraid of knowledge spillovers and the firm's decision-makers and employees are less likely to protect themselves against opportunistic behaviour by their partners (Inkpen and Tsang, 2005; Newell and Swan, 2000; Swan and Scarbrough, 2005).

Commitment is 'the form of a moral obligation as opposed to a concern for individual gratification' (Muthusamy and White, 2005: 419). It is a necessary mechanism for knowledge sharing: it ensures the stability of the relationship and creates the conditions for network members to be loyal enough to share knowledge (Hardy et al., 2003; Newell and Swan, 2000). Although it seems clear that commitment is an enabler for knowledge sharing in a network, commitment itself can hardly be designed. Commitment is a result of fragmented and incidentally taken decisions and choices (Knight and Pye, 2005).

Network Identity

Having a shared identity means that individuals share a sense of purpose and belonging with other members of a collective (Kogut, 2000). Such a shared identity can also develop within a network of organizations.

Knowledge is most effectively shared by individuals who identify with a larger collective and consider other network members to be 'one of us'. When people feel themselves to be part of a larger collective, they become motivated to contribute to that collective and to share even tacit or core knowledge (Dyer and Nobeoka, 2000; Kogut, 2000). Furthermore, Dyer and Nobeoka (2000) argue that a shared identity establishes explicit and tacit rules of coordination. People sharing a network identity know what to expect from each other.

CONTINGENCY FACTORS

It is unlikely that solutions are equally effective across a range of different situations. In this chapter we discuss two groups of contingency factors that may affect the effectiveness of the identified solution concepts. First, we explore the moderating effect of the type of knowledge that is being shared in a network. Second, we explore the impact of the type of network.

Tacit and Explicit Knowledge

A basic distinction is often made between tacit and explicit knowledge. Tacit knowledge refers to knowledge that we use without being fully aware of it (Polanyi, 1958). It enables us to do things without being able to tell exactly how. Tacit knowledge is usually difficult to codify, and resides, for instance, in routines, skills and competences (Nonaka, 1994). Nonaka and Takeuchi (1995) distinguished two dimensions of tacit knowledge: a technical one and a cognitive one. The first embodies know-how: the skills and behaviour of a person. The latter consists of mental models: ideas and values. Explicit knowledge is the type of knowledge that can be expressed in codified symbols, language or otherwise. For example, a manual contains explicit knowledge. Brown and Duguid (2001) argue that to understand explicit knowledge, tacit knowledge is necessary. Because of the importance of tacit knowledge, we prefer the term 'knowledge sharing' over 'knowledge transfer'. The latter presupposes that knowledge is like a package or a concrete thing (Soekijad, 2005: 18). This may be applicable to explicit knowledge or information, but definitely not to tacit knowledge. Knowledge sharing occurs through multiple actions and processes, like co-working, talking, sharing documents and so on.

Research within organizations has found that the codifiability of knowledge influences the effectiveness of solution concepts (Hansen, 1999). Two aspects influence the fit of solution concepts with tacit or explicit knowledge: the formality of the solution concept and richness of

Table 3.1 Tangible solution concepts for codified and tacit knowledge

Knowledge type	Solution concept
Mainly *codified knowledge*	Rules and agreements Goal alignment Printed and electronic media
Both *codified* and *tacit knowledge*	Knowledge brokers
Mainly *tacit knowledge* sharing	Personnel transfer Direct communications Interpersonal relationships Partner selection

the communication media. Makhija and Ganesh (1997) argue that formal mechanisms enhance predictability of events and standardization of processes. Using these mechanisms for knowledge sharing assumes that the knowledge is separable from the individual who possesses it, which is not applicable to tacit knowledge. Formal mechanisms are more feasible for sharing codified knowledge and less for sharing non-codifiable knowledge. Because tacit knowledge is highly personal it cannot easily be communicated to a different person or context (Nonaka, 1994). The personal component requires human (face-to-face) interaction for sharing tacit knowledge. Solution concepts that allow for richer communication are more suited to sharing tacit knowledge (Nonaka, 1994). Solution concepts that only support low-context and impersonal interaction are less suited to sharing tacit knowledge.

Taking these aspects into account, the appropriateness of the solution concepts for sharing codified and non-codified knowledge can be discussed (see Table 3.1). In this discussion, we focus on the tangible concepts because they are more manageable. First, reports and information systems are mainly feasible for sharing codified knowledge (but to interpret this knowledge, common (tacit) knowledge is necessary, according to Brown and Duguid, 2001). Also rules and agreements and goal alignment are more likely to enhance the sharing of codified knowledge than of tacit knowledge, because of the high formality of these solution concepts. Second, knowledge brokers could, to some extent, enable the sharing of both types of knowledge. They have the explicit role to bridge boundaries and to translate the languages of disjoint practices. Third, the solutions that involve rich personal interaction enable tacit knowledge sharing. The deeper the interaction, like interpersonal relations or co-working in a co-located team, the better tacit knowledge can be shared (Hansen, 1999; Reagans and McEvily, 2003). Thus, personnel transfer, direct communication and interpersonal relationships are effective at sharing tacit knowledge. Also partner selection may enable the sharing of tacit knowledge, although this may seem to be a formal mechanism. But, by choosing a trustworthy partner with a shared practice, common knowledge and absorptive capacity can be constituted, thus enabling sharing tacit knowledge.

Coreness of Knowledge

The coreness of knowledge refers to the importance of knowledge for the firm's core competences. Core knowledge is that particular kind of knowledge that creates the core competences of a firm (Blaauw, 2005). These core competences form the basis for the sustainable competitive advantage of a firm (Prahalad and Hamel, 1990). Two consistent themes appear in the literature about competencies: the source is always internal to the firm and a competency is produced by the use of the firm's internal skills and resources (Reed and DeFillippi, 1990). When firms are cooperating, they share their non-core knowledge rather than their core knowledge. Obviously they prefer to maintain their competitive advantage. Especially when the cooperating firms are competitors, there is likely to be a tendency to protect core knowledge. Thus, the motivation dilemma will be particularly strong if core knowledge is involved. Solution concepts that are able to deal with this dilemma are very important if core knowledge has to be shared.

The first solution concept that might overcome the reluctance to share core knowledge is trust (Newell and Swan, 2000). Soekijad and Andriessen (2003) assessed conditions and mechanisms for knowledge sharing in co-opetitive partnerships. They conclude that the creation of trust lowers the tendency to protect knowledge, as it involves the conviction that others will not abuse openness. According to Kale et al. (2000), mechanisms that constitute mutual trust, friendship and respect reduce the protection of core knowledge. Following this reasoning, interpersonal relationships and other solution concepts that effectuate trust (knowledge brokers, rules and agreements, goal alignment, partner selection) are able to reduce knowledge protection and thus enable the flow of core knowledge. Relationships establish their own norms and these norms are even more stable than contractual norms (Liebeskind et al., 1996). Agreements can also express commitment at the managerial level and can include property rules that provide clarity about the status of knowledge and the expected sharing behaviour (Dyer and Nobeoka, 2000). The expected sharing behaviour can furthermore be improved by rewarding rules for knowledge sharing (Dyer and Nobeoka, 2000; Mody, 1993; Orlikowski, 2002; Spekman et al., 2002).

Another solution concept that enables sharing core knowledge is network identity. When partners and employees identify with the larger collective, they become motivated to share even their core knowledge (Dyer and Nobeoka, 2000). Thus, it can be expected that the solution concepts for network identity, personnel transfer and direct communications enable the sharing of core knowledge.

Network Centrality

What is the effect of centrality or decentrality on the feasibility of the identified solution concepts? Powell et al. (1996) examined the effect of centrality on learning in interorganizational networks in the bioindustry in the US. They found that a firm's centrality in a network enhances knowledge sharing and learning because it intensifies the firm's commitment and facilitates common understanding (because of frequent interactions) and shared principles of cooperation. In a more centralized network, knowledge-sharing mechanisms can be more formally implemented, as has been shown in a number of case studies (Dyer and Nobeoka, 2000; Knight and Pye, 2004, 2005; Soekijad and Andriessen, 2003; Swan and Scarbrough, 2005; van Baalen et al., 2005). However, in a decentralized network, agreements and rules can be made in dyadic relationships within the network, but seldom at the network level. In decentralized networks, power and commitment have less to do with authority because there is no single firm that is able to exert power over the other partners. Power in such a network setting is more reputational and relational; it has to do with expertise and social bonds and close relationships (Achrol, 1997). Therefore, to enable knowledge sharing in decentralized networks, informal mechanisms are crucial.

Single versus Multiple Innovations

In the literature reviewed, no difference is found between networks that aim to perform one single innovation and networks that aim for continuous collaboration in order to establish multiple innovations. One reason may be that most studies concentrate on long-term innovations, or because longitudinal studies are scarce and therefore the effect of time is not examined. On the one hand, if cooperation lasts longer, the need to solve dilemmas becomes stronger because these problems are likely to become more severe (Das and Teng, 2002). On the other hand, a number of authors recommend that a long-term orientation in interorganizational collaboration is beneficial because it reduces opportunistic behaviour and long-lasting relationships can be built (Lorenzoni and Lipparini, 1999; Walker et al., 1997; Ring and van de Ven, 1994). When network partners know that they are going to cooperate for a longer period, opportunistic behaviour (like free-riding and knowledge protection) is reduced. Ongoing network collaboration enables the building of learning mechanisms like strong ties and social norms (Dyer and Nobeoka, 2000). Because trust is partly built on ongoing interactions, a continuous collaboration seems to be a context where this mechanism can flourish more than in a one-off collaboration.

DISCUSSION AND CONCLUSIONS

In this literature review, we took a design-oriented approach to reviewing the literature on knowledge sharing in networks. This approach was helpful to integrate findings and to articulate insights into the moderating effects of knowledge and network type.

This review has also exposed some limitations in the existing literature. First, most of the research on managing knowledge sharing in networks takes a positive approach. The positive effects of solution concepts are extensively examined, but the limitations of these concepts are not investigated. For example, the positive effects of interpersonal relationships are frequently established, but potential negative effects, like conflicts and groupthink, are scarcely examined. If performance is below expectations, this is often blamed on inaccurate implementation and not on the inappropriateness of a solution concept itself. Furthermore, the costs of implementing particular solutions are seldom taken into account. A second weakness in the literature is that there is a tendency towards 'more is better' with regard to knowledge sharing in networks. Knowledge sharing and cooperation are usually assumed to be beneficial (as we have implicitly assumed in this chapter). In the literature about knowledge sharing in interorganizational networks, the dark sides and the risk factors of these cooperations have received less attention. In this regard, the literature about supplier involvement in innovation processes can be a source of complementary insight. This literature has investigated risk factors such as the probability that a supplier capability will fail to meet a customer's requirements (Huang et al., 2003). The third weakness is the lack of studies that take contextual factors into account. The moderating effects of environmental factors, knowledge types and network characteristics are hardly examined.

This review itself has some limitations as well. Due to its broad scope, the solution concepts could not be explored in great depth. A complicating factor was that the case studies presented in the literature often do not describe managerial interventions in full detail. Again, the literature on supplier involvement may be a source of additional insight. For example, Wynstra et al. (2003) proposed a framework for supplier interface management in new product development which incorporates many of the elements presented in this chapter. This framework covers activities across four management levels of interfirm cooperation and knowledge sharing. The solution concepts are described in more detail and depth and become more practical to implement in a real business situation. The case studies presented in the other chapters also serve to provide further detail with regard to the different solution concepts presented in this chapter.

SUMMARY

For many companies, managing knowledge sharing in interorganizational networks is important for their competitive advantage. Knowledge management has to deal with four potential problems: motivation, free-riding, efficiency and boundaries. We found several solution concepts that can be applied to prevent and reduce these problems. A number of tangible, manageable mechanisms are found in the literature: personnel transfer, printed and electronic media, knowledge brokers, direct communication, goal alignment, interpersonal relationships, rules and agreements, and partner selection. Besides this, there are other, less tangible means: absorptive capacity, trust and commitment, and network identity. The effect of these solution concepts depends on contextual elements, including the type of knowledge, the coreness of knowledge, and network and innovation characteristics.

REFERENCES

Achrol, R.S. (1997), 'Changes in the theory of interorganizational relations in marketing: toward a network paradigm', *Journal of the Academy of Marketing Science*, **25** (1), 56–71.

Ahuja, G. (2000), 'Collaboration networks, structural holes, and innovation: a longitudinal study', *Administrative Science Quarterly*, **45** (3), 425–54.

Berends, H. (2003), *Knowledge Sharing in Industrial Research*, Dissertation, Eindhoven: Eindhoven University Press.

Berman, S.L., J. Down and C.W.L. Hill (2002), 'Tacit knowledge as a source of competitive advantage in the National Basketball Association', *Academy of Management Journal*, **45** (1), 13–31.

Blaauw, G. (2005), *Identificatie van Cruciale Kennis*, Dissertation, Ridderkerk: RU Groningen.

Brown, J.S. and P. Duguid (2001), 'Knowledge and organization: a social-practice perspective', *Organization Science*, **12** (2), 198–213.

Carlile, P.R. (2004), 'Transferring, translating, and transforming: an integrative framework for managing knowledge across boundaries', *Organization Science*, **15** (5), 555–68.

Chesbrough, H.W. (2003), *Open Innovation*, Boston, MA: Harvard Business School Press.
Cohen, W.M. and D.A. Levinthal (1990), 'Absorptive capacity: a new perspective on learning and innovation', *Administrative Science Quarterly*, **35** (1), 128–52.
Daghfous, A. (2004), 'Organizational learning, knowledge and technology transfer: a case study', *The Learning Organization*, **11** (1), 67–83.
Das, T.K. and B.-S. Teng (2002), 'Alliance constellations: a social exchange perspective', *Academy of Management Review*, **27** (3), 445–56.
Denyer, D. and D. Tranfield (2005), 'Developing technological rules from a synthesis of the science base', Paper presented at Euram conference 2005.
Drucker, P.F. (1993), *Post-capitalist Society*, Oxford: Butterworth-Heinemann.
Dubois, A. and H. Håkansson (1999), 'Relationships as activity links', in M. Ebers (ed.), *The Formation of Inter-organizational Networks*, Oxford: Oxford University Press, pp. 43–65.
Duysters, G., A.P. de Man and L. Wildeman (1999), 'A network approach to alliance management', *European Management Journal*, **17** (2), 182–7.
Dyer, J.H. and K. Nobeoka (2000), 'Creating and managing a high-performance knowledge-sharing network: the Toyota case', *Strategic Management Journal*, **21**, 345–67.
Ebers, M. (1999), 'Explaining inter-organizational network formation', in M. Ebers (ed.), *The Formation of Inter-organizational Networks*, Oxford: Oxford University Press, pp. 3–40.
Gittel, J.H. and L. Weiss (2004), 'Coordination networks within and across organizations: a multi-level framework', *Journal of Management Studies*, **41** (1), 127–53.
Grandori, A. and G. Soda (1995), 'Inter-firm networks: antecedents, mechanisms and forms', *Organization Studies*, **16** (2), 183–214.
Grant, R.M. and C. Baden-Fuller (2004), 'A knowledge accessing theory of strategic alliances', *Journal of Management Studies*, **41** (1), 61–84.
Hamel, G. (1991), 'Learning in international alliances', *Strategic Management Journal*, **12**, 83–103.
Hansen, M.T. (1999), 'The search-transfer problem: the role of weak ties in sharing knowledge across organization subunits', *Administrative Science Quarterly*, **44** (1), 82–111.
Hardy, C., N. Phillips and T.B. Lawrence (2003), 'Resources, knowledge and influence: the organizational effects of interorganizational collaboration', *Journal of Management Studies*, **40** (2), 321–47.
Huang, G.Q., K.L. Mak and P.K. Humphreys (2003), 'A new model of the customer-supplier partnership in new product development', *Journal of Materials Processing Technology*, **138** (1), 301–5.
Inkpen, A.C. (1998), 'Learning and knowledge acquisition through international strategic alliances', *Academy of Management Executive*, **12** (4), 69–80.
Inkpen, A.C. (2000), 'Learning through joint ventures: a framework of knowledge acquisition', *Journal of Management Studies*, **37** (7), 1019–43.
Inkpen, A.C. and A. Dinur (1998), 'Knowledge management processes and international joint ventures', *Organization Science*, **9** (4), 454–68.
Inkpen, A.C. and E.W.K. Tsang (2005), 'Social capital, networks, and knowledge transfer', *Academy of Management Review*, **30** (1), 145–65.
Jones, C., W.S. Hesterly and S.P. Borgatti (1997), 'A general theory of network governance: exchange conditions and social mechanisms', *Academy of Management Review*, **22** (4), 911–45.

Kale, P., H. Singh and H. Perlmutter (2000), 'Learning and protection of proprietary assets in strategic alliances: building relational capital', *Strategic Management Journal*, **21** (3), 217–37.

Knight, L. and A. Pye (2004), 'Exploring the relationships between network change and network learning', *Management Learning*, **35** (4), 473–90.

Knight, L. and A. Pye (2005), 'Network learning: an empirically derived model of learning by groups of organizations', *Human Relations*, **58** (3), 369–92.

Kogut, B. (2000), 'The network as knowledge: generative rules and the emergence of structure', *Strategic Management Journal*, **21**, 405–25.

Lane, P.J. and M. Lubatkin (1998), 'Relative absorptive capacity and interorganizational learning', *Strategic Management Journal*, **19** (5), 461–77.

Larsson, R., L. Bengtsson, K. Henriksson and J. Sparks (1998), 'The interorganizational learning dilemma: collective knowledge development in strategic alliances', *Organization Science*, **9** (3), 285–305.

Levinthal, D. and J. March (1993), 'The myopia of learning', *Strategic Management Journal*, **14** (Winter Special Issue), 95–112.

Liebeskind, J.P., A.L. Oliver, L. Zucker and M. Brewer (1996), 'Social networks, learning, and flexibility: sourcing scientific knowledge in new biotechnology firms', *Organization Science*, **7** (4), 428–43.

Lorenzoni, G. and A. Lipparini (1999), 'The leveraging of interfirm relationships as a distinctive organizational capability: a longitudinal study', *Strategic Management Journal*, **20** (4), 317–38.

Makhija, M.V. and U. Ganesh (1997), 'The relationship between control and partner learning in learning-related joint ventures', *Organization Science*, **8** (5), 508–27.

March, J.G. (1991), 'Exploration and exploitation in organizational learning', *Organization Science*, **2** (1), 71–87.

Mody, A. (1993), 'Learning through alliances', *Journal of Economic Behavior and Organization*, **20**, 151–70.

Mowery, D.C., J.E. Oxley and B.S. Silverman (1996), 'Strategic alliances and interfirm knowledge transfer', *Strategic Management Journal*, **17**, 77–91.

Muthusamy, S.K. and M.A. White (2005), 'Learning and knowledge transfer in strategic alliances: a social exchange view', *Organization Studies*, **26** (3), 415–41.

Newell, S. and J. Swan (2000), 'Trust and inter-organizational networking', *Human Relations*, **53** (10), 1287–328.

Nonaka, I. (1994), 'A dynamic theory of organizational knowledge creation', *Organization Science*, **5** (1), 14–37.

Nonaka, I. and H. Takeuchi (1995), *The Knowledge Creating Company: How Japanese Companies Create the Dynamics of Innovation*, New York: Oxford University Press.

Orlikowski, W.J. (2002), 'Knowing in practice: enacting a collective capability in distributed organizing', *Organization Science*, **13** (3), 249–73.

Peña, I. (2002), 'Knowledge networks as part of an integrated knowledge management approach', *Journal of Knowledge Management*, **6** (5), 469–78.

Podolny, J.M. and K.L. Page (1998), 'Network forms of organization', *Annual Review of Sociology*, **24**, 57–76.

Polanyi, M. (1958), *Personal Knowledge*, London: Routledge and Kegan Paul.

Powell, W.W., K.W. Koput and L. Smith-Doerr (1996), 'Interorganizational collaboration and the locus of innovation: networks of learning in biotechnology', *Administrative Science Quarterly*, **41** (1), 116–45.

Prahalad, C.K. and G. Hamel (1990), 'The core competence of the corporation', *Harvard Business Review*, **68** (3), 79–92.

Reagans, R. and B. McEvily (2003), 'Network structure and knowledge transfer: the effects of cohesion and range', *Administrative Science Quarterly*, **48**, 240–67.

Reed, R. and R.J. DeFillippi (1990), 'Causal ambiguity, barriers to imitation, and sustainable competitive advantage', *The Academy of Management Review*, **15** (1), 88–102.

Ring, P.S. (1999), 'Processes facilitating reliance on trust in inter-organizational networks', in M. Ebers (ed.), *The Formation of Inter-organizational Networks*, Oxford: Oxford University Press, pp. 113–45.

Ring, P.S. and A.H. van de Ven (1994), 'Developmental processes of cooperative interorganizational relationships', *Academy of Management Review*, **19** (1), 90–118.

Romme, A.G.L. (2003), 'Making a difference: organization as design', *Organization Science*, **14** (5), 558–73.

Romme, A.G.L. and G. Endenburg (2006), 'Construction principles and design rules in the case of circular design', *Organization Science*, **17** (2), 287–300.

Simonin, B.L. (1999), 'Ambiguity and the process of knowledge transfer in strategic alliances', *Strategic Management Journal*, **20** (7), 595–623.

Singh, J. (2005), 'Collaborative networks as determinants of knowledge diffusion patterns', *Management Science*, **51** (5), 756–70.

Soekijad, M. (2005), *Dare to Share: Knowledge Sharing Professionals in Co-opetitive Networks*, Dissertation, Delft: TU Delft.

Soekijad, M. and E. Andriessen (2003), 'Conditions for knowledge sharing in competitive alliances', *European Management Journal*, **21** (5), 578–87.

Spekman, R.E., J. Spear and J. Kamauff (2002), 'Supply chain competency: learning as a key component', *Supply Chain Management*, **7** (1), 41–55.

Steensma, H.K. and K.G. Corley (2000), 'On the performance of technology-sourcing partnerships: the interaction between partner interdependence and technology attributes', *Academy of Management Journal*, **43** (6), 1045–67.

Swan, J. and H. Scarbrough (2005), 'The politics of networked innovation', *Human Relations*, **58** (7), 913–43.

van Aken, J.E. (2004), 'Management research based on the paradigm of the design sciences: The quest for field-tested and grounded technological rules', *Journal of Management Studies*, **41** (2), 219–46.

van Aken, J.E. and M.P. Weggeman (2000), 'Managing learning in informal innovation networks: overcoming the Daphne-dilemma', *R&D Management*, **30** (2), 139–49.

van Baalen, P., J. Bloemhof-Ruwaard and E. van Heck (2005), 'Knowledge sharing in an emerging network of practice: the role of a knowledge portal', *European Management Journal*, **23** (3), 300–14.

Walker, G., B. Kogut and W. Shan (1997), 'Social capital, structural holes and the formation of an industry network', *Organization Science*, **8** (2), 109–25.

Winter, S.G. (1987), 'Knowledge and competence as strategic assets', in D.J. Teece (ed.), *The Competitive Challenge*, Cambridge, MA: Ballinger.

Wynstra, F., M. Weggeman and A. van Weele (2003), 'Exploring purchasing integration in product development', *Industrial Marketing Management*, **32** (1), 69–83.

APPENDIX: LITERATURE ABOUT KNOWLEDGE SHARING IN A NETWORK

For each solution concept, we present the papers that support the application of this concept to enable knowledge sharing in a network. We also show the kind of evidence that a paper presents: case study results (C), quantitative results (i.e. surveys and patent counts) (Q), literature reviews (L) and theory development without empirical evidence (T).

Table 3.2 Literature about knowledge sharing in a network

Solution concept	Article
Personnel transfer	C Dyer and Nobeoka (2000), Inkpen and Dinur (1998) T Inkpen (1998), Inkpen (2000), Inkpen and Tsang (2005)
Printed and electronic media	C Gittel and Weiss (2004), Newell and Swan (2000) Q Spekman et al. (2002), van Baalen et al. (2005)
Knowledge brokers	C Dyer and Nobeoka (2000), Gittel and Weiss (2004), Inkpen and Dinur (1998), Soekijad and Andriessen (2003), Swan and Scarbrough (2005) L Grandori and Soda (1995) Q van Baalen et al. (2005) T Inkpen (2000)
Direct communication	C Carlile (2004), Daghfous (2004), Dyer and Nobeoka (2000), Gittel and Weiss (2004), Inkpen and Dinur (1998), Newell and Swan (2000), Orlikowski (2002), Soekijad and Andriessen (2003) L Ring and van de Ven (1994) Q Hansen (1999), Liebeskind et al. (1996), Spekman et al. (2002) T Inkpen (1998), Inkpen (2000), Jones et al. (1997), Ring (1999)
Goal alignment	C Knight and Pye (2004), Knight and Pye (2005), Newell and Swan (2000), Soekijad and Andriessen (2003), Swan and Scarbrough (2005) L Das and Teng (2002), Grandori and Soda (1995) Q Mowery et al. (1996), Muthusamy and White (2005), Reagans and McEvily (2003), Spekman et al. (2002) T Inkpen (1998), Inkpen (2000), Inkpen and Tsang (2005), Jones et al. (1997), Larsson et al. (1998), Ring (1999)
Interpersonal relationships	C Dubois and Håkansson (1999), Hamel (1991), Hardy et al. (2003), Lorenzoni and Lipparini (1999), Newell and Swan (2000), Orlikowski (2002), Soekijad and Andriessen (2003), Swan and Scarbrough (2005)

Table 3.2 (continued)

Solution concept	Article
	L Das and Teng (2002), Grandori and Soda (1995), Inkpen and Tsang (2005), Ring and van de Ven (1994) Q Ahuja (2000), Kale et al. (2000), Liebeskind et al. (1996), Muthusamy and White (2005), Powell et al. (1996), Reagans and McEvily (2003), Simonin (1999), Singh (2005), Steensma and Corley (2000) T Brown and Duguid (2001), Duysters et al. (1999), Ebers (1999), Inkpen (2000), Jones et al. (1997), Mody (1993), Powell et al. (1996), Ring (1999), van Aken and Weggeman (2000)
Rules and agreements	C Dyer and Nobeoka (2000), Muthusamy and White (2005), Newell and Swan (2000), Orlikowski (2002), Soekijad and Andriessen (2003), Swan and Scarbrough (2005) L Grandori and Soda (1995) Q Muthusamy and White (2005), Peña (2002), Spekman et al. (2002), Steensma and Corley (2000) T Inkpen (1998), Inkpen (2000), Inkpen and Tsang (2005), Jones et al. (1997), Larsson et al. (1998), Mody (1993), Ring (1999)
Partner selection	C Carlile (2004), Daghfous (2004), Hamel (1991), Inkpen and Dinur (1998), Knight and Pye (2004), Newell and Swan (2000), Orlikowski (2002), Soekijad and Andriessen (2003) L Grandori and Soda (1995), Podolny and Page (1998) Q Lane and Lubatkin (1997), Mowery et al. (1996), Muthusamy and White (2005), Powell et al. (1996), Reagans and McEvily (2003), Simonin (1999), Spekman et al. (2002) T Brown and Duguid (2001), Duysters et al. (1999), Grant and Baden-Fuller (2004), Inkpen (1998), Inkpen (2000), Larsson et al. (1998), Powell et al. (1996)
Absorptive capacity	C Carlile (2004), Daghfous (2004), Hamel (1991), Inkpen and Dinur (1998), Knight and Pye (2004), Knight and Pye (2005), Orlikowski (2002), Soekijad and Andriessen (2003), Swan and Scarbrough (2005) L Grandori and Soda (1995), Podolny and Page (1998) Q Lane and Lubatkin (1997), Liebeskind et al. (1996), Mowery et al. (1996), Reagans and McEvily (2003), Simonin (1999), Spekman et al. (2002) T Brown and Duguid (2001), Duysters et al. (1999), Grant and Baden-Fuller (2004), Inkpen (1998), Inkpen (2000),

Table 3.2 (continued)

Solution concept		Article
		Inkpen and Tsang (2005), Jones et al. (1997), Larsson et al. (1998), Powell et al. (1996), Ring (1999)
Trust and commitment	C	Dyer and Nobeoka (2000), Knight and Pye (2005), Newell and Swan (2000), Orlikowski (2002), Soekijad and Andriessen (2003), Swan and Scarbrough (2005)
	L	Das and Teng (2002), Grandori and Soda (1995), Ring and van de Ven (1994)
	Q	Hansen (1999), Kale et al. (2000), Liebeskind et al. (1996), Mowery et al. (1996), Muthusamy and White (2005), Peña (2002), Powell et al. (1996), Reagans and McEvily (2003), Spekman et al. (2002), Steensma and Corley (2000)
	T	Duysters et al. (1999), Inkpen (2000), Inkpen and Tsang (2005), Jones et al. (1997), Larsson et al. (1998), Mody (1993), Ring (1999)
Network identity	C	Dyer and Nobeoka (2000), Orlikowski (2002), Soekijad and Andriessen (2003)
	Q	Hansen (1999)

4. Meeting Moore's law: high velocity knowledge development in the supplier network of ASML[1]

Irene Lammers, Pim Eling, Ard-Pieter de Man and Arjan van Weele

SUMMARY

One of the reasons for the success of ASML, a producer of lithography systems headquartered in The Netherlands, is its management of its extensive supplier network. ASML works with about 500 firms that supply about 90 per cent of the costs of a lithography system, leaving ASML with the task of integrating these modules and parts into the final tool. In order to meet the technology roadmap of the high velocity semiconductor industry (Eisenhardt, 1989b), the pace of innovation in the ASML network is high. An important approach that ASML uses to secure innovation as well as to spread the risk of development in the network is their supply chain management philosophy of value sourcing. This philosophy implies that for each technological competence, multiple suppliers are used to decrease dependencies. Existing partners are constantly monitored in terms of improvements in their knowledge base, as well as their control of processes. These and other practices have enabled ASML to develop into the technology leader in the chip lithography market. By drawing on four embedded case studies of innovation projects conducted within ASML's supplier network, we present both the theory and the practice of ASML's supply chain management approach. We conclude that ASML's approach to managing its network of suppliers is notably different from approaches in less dynamic industries such as the automotive industry (Dyer and Nobeoka, 2000). The modularization of the network means that knowledge is integrated in separate projects, each involving a limited number of partners. As a consequence, ASML is able to innovate with a large number of partners without implementing numerous knowledge management mechanisms across the entire supplier network. However, this approach has its limitations. It only works when the partners in the network have high managerial and technological skills. Where these skills are absent, difficulties occur.

INTRODUCTION

> You can quote me on this: wow! (Eric Meurice, CEO of ASML, expresses his enthusiasm over the results of ASML in 2006).

ASML is a leading provider of advanced technology systems for the semiconductor industry. The company produces a portfolio of lithography systems, mainly for manufacturing complex integrated circuits ('semiconductors', 'ICs' or 'chips'). The chips that are made with these lithography systems are found in numerous consumer products, such as phones, hand-held mobile computers (PDAs), digital television, and DVD players. Headquartered in Veldhoven, The Netherlands, ASML delivers to IC manufacturers in the United States, Asia and Europe. Besides lithography systems, ASML also provides its customers with a range of support activities and products, including process and product software applications, advice and service support. Figure 4.1 shows one of ASML's products.

Figure 4.1 ASML's TWINSCAN

Meurice's enthusiasm about the results of ASML can be understood when one takes a look at the company's impressive performance. In 2006 ASML had a turnover of €3.6 billion with a net income of €625 million and saw an increase in market share, from 57 per cent in 2005 to 63 per cent in 2006 (ASML, 2006, based on independent research firms). These results can be added to a long list of impressive results from its founding in 1984 to the market leadership position its holds today. While the chip lithography market grew from €463 million in 1984 to €4800 million in 2006 worldwide (ASML/DeYoung, 2007), the market share of ASML's major competitors, Nikon and Canon, decreased from respectively 45 per cent and 29 per cent in 1995 to 21 per cent and 16 per cent in 2006. ASML ships 83 per cent of its products to Asia (ASML/Borggreve, 2006).

ASML is also technologically successful. It ranked 167th on the list of companies granted the most patents in 2005 and was the third most active in patents in The Netherlands following Philips and Unilever, firms many times ASML's size (IPO, 2005).

Of the 20 largest semiconductor manufacturers ranked by capital expenditure, 17 were customers of ASML in 2005 (ASML/Borggreve, 2006). ASML also further penetrated the Japanese market, the homeland of Canon and Nikon, gaining six new Japanese customers in 2005 (ASML/Borggreve, 2006). This result is particularly impressive taking into account that mere survival in this industry is virtually a miracle: 20 years ago there were eight manufacturers of wafer steppers. In 2005 only three were left (see Figure 4.2).

In this chapter, we seek to explain the impressive results of ASML by looking at the way ASML manages and operates the networks in which the company is embedded. ASML works with about 500 suppliers, whose supplies make up about 90 per cent of the total costs of its lithography systems (ASML, 2006). In terms of the conceptual model (see Chapter 1), the supplier network of ASML can be characterized as a geographically dispersed network. Although ASML's most important suppliers are situated in the south of the Netherlands and the Ruhr area of Germany, the network also involves suppliers from other EU countries, the United States and Canada. The supplier network of ASML is a centralized network: owing to its capacity to give or withdraw business, ASML has an important say in the companies in the supplier network. ASML shares this central position with some of its strategic partners, like Carl Zeiss SMT and Philips Electronics.

We will study the knowledge-sharing dynamics in ASML's supplier network by analysing the developments in four innovation projects. These projects, operating in different technological areas and with varying degrees of success, cast an interesting light on the theory and practice of ASML's supply chain management.

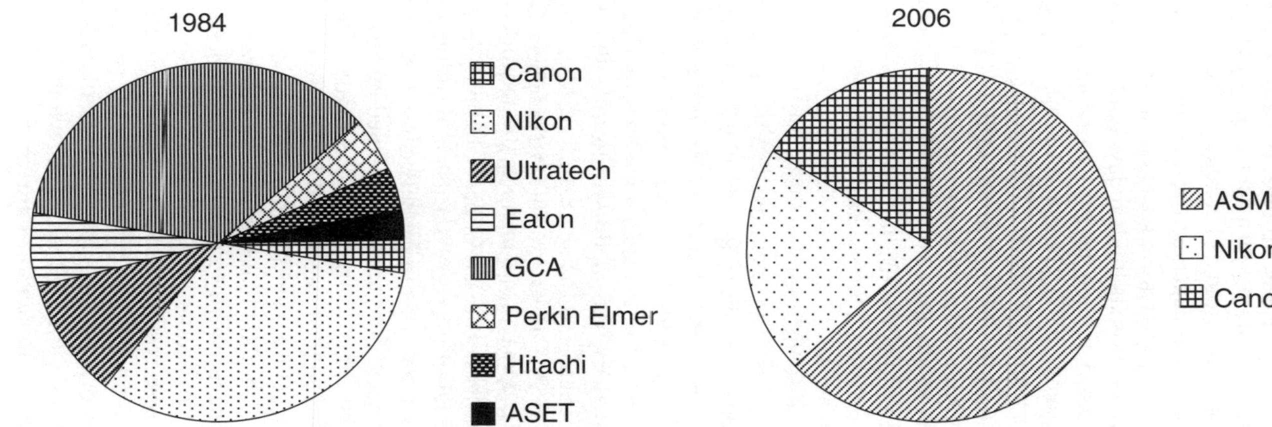

Source: ASML, 2007.

Figure 4.2 Chip lithography market in 1984 and 2006

In ASML's supplier network, several kinds of product and process innovations are being pursued. ASML and its network partners produce a new type of lithography machine every six months. While every new type has a better performance due to incremental improvements, some types feature radical innovations in the underlying technologies. Beside these developments in the core technologies in the lithography machines, the network improves its working processes continuously, in order to shorten development cycles and to improve the controllability of the processes of development, logistics and production. To facilitate these innovations, a wide variety of knowledge is exchanged between ASML and its network partners. These exchanges include both explicit and tacit knowledge, and core and not-so-core knowledge. Explicit knowledge exchange includes project plans, production plans, procedures and policies of ASML, for instance at periodical meetings between a supplier and the account management team of ASML. Tacit knowledge is also exchanged, for instance when engineers from ASML and suppliers in close collaboration strive to solve a technological problem.

In general, the case study concludes that the problems regarding knowledge sharing in networks that were mentioned in the literature (e.g. free-riding, a lack of motivation to share, a lack of efficiency in knowledge localization and knowledge transfer, and the problem of how to cross boundaries) were addressed by implementing a number of solution concepts. These include partner selection, agreement on value distribution, the possibility of using sanctions, the modularization of the network and direct communication. Thanks to the success of ASML, involvement in the supplier network of ASML means business to suppliers. Some suppliers would cease to exist if ASML stopped buying their products, so membership of ASML's supplier network is of crucial importance. The power of ASML to select and reject partners is a mechanism that assures goal alignment between ASML and its suppliers. Because high interests are at stake, most collaboration activities are accompanied by formal contracts, in which agreements on value distribution are made when necessary. Another factor that helps to facilitate effective knowledge sharing in the network is its modular structure. The lithography machines of ASML have a modular nature. Each module is developed by a subset of suppliers within the network. While nobody oversees the entire supplier network of ASML, within a network module only a limited number of companies operate. The people in these companies know each other and collaborate in a number of ways, facilitated by the generally long-term nature of these relationships. In this network, personal relationships and direct communication play an important role, and obstructive behaviour by suppliers, such as free-riding, would cause reputation damage or even withdrawal of (future) business.

Our research indicates that there are significant differences between the 'theory' and the 'practice' of ASML's supply chain management practices. The time pressure in the innovation trajectories, the number of relationships involved, and differences in the managerial and technological quality of the partners cause communication errors and create knowledge-sharing barriers between ASML and its network partners. For weaker partners in particular, this makes it difficult to participate in the ASML network.

In the remainder of this chapter we will first describe the microlithography technology, the semiconductor industry and the technological challenges ASML and its supplier network face. Next we describe ASML's strategies in creating technological leadership in and through its supplier network. We illustrate the day-to-day implications of these strategies by describing four technological projects indepth. Subsequently, we analyse knowledge sharing in this network. We present an overview of the knowledge-sharing problems and discuss the solution concepts that were applied. We conclude our analysis by discussing interesting findings.

MICROLITHOGRAPHY

Making Chips

ASML concentrates on the development and production of lithography systems. These are complex machines that are critical to the production of integrated circuits (IC) or chips. Chips are small pieces of silicon that have integrated circuits printed on them. The production process for a chip (see Figure 4.3) starts with slicing a bar of silicon into thin plates called wafers. This wafer undergoes a process of polishing, followed by repeated steps of coating, lithographic printing of the circuit, developing and baking, etching and ion implantation and removal of the photo-resist layer. Steps 3 to 8 in Figure 4.3 are repeated between 20 and 50 times, building up layers on top of each other which, through relative positioning and patterns, give the IC its characteristics. Finally, when all layers have been completed, the finished wafer is cut into individual dies, the separate identical chips. The machines of ASML are useful for one crucial step in this production process: the lithographic printing of the circuit on a wafer (step 5 in Figure 4.3).

A microlithography machine is made up out of the following units (see Figure 4.4). There is a light source or light-generating unit, like a laser; an illumination unit that controls the light and brings it to the reticle or photomask; a reticle stage on which the reticle is placed; a projection lens unit that projects light passing through the reticle to make an image upon the

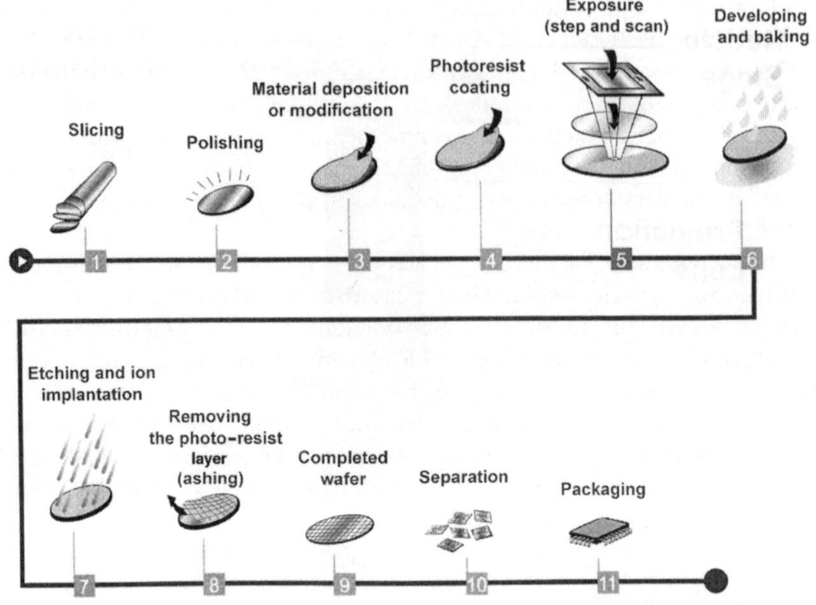

Note: Steps 3–8 can be repeated numerous times

Source: ASML, 2006.

Figure 4.3 The production process of integrated circuits

silicon wafer on which resist or photosensitizer has been applied; a wafer stage upon which a silicon wafer is placed; loading units that convey reticles and wafers to the stages and install them; an alignment (scope) unit that adjusts the stages and other units which are auto-focused along the optic axis when exposed; and a body unit that holds all the above elements. Currently, there are two basic types of microlithography system: the stepper (step and repeat) and a scanner (step and scan). A stepper uses the projection lens to project and expose the IC patterns in a photomask while reticle and wafer stand still. By stepping over the wafer between exposures, the entire wafer is filled with patterns. A step and scan system exposes while the reticle and wafer move (or scan) in opposite directions, and uses a smaller part of the lens to transfer the IC patterns to the wafer. By stepping over the wafer between exposures, the entire wafer is filled with patterns.

The challenge in microlithography is to make chips as small as possible. Where the first IC, made in 1958, held only one transistor, three resistors and a capacitor on a surface the size of an adult's little finger, today an IC

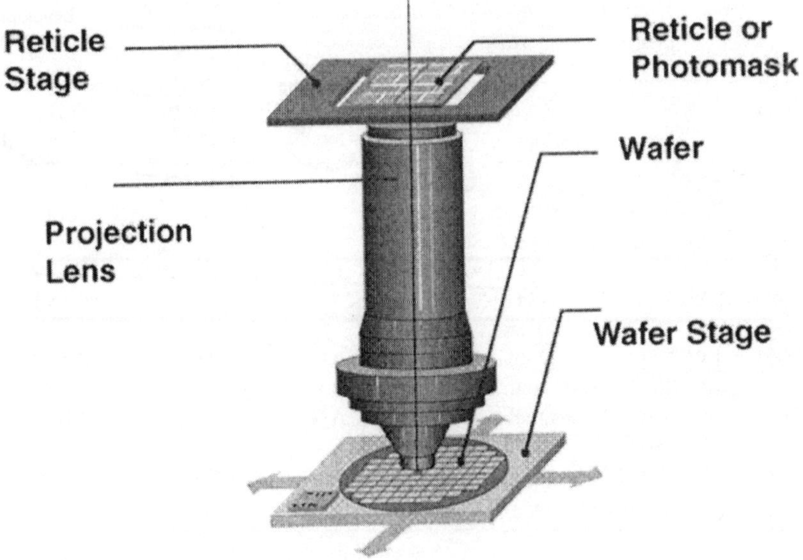

Source: Chuma, 2006.

Figure 4.4 Bare-bone structure of microlithography

smaller than the smallest coin can hold more than 125 million transistors (ASML, 2004, p. 13). The need for miniaturization in the industry follows a pattern, usually referred to as 'Moore's law', based on the observation of INTEL co-founder Gordon Moore who predicted as early as 1965 that the number of transistors on a chip would double every 18 months. What once was an observation now acts as an industry-wide technological roadmap: manufacturers like ASML are striving to make Moore's law a reality. Microlithography is the key enabling technology for this increasing miniaturization of electronics. Currently, ASML's latest lithography equipment (TWINSCAN XT1900i) sets the industry standard in terms of precision and accuracy: it is able to make patterns with a precision of 40 nanometres (0.0000040 mm), which are positioned layer-to-layer with a close control accuracy of 6 nanometres and reach a productivity of 2500 wafers per day. It is indeed as Chuma (2006, p. 395) puts it, 'the ultimate precision tool in human history'. For IC manufacturers, the benefits of further miniaturization are enormous. When chips get smaller, they also work faster because electrons in current have a shorter distance to travel. Smaller chips also require less energy and become cheaper. The costs of operation decrease exponentially, as does the need for temperature control.

Table 4.1 Performance of ASML's PAS products and TWINSCAN products over time

Year	Machine	Key technology	Wave length (nm)	Precision (1000 micron)
1986	PAS 2500		436	0.90
1988	PAS 5000/50	UV light source	365	0.50
1998	PAS 5500	Step & Scan AERIAL illuminator	193	0.28
1999	PAS 5500/700	ATHENA alignment system	193	0.15
2001	TWINSCAN AT 750T	Dual-stage TWINSCAN with KrF light source	248	0.13
2001	TWINSCAN AT 1100	Dual-stage TWINSCAN with ArF light source	193	0.09
2005	TWINSCAN XT 1150i	Immersion	193	0.045

Source: ASML, 2004 and annual reports.

Past and Future Technological Progress

In order to meet their customers' demands for further miniaturization, lithography producers focus on three major performance criteria: imaging, overlay accuracy and throughput productivity. Imaging concerns the precision of the projection of the IC patterns on to the photographic mask. An important way of measuring this is the minimal feature size that the equipment is able to produce. The overlay process concerns the precision in positioning the wafer in relation to the reticle and previous layers, and the quality of the lens. Productivity is measured in terms of wafers per hour, and is determined by the light intensity of the projector, and the speed with which wafers are brought into position, aligned and projected.

Since its founding in 1984, ASML has repeatedly developed different generations of machines to meet rising performance demands. Since the development and production of its first machine, the PAS 2000 in 1985, ASML has developed about 50 new versions of their machines. ASML is currently working on the development and production of two types of machines, the PAS 5500 series and the TWINSCAN series. Table 4.1 provides an indication of the improving performance of this lithography equipment.

The improving performance of the lithography equipment over time has been made possible by a number of new technological developments. Important inventions are the dual-stage system and the immersion technology. The dual-stage system permits the exposure of one wafer while another wafer is being prepared for exposure. This significantly increases the productivity of ASML's systems. With immersion technology, the air flow over the wafer during projection is replaced by purified water. This improves lens resolution by approximately 40 per cent (ASML/Borggreve, 2006).

PARTNERING AS A SOURCE OF COMPETITIVE ADVANTAGE FOR ASML

Developing Core Technological Capabilities

Clearly, lithography equipment is a complex technology. For ASML, control and further development of the key technological competences needed to build the current and new generations of lithography equipment is essential for its survival in the long run.

ASML pursues a number of avenues to secure and develop relevant technological expertise. The foundation of ASML's knowledge base consists of its own R&D employees. About 25 per cent of its total employees are considered to be R&D staff (1244 R&D workers out of 5055 total employees in 2006 (ASML, 2006)), the majority of them (85 per cent) working in Veldhoven, ASML's headquarters. The education level of the R&D workers is high: a substantial number hold a Ph.D. in one of the technological disciplines. ASML also invests heavily in research and development (R&D). In 2005 it invested about €348 million, significantly more (in absolute terms as well as compared to the total number of sales) than its main competitors Nikon and Canon. ASML also draws upon research findings from their relations with top universities and institutes around the world, including Massachusetts Institute of Technology (MIT), Institute for applied scientific research (TNO), IMEC (a research organization aiming to perform R&D, 3 to 10 years ahead of industrial needs, in microelectronics, nanotechnology, design methods and technologies for ICT systems) and Eindhoven University of Technology.

However, the technological leadership of ASML does not only reside in its in-house capabilities. It also draws heavily on technological expertise that is provided by other companies. First, ASML has strategic alliances with firms possessing complementary expertise such as Carl Zeiss SMT and Philips. For instance, Zeiss, a specialist in precision optics and mechanics, designs and produces optical components for the lithography systems such as the project lens. These long-term relationships have enabled ASML to pursue crucial knowledge development in close collaboration with other firms. Second, ASML takes over companies that are considered to have crucial expertise. For instance, in March 2007 ASML acquired Brion Technologies, Inc., a US firm that claims to be the technology leader in computational lithography, which encompasses design verification, reticle enhancement technologies and optical proximity correction. According to CEO Eric Meurice, this will increase the imaging quality and the yield of wafer manufacturing equipment (Meurice, 2007). Third, ASML focuses on the design of lithography equipment from a system integration perspective. The task of actually making the components is, as far as possible, handed over to ASML's supplier base. ASML estimates that 90 per cent of the costs of a lithography system are being supplied by external partners. Its degree of outsourcing is significantly higher than its main competitors Nikon and Canon (see Table 4.2). ASML works with over 500 suppliers (+/− 300 from The Netherlands, 100 from the rest of Europe and another 100 suppliers outside the EU, mostly from the US).

The partnering strategy offers several distinct advantages for ASML. Partnering allows ASML fast access to the latest technological know-how without the requirement of having to be world champion in all areas. These partners make crucial investments in developing new knowledge and capabilities. Also, as technological demands change over time, part-

Table 4.2 Extent of outsourcing of ASML, compared with Nikon and Canon

Components	ASML	Nikon	Canon
Projection lens (development and design)	Zeiss	In-house	In-house
Stage development and design	Philips	In-house	In-house
Light sources			
– Mercury lamp	Ushio	Ushio	Ushio
– DUV	Cymer, Giga Photon	Cymer, Giga Photon	Cymer, Giga Photon
– Body (development and fabrication)	Philips	In-house	In-house
Alignment system	In-house, Philips	In-house	In-house
Software			
– system design	In-house	In-house	In-house
– software development	others	others	others

Source: Adapted from Chuma, 2006.

nering also provides a way to spread the risk of obsolete knowledge as it provides the flexibility to make the necessary adjustments in the supplier base. Lastly, by depending on suppliers to produce a substantial part of its lithography systems, ASML can focus on customer requirements and system integration.

Challenges for Managing Supplier Relations

How to manage supplier relations with over 500 external suppliers? In essence, ASML's strategy is to translate the demands of the semiconductor market into demands on their suppliers. For instance, as the customer expects equipment that is highly reliable and operates virtually fault-free, ASML translates this into demand for high quality components, secured by high degrees of product and process control. The motto here is: 'What our customer expects us to perform is what we expect our suppliers to perform' (ASML/GWO Procurement, 2004).

ASML recognizes four important customer expectations that guide their supply chain management approach:

- Meeting the technological challenges and timelines that arise from the technology roadmap derived from 'Moore's law'. Past experiences have shown that not all suppliers are equally able to change their engineering practices and produce a partly or entirely new product within a short time period;
- Securing the level of quality of the products. A lithography machine that isn't working at the customer site may cause a whole manufacturing site to be down: a very costly situation. 'Zero defects' for the components of lithography equipment is therefore the rule;
- Logistics is another important focus that arises from the characteristics of the semiconductor industry. The semiconductor industry is highly cyclical: at times, the order book may be more than full, at other times, the number of orders is at a much lower level. This makes managing the supply chain a challenging task. In terms of logistic management, it is important that the supply of modules, components and parts is reliable in all situations. Agreements have to be made about the level of components that are being held in stock by the first- and second-tier suppliers, and even further down the supply chain. Furthermore, it is important that suppliers are able to enlarge or shrink their production capacity if customer demand rises. Lastly, both costs and risks of over- or underproduction in the supply chain in case of changes in demand decrease when the production lead time throughout the entire supply chain is as short as possible. Shortening

lead times is therefore another focus in the supply chain management approach.

- Managing costs. The increasing complexity of the equipment has driven up prices. In 2004, the average selling price of new lithography equipment was about €9 million versus about €14 million in 2007 (ASML/DeYoung, 2007). ASML sells its machines by arguing that these high prices are competitive and worth their money due to the enhanced technological possibilities they bring. ASML also has an extended customer support programme to enhance the 'value of ownership' of machines for their customers. In their supply chain, ASML negotiates reasonable prices with their suppliers, to secure the margins of both parties. A critical aspect in these negotiations is which party carries the risk of cancellation of orders by customers or the additional costs of orders rising above the current production capacity. ASML's policy is to equally share the risks and costs associated with these circumstances.

Value Sourcing: Principles and Practices

In a strategy meeting in October 2004 ASML's procurement mission was formulated as follows:

> Create, maintain and qualify a global supplier network that enables the execution of the ASML development, production and customer support plans and operates according to the principles of value sourcing. (ASML/GWO Procurement, 2004)

Value sourcing involves managing the outsourcing process at three levels. At the strategic level, decisions have to be made about which activities will be considered for outsourcing and which will not. An important consideration here is the question whether this activity, and its underlying resources or capabilities, are crucial for ASML's competitive advantage. These decisions are being made by the make-buy board, which operates under the direct supervision of the board of ASML.

At the tactical level, a reliable supply chain for each product family has to be identified and optimized. Cross-functional 'Product family teams', consisting of representatives from Technology, Procurement, Quality, Logistics, Production and Finance, define a supply chain strategy for each product family, based on actual market knowledge and insights into the current suppliers of these product families. Product family teams define the desired performance profile for suppliers of this type of product in terms of quality, logistics, technology and costs ('QLTC'), and evaluate the supply chain in these terms. For some products, state-of-the-art knowledge and the innovation potential of suppliers are of crucial importance, thus suppliers will be evaluated with particular reference to their technological potential. For other more routine products, relevant supplier performance will be formulated in terms of logistics and cost control. The aim of a product family team is to identify a small group of preferred suppliers (with a satisfying performance) for the product line and to develop and maintain long-term relationships with them, by sharing risks and rewards. These long-term relationships are necessary due to the cost and time loss incurred when switching suppliers. A second aim, partly in conflict with the first aim, is the desire of ASML to minimize dependencies. ASML therefore aims for a 'dual sourcing of knowledge, globally, together with the suppliers, and a single, dual, or multiple sourcing of products, where possible or required' (Dijkhuis, 2006). ASML has several reasons to minimize its dependency on suppliers: decreasing dependency means spreading the risk that a supplier won't perform as expected or goes out of business. Decreasing dependency also maintains ASML's dominance in supplier relations, thus enhancing ASML's possibilities for control over the network. Lastly, decreasing dependency is also necessary for the long-term survival of ASML. At the time of our research (2006–7), several suppliers had a very high dependence on ASML; ASML sometimes provides over 50 per cent of the business volume of a supplier. The industry downturn in 2002, when ASML had to cancel over 40 per cent of its orders as customers cancelled theirs, pushed several of these high dependence suppliers into bankruptcy, endangering the survival of the entire supply chain. Therefore it is an important aim of ASML to decrease the level of dependence of suppliers to below 25 per cent.

In a strategic alignment process, ASML seeks to have the strategy of preferred suppliers aligned with its own. Preferred suppliers must be able to handle the characteristics of the semiconductor market, for example to expand or decrease their production capacity. Performance criteria in terms of quality, logistics, technology and costs are critical, so suppliers must agree to work on any deficiency they have in these respects. ASML also wants suppliers to develop their production process technologies to address current and future innovations. Lastly, they should be able to be a preferred supplier for all the products they offer. The alignment of their business plans with ASML's needs secures long-term commitment to ASML. Where necessary, suppliers are being encouraged to use the competences and good reputation they acquire by working for ASML to identify and develop new markets in other segments and thus further decrease their dependence on ASML.

Lastly, at the operational level ASML recently installed Supplier Account Teams that focus on monitoring and improving the performance of a single supplier. The supplier account team consists of a cross-functional team of ASML staff (e.g. technology, purchasing, logistics, customer support, finance) together with their counterparts from the supplier. The starting point for the activities of the Supplier Account Team is the supplier profile, created by the responsible ASML purchaser and discussed with the supplier's management, describing the actual and desired profiles of a supplier in terms of quality, logistics, technology and total cost (QLTC). In case of underperformance on a certain criterion, for example 'delivery reliability', an improvement project is defined to address the issue. If the performance of these suppliers does not improve, the relationship is not immediately terminated. Only if the supplier is structurally not capable of improving its performance will sanctions follow.

SUPPLY CHAIN MANAGEMENT IN PRACTICE: FOUR INNOVATION PROJECTS

Selection of Case Studies

In this section, we discuss the results of our empirical investigation into the day-to-day practice of managing innovation trajectories in the ASML network. For practical reasons, our focus has been on the regional supplier network of ASML. We have selected four innovation projects, conducted in collaboration with four different key suppliers. These innovation projects were selected to cast light on the opportunities as well as the limitations of ASML's supply chain management approach. Thus, our sample includes one highly successful project, one disappointing project and two projects that were successful, but for which some network characteristic problems had to be overcome. So the sample was chosen in order to learn from the contrast between smoothly running projects and more challenging ones; it was not chosen to be representative of all ASML projects. Three or more organizations were involved in each of these projects. Table 4.3 shows the characteristics of these four projects. Each project will be discussed in detail. We will subsequently discuss the knowledge processes and knowledge management solutions that we found in use in ASML's supplier network. We will conclude this section by reflecting on the effectiveness of ASML's supply management approach, as indicated by our case studies.

Four Innovation Projects

Project 'Precision motor 3' and supplier High Gear

The first innovation project concerns a project aimed at the development of a short stroke precision motor for the TWINSCAN XT 1700i. This motor

Table 4.3 Characteristics of the four innovation projects

	Project 'Precision motor 3'	Project 'Moving diaphragm'	Project 'Qualification tool'	Project 'Power amplifier'
Lead Supplier	High Gear	Mechatron	Tooler	Power Electronics
Age	9 years	50 years	85 years	13 years
Partnership	22 years	11 years	22 years	9 years
Dependence	50%	15%	38%	60%
Employees	100	188	135	130
Proximity	175 km	4 km	58 km	15 km
Other parties	4	6	1	1
Project name	Precision motor	Moving diaphragm	Qualification tool	Power amplifier
Goal	New short stroke motorto bring wafers into position	New system to let the reticle move while scanning	Tool to test quality of beam measurement unit	Improved power amplifier for short stroke motor
Duration	8 months	24 months	8 years	9 months
Outsourced project management selection tasks	Project Mgmt Production Logistics	Project Mgmt Supplier selection Production Logistics	Project Mgmt Production	Design Project Mgmt Supplier selection Production Logistics

is part of the mechanics that takes care of the positioning of the reticle stage in relation to the wafer stage. As precision in positioning is of crucial importance for the performance of the lithography equipment, ASML has identified the discipline 'motion' behind such positioning as a core competence for ASML. Motors permitting sub-micron precision are very specialized devices.

The key supplier involved is High Gear, a Philips spin-off specialized in the production of precision motors. High Gear has worked with ASML since ASML's founding in 1984. High Gear employs about 75 people in The Netherlands and another 25 in a second production plant in China. Coming from a dependency of over 80 per cent in 2002, High Gear has reduced ASML sales to the current 50 per cent by opening up new markets and finding new customers for its technological solutions, for instance in the medical equipment market. This is difficult due to the highly specialized nature of its products. High Gear also illustrates the degree to which the ASML industrial complex is interconnected, since some of High Gear's new customers are suppliers to ASML: so, indirectly, High Gear's dependency on the semiconductor market remains. At the same time, ASML has decreased its dependency on High Gear by involving two other suppliers of precision motors. Since the involvement of other suppliers, a product family team for linear motors is in the process of being defined (instead of a single-company-focused supplier account team). As ASML considers precision motor design to be a core competence, they outsource the building of precision motors but not the design of these motors.

The design process for 'Precision motor 3' started in October 2005 as a project executed by the engineering department of ASML. When the design of this motor was finished, at the end of January 2006, the design was transferred to High Gear. Between February and April 2006, High Gear and ASML engineers worked together on the realization of the first prototype. After that, High Gear had about six weeks to realize the first pilot production. As High Gear engineers had not been involved in the design phase, and the first prototype was not perfect, they faced difficulties in translating the first prototype into a product that could be produced in series. High Gear was also in charge of the logistics for this item, purchasing specialized and standard items from other suppliers, and developing logistic plans over the rest of the supply chain. The time available for these tasks appeared to be rather short: High Gear was unable to meet certain important deadlines, which led to aggressive control actions by ASML.

This case study poses some interesting questions about the supply chain management practice of ASML. First, why was High Gear, a known supplier, not involved in the design phase? This would probably have increased the manufacturability of the motor right from the beginning, and would have prevented the problems in the crucial phase in the spring of 2006. This point has already been noted by ASML and the engineers of High Gear are now involved at an early stage in a new innovation project. Second, as ASML strives to create 'preferred suppliers' and the technological capability of High Gear surpasses its main competitors, the question arises why ASML does not enable High Gear to be such a preferred supplier. According to ASML, this is due to the fact that, although High Gear and other suppliers realize good technological performance for their product, this is only a part of what needs to be done. These suppliers are not able to meet ASML's total custom demands for 'motion'.

> If we look at the performance that we deliver to the market in the area of motion, we acknowledge that there is no supplier that has complete fit with ASML in this area. They do so in parts, but there's no 100% fit on a technology. This explains the differences of opinion between these suppliers when we talk about their technological competence. The lack of technological competence in this area is a development constraint. We need to transfer a lot of information to get the supplier up to a level that is needed to realize our machine specifications. (ASML's procurement account manager for High Gear)

Project 'Moving diaphragm' and supplier Mechatron

The second innovation is the project 'Moving diaphragm', also an innovation for the TWINSCAN XT 1700i. The moving diaphragm is a solution for deformation that occurs at the edges of the lighting areas when light is shone through the mask to expose a wafer. The innovation process for this product involves a number of suppliers, with 'Mechatron' as a lead supplier. Mechatron is part of an international holding company. It designs, develops and produces complex machine parts, based on precision mechanics, historically for the defence industry. Mechatron has existed for over 50 years and has been an ASML supplier for about 11 years. Its dependency on ASML is limited, a little over 15 per cent. ASML's relationship with Mechatron is managed via a supplier account team.

The 'Moving diaphragm' project started in May 2004 and finished two years later, in May 2006. In the first year, the product design was created by ASML in close collaboration with an engineering firm that used to be a part of Philips. This choice was due to the fact that Mechatron did not have the technological capability to take care of the entire design for the module, although it would have been able to design parts of it. Mechatron did participate in the design trajectory as producer of the new system and monitored the manufacturability of the new design and the need for tools. They also proposed a number of second-tier suppliers for parts of the module, including the aforementioned supplier High Gear. In May 2005 ASML ordered the delivery of the first five prototypes. At the same time, both at ASML and at Mechatron, the project leaders for this project changed. Soon, the first problems arose in the project. It appeared that the design made by the engineering agency posed a number of unforeseen production problems for Mechatron. In addition to this, the second-tier suppliers raised a number of questions about the functionality of the components they had to deliver, which the new project leader at Mechatron was not able to address or manage properly. Nor did the ASML project leader take appropriate action, which led two ASML group leaders to take over responsibility for the project in October 2005. When the first prototypes were realized, a number of problems arose with regard to the quality of components. For a long time, it was unclear what the root causes of the problems were. Problems mounted to such an extent that the introduction of the new TWINSCAN was endangered. This led ASML to change the entire supplier account team and install a completely new multidisciplinary team, which, together with Mechatron and the second-tier suppliers, worked to rescue the project. This so-called 'tiger team' was introduced in February 2006 and worked until May 2006. The tiger team met with the management of Mechatron each day to discuss what had been done the previous day and the steps to be taken the following day. Along with Mechatron's engineers, ASML engineers visited the second-tier supplier that had been the cause of the quality problems and solved them. The tiger team also made design changes to improve the manufacturability of the product and analysed the lead times in the supply chain for the product. At the same time, there were further changes in specifications for the entire module, overhauling the discussions concerning the quality of the prototypes. Eventually, the first pilot production was realized in June 2006, while release for volume production was realized in October 2006.

This case study casts an interesting light on the actual supply chain management practices of ASML. The problems in this project can be traced back to two root causes. First, although ASML has tried to outsource this project as far as possible, a number of problems arose from the insufficient technological capability of the supplier to make the required design, necessitating the hiring of a separate engineering agency. Second, technological complexity and the number of parties involved in the production of this module required skilful and consistent project leadership. But personnel changes and the inadequate experience of the project leaders involved (at Mechatron as well as ASML) in the second part of the project led to unsolved problems and delays that threatened the entire project. Although ASML initially contributed to the problems, when the urgency of the problems was finally recognized, the 'tiger team' displayed effective problem-solving behaviour to 'save' the project in the end.

Project 'Qualification tool' and supplier Tooler

Qualification tools are needed to test several modules of the lithography equipment to determine whether the module meets the specifications. The qualification tool in this project is a tool developed to test, fine-tune and qualify a beam-measuring unit (BMU) for beams with 248 nanometres wave-length. The tool is also used for the 193 nanometres BMUs, but is only capable of measuring parts of this module.

The main supplier involved was Tooler, a family-owned business that originally worked for the defence industry. Tooler's core competence is the design, production and testing of optical mechanical products. Although optical and electronical components are usually supplied by third parties,

Tooler's specialism lies in providing high-tech assemblies in a clean room environment. Tooler has worked with ASML for quite a long time: 22 years. In the majority of cases, it produces designs made by ASML. As its dependency of ASML is around 38 per cent, Tooler seeks to expand its business to other suppliers. At the same time, ASML is looking for other suppliers of optical-mechanical products.

The qualification tool project started in 1998, when a third-party engineering company was asked to design a new tool. In 1999, the tool was built at ASML and was used to measure the quality of the BMUs. As the BMUs were produced by Tooler, in 2001 ASML decided to hand over the qualification tool as well as the test responsibility to Tooler to enable Tooler to deliver tested BMUs. Tooler was expected to further develop the qualification tool, to develop test protocols and test the BMUs. Unfortunately, the transfer was not accompanied by clear agreements on the development process of the tool, the financial aspects of the project, how communication about the project should run or other key details. In essence, ASML did not want to devote any more resources to the project, as the BMUs functioned reasonably well and resources were needed for other, more pressing problems. Tooler did not know how to improve the qualification tool or develop test protocols, and were not paid to work on it, so they continued to work with the underdeveloped tool as provided by ASML. By 2004, however, assembly of the BMUs appeared to be taking too long in ASML's production department. In addition, several BMUs operating in lithographic systems at customer sites were causing problems. Lastly, BMUs that were held in stock also appeared to have quality problems. The defective BMUs were returned to Tooler, which tested them with the unfinished qualification tool. As Tooler did not find any problems, the BMUs were sent back to ASML, which again found problems. These events made the need for a validated qualification tool apparent. It took almost another year before the urgency was recognized, but in 2005 a project leader at ASML started working again on this project. In mid-2006, the qualification tool was finished for the BMU for wavelength 248. The project included the necessary process changes at Tooler to assure the quality of this type of BMUs. The project took much longer than was expected, due to limited attention from ASML engineers and Tooler's inability to optimize the functioning of the qualification tool, the frequent withdrawal of resources at both parties due to more pressing problems, a lack of technological capability at Tooler to address emerging difficulties and engineering change management problems.

This project casts an interesting light on what happens to projects that are not considered to be of strategic relevance. In essence, in this project there was no high-level technological challenge to be met; in the words of ASML's procurement account manager for Tooler: 'The ball was right in front of the goal and only needed to be kicked in'. The long timeline for this project can be traced back to the lack of project priority, insufficient project management attention and resource withdrawals. The issues in this project were apparently also missed by the procurement account manager and the supplier account team. Although the project had a low priority for most of its duration, the lack of an adequate qualification tool caused serious quality problems for the BMUs at the customers' sites, leading to costly downtime for the lithography equipment for the customer, as well as costly repair actions for ASML. Apparently, ASML's successful focus on high velocity technological innovation comes at the cost of quality problems and high repair costs when underlying tools are not available and development of them is not actively managed.

Project 'Power amplifier' and supplier Power Electronics

The fourth innovation project concerns a project aimed at the development of a switching amplifier with digital control for the power supply of the short stroke precision motor 3 in the TWINSCAN XT 1700i. Although power amplifiers can be bought in the market, the combination of high power levels with nanometer accuracy requires that amplifiers and power supplies are tailor-made for each new type of lithography equipment.

The main supplier involved was Power Electronics, a young company (13 years old) that started as a spin-off from Eindhoven University of Technology but now employs about 130 people. Power Electronics develops technological solutions in fields like motion control, digital processing and power electronics. Since 1999 it has also produced the technological solutions it designs, made possible by the necessary investments in production machinery and a production site. Both the production site and the development departments are conveniently located at a 15 km distance from ASML. Power Electronics has invested significant time and money in optimizing its design and production processes. It is therefore capable of developing new designs 'the first time right' resulting in products with a 100 per cent level of quality, all within reliable timelines. Collaboration with ASML started nine years ago.

Since then, collaboration between Power Electronics and ASML has increased significantly. Power Electronics was one of the first suppliers of ASML to sign a long-term agreement, which covers among other things agreements on the preferred supplier status, the supplier performance, intellectual property and the non-hiring of each other's employees. In 2007, Power Electronics was dependent on ASML for nearly 60 per cent of its turnover. As this is well beyond the 25 per cent dependence ASML aims for, both parties strive to decrease this dependency while maintaining their good relationship. Power Electronics is highly active in the development of new products and markets, such as control components for other types of high-tech equipment and robotics for consumer applications. ASML has approached some other power electronics suppliers to outsource the production of some components and hopes to be able to involve these parties in design issues in the next few years. In the mean time, the relationship with Power Electronics is managed by a supplier account team.

In contrast to the previous three suppliers, Power Electronics has the privilege to participate in new development projects at a very early stage. This was also the case in the innovation project aimed at the development of a switching amplifier with digital control for the power supply of the short stroke precision motor 3. The start of the project in the autumn of 2005 went smoothly. Based on the performance characteristics of the new lithography equipment, ASML engineers developed the elementary design specifications for the new amplifier. The joint design process that followed involved brainstorm meetings and design activities conducted by both parties. When a general design was approved, Power Electronics made the product design, a first prototype and the first small series. ASML reviewed the several mid-term deliverables and monitored the design process in terms of cost efficiency, the realization of design criteria and the fit with the final TWINSCAN equipment. Small changes in requirements were made during the process, which is common for this kind of project. ASML tested the amplifier for the first time in the machine in the autumn of 2006 and then started to assemble the first TWINSCAN 1700i machines. At this point in time, a major problem came to light. The designers of ASML had overlooked one specification element, regarding the linearity of the amplifier. Although the exact specifications of the amplifier had been agreed upon two years before, initial testing now revealed that the amplifier needed to be 40 times as precise for the improved performance of the new TWINSCAN machine to be possible. The project leader at Power Electronics said:

> What popped up was core. Look, a factor 2 can be reached by optimizing things, but a factor 40 or more has quite some impact. Anyway, ASML's story was also very clear: we need this improvement by factor 40 or we cannot build the new machine. We recognized that too, and saw it as a challenge. You see, our goal is to make sure that those machines leave ASML in time. So we took a look inside to see what was possible.

In open deliberation with the TWINSCAN 1700i steering committee, ASML and Power Electronics agreed that Power Electronics would design, develop, produce and test a new version of the amplifier within little more than six weeks. The normal production time for a device like this would be about 12 weeks. In order to make this timeline, Power Electronics had to make significant efforts to develop a new design, reserve production capacity, organize new components (which in some cases also had to be newly developed) and so on. When Power Electronics foresaw that they would not make it within this tight deadline, ASML and Power Electronics agreed that Power Electronics would send out 'preprotos': first prototypes that are only tested to a limited extent, but that allowed ASML engineers to start testing the complete machine. Until the new amplifier was fully developed and tested, Power Electronics and ASML worked with two activity lines: producing the original amplifier, and one stream of activity aimed at developing, testing and producing the newly developed amplifier. This enabled ASML to send out their new machines as agreed upon with their customers.

This project casts an interesting light on the achievements of two organizations that are able to collaborate closely. The relationship with Power Electronics differs from the relationship with other partners in a number of ways. First, Power Electronics is highly competent technologically. According to their supply chain manager at ASML, Power Electronics has earned a privileged position within ASML due to past performance. Their technological competence in power electronics is very high and so is their level of logistic process control and quality control. Second, unlike the other three cases, Power Electronics is involved in the design process of new generations of machines, right from the point where the specifications for the new machine have become clear. Third, Power Electronics is allowed to choose its own suppliers, and manages its own library of components. ASML trusts Power Electronics to such an extent, that it allows Power Electronics to work on a critical component on the basis of 'best effort'. Fourth, the communication with Power Electronics is better structured and more intense than with the other partners.

The level of trust between these two companies has huge benefits for both companies. ASML is able to outsource nearly all design and production activities in this area to Power Electronics. It can rely on the competence of Power Electronics to make the next generation of designs and even to solve problems produced by ASML itself. Power Electronics derives significant business from ASML. It learns from ASML's way of managing supplier relations and is able to maintain its high level of process control due to the early supplier involvement it has gained with ASML. This case can therefore be seen as exemplary, both in terms of the way ASML works with this supplier and in terms of the benefits the close collaboration brings.

In fact, for ASML it is a point of debate to what extent it can allow another organization such as Power Electronics to take over responsibilities. In order to maintain ASML's competence in the area of power electronics, another design in this area has been developed by ASML independently. However, the design has been reviewed by Power Electronics engineers and the production of this component has been outsourced to Power Electronics.

KNOWLEDGE MANAGEMENT PROCESSES AND SOLUTIONS IN THE ASML SUPPLIER NETWORK

To what extent was knowledge shared in the ASML network and which solution concepts to facilitate these processes appeared to be in place? Here we follow the research framework that was described in Chapter 1.

Type of Knowledge Exchanged

In the ASML network, the organization of knowledge exchange seems not to be a goal in itself. Knowledge exchange actually happens as a by-product of other types of interactions. We have noted some exceptions to this rule. For instance, Power Electronics and ASML organized bilateral competence meetings to exchange specific technological knowledge and Mechatron has invested in multiple site visits to ASML to increase its understanding of ASML's production processes. In both cases, tacit as well as explicit knowledge was exchanged.

In the majority of cases, however, core technological knowledge is exchanged to a limited extent. ASML and its suppliers try to integrate their knowledge. They try to use each other's knowledge as building blocks to realize something that neither of them would have been able to do on their own. ASML is the provider of innovative designs, but needs the production expertise of its suppliers to translate the design into a physical product. Exchanges between suppliers themselves follow the same logic. Each network partner maintains, develops and protects its own technological competence base. Agreements protecting intellectual property are in use to make sure that technological knowledge does not accidentally spill over to competitors. Yet formal knowledge exchange practices are not standard practice.

Explicit knowledge exchange includes several innovation process milestone documents, 'elementary product specification', 'elementary design specification' and the 'technical product specification'. The technical product specification contains the final design of the product that guides the production process. When products are taken into volume production, two information systems (the Q-portal and the L-portal) are used. Logistic information on forecasting and expediting is exchanged within the L-portal. Quality information on non-conforming products, such as defect products, is exchanged within the Q-portal. ASML also provides a machine production plan as well as a forecast of future production on a weekly basis. The suppliers use these plans and forecasts to plan their own production, stocks and purchasing decisions. This is how explicit knowledge is transferred and exchanged between parties.

In the cases that were studied we documented several interventions by ASML to address specific problems. The 'tiger team' at Mechatron is the most notable example here. Close collaboration between ASML and Mechatron to address the problems in the moving diaphragm project permitted in-depth knowledge exchange about the managerial challenges of Mechatron and techniques to address these. ASML's focus on supplier performance also partly serves as a learning vehicle. ASML expects to get insight into the supplier network of the supplier and requires suppliers to write a technological competence development plan. It also stimulates partners to look for new markets for their technological solutions, so that their dependency on ASML is reduced. In this sense, ASML provides a strong learning trigger for its suppliers. However, this is where ASML stops. It signals the required actions a supplier needs to take, but it does not transfer management best practices to them that might help them implement the desired action. In ASML's view, this is the supplier's responsibility.

Impact of Network Type

The ASML supplier network has brought forth multiple innovations. Most partners have long-term relationships with ASML, even though ASML gives no guarantees that partners will be involved in the next project. The many long-term relationships in the ASML network, as well as the cultural and physical proximity between most suppliers, enables efficient knowledge exchange. This is illustrated by many stories about problematic exchanges with new foreign suppliers: new suppliers have great difficulty in understanding the ways of working within ASML, which leads to miscommunication and a lack of responsiveness, for instance about the need to change specifications late in a project. An important element in the network success is ASML's power: the network is highly centralized, with ASML dictating to the partners. The effect is that knowledge sharing is essentially centralized and controlled by ASML. Direct knowledge sharing between other partners in the network does not appear to take place unless they are working on a module together.

Occurrence of Knowledge-sharing Problems and Knowledge Management Solutions

In the literature, four problems with knowledge sharing in networks are reported: a lack of motivation to share knowledge, free-riding on each

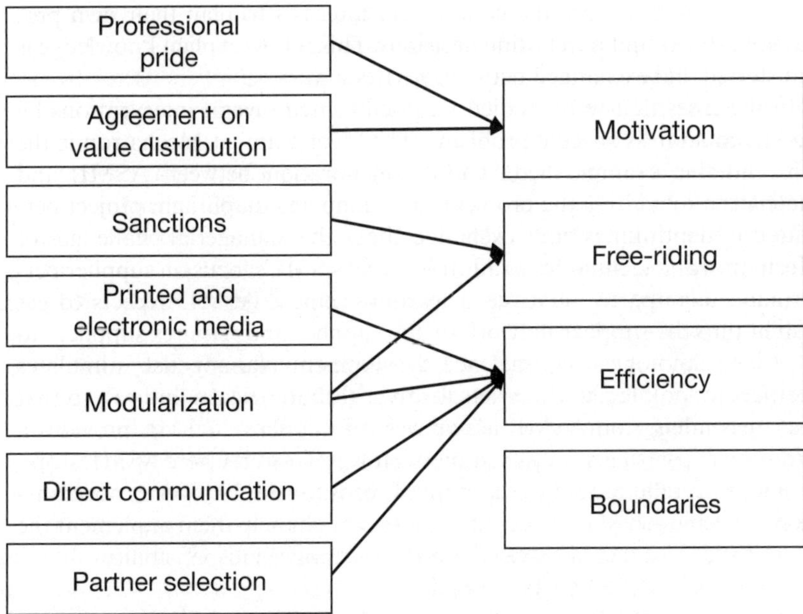

Figure 4.5 Solution concepts in the ASML network

other's knowledge, problems with efficiently finding and sharing knowledge and the problem of crossing physical or cultural boundaries. These problems may be overcome by implementing multiple knowledge management solutions. Figure 4.5 shows which solution concepts are applied in the ASML network.

Based upon our case studies, only a few problems regarding the motivation to share knowledge were observed. The main reason for this is that the parties' economic interest in sharing knowledge when necessary is high. The professional pride that the technicians in the ASML network have also contributes to a high motivation to share knowledge. Having ASML as a client improves the supplier's and technician's reputation and competences considerably, making it easier to gain new clients for the supplier. Another enabling factor is the clear agreements on value distribution. Contracts about supplies, organizational performance and intellectual property make it very clear which knowledge and products should be supplied by which partner. Where this was not clear, as in the qualification tool project, difficulties arose.

The free-rider problem seems to be only a minor problem in the ASML network. The modular structure of the network makes it difficult for suppliers to free-ride on the achievements of other partners, because in many cases suppliers are individually responsible for the module they have to deliver. Free-rider behaviour may occur when suppliers use or transfer knowledge developed together with ASML or other network partners for the products of competitors. However, the long-term relations and mutual dependence between ASML and its key suppliers, as well as contracts on intellectual property rights, make free-riding less likely. The main sanction against free-riding is that ASML has the possibility to exclude the supplier from further business. In connection with this, there is also a chance of reputation damage, as most suppliers know each other and may need each other on a future occasion.

Like free-riding, efficiency of knowledge transfer appears not to be an important problem at the network level. Modularization limits the need to set up communication channels between all suppliers in the entire network: relationships usually only exist between suppliers that participate in developing a specific module. It is a small world: most supplier organizations know each other very well and in most cases have worked together before. The small world is illustrated by the different kinds of relationships in the network: some first-tier suppliers to ASML (e.g. High Gear) are also second-tier suppliers to another first-tier supplier (e.g. Mechatron). Some second-tier suppliers of ASML produce components with the aid of a lithography system supplied by ASML and are both customer and supplier.

The efficiency of knowledge exchange in the network is further enabled by some other solution mechanisms. These include the use of electronic media (to exchange documents with technical and logistical information), direct communication (especially the exchange of information when a design is handed over to a supplier and communication in the supplier account teams) and partner selection (aiming to find partners with such competences so as to minimize the required communication). The efficiency of knowledge transfer between ASML and partners is clearly hampered by regular personnel changes at ASML and the suppliers. This requires new personal relationships to be built up frequently.

The most important boundary to be crossed in the ASML network is the difference caused by diverse technological knowledge and capabilities of different partners. As ASML makes a distinction between knowledge for development and knowledge for manufacturing, there is automatically a difference in the types of knowledge suppliers have. In addition, there is a difference in education levels: ASML staff are mainly university trained, whereas suppliers employ few people with a university background. Important problems, however, are not always of a technological nature: the managerial capabilities of some suppliers are not always up to standard. For example, not all suppliers are capable of managing their own suppliers.

ASML has no knowledge management mechanism in place to remedy this situation, other than evaluating the suppliers on these issues and communicating what their performance is. Cultural problems appear limited, because a substantial section of ASML suppliers (and the cases that we studied) are located in the same region as ASML, facilitating communication. ASML's strategy to extend and internationalize the supplier base to limit dependency could make this problem more pressing in the future.

When comparing ASML's network management policy with the reality of these cases some points come to light. First of all, not all elements of ASML's network management approach are implemented in all cases. Supplier account teams or product family teams did not exist in some cases, although the need for them was recognized and articulated. This may be explained by the timing of our study, as the full implementation of the value sourcing strategy was still a work in progress. Another aspect is the lack of early supplier involvement. The cases of High Gear and Mechatron illustrate that not involving suppliers in the design phase may generate problems in the pilot phase, when the manufacturability of components comes to a first test. Finally, considering the need to constantly enhance both the technological and the managerial capabilities in ASML's supplier network, it is surprising to see how few explicit knowledge-leveraging initiatives exist in the network. Only Power Electronics mentioned the use of effective knowledge exchange practices such as competence meetings and collaborative design meetings with ASML's engineers.

CONCLUSION

ASML is a highly successful organization that depends to a large extent on its supplier network. In order to manage its supplier network, ASML uses a value-based sourcing strategy. This is an approach centred around the idea of leveraging the performance of suppliers as well as decreasing dependency on the network. Our research has focused on the theories and realities of this network approach, with particular attention to the knowledge management practices.

Our research revealed that ASML is successful even though the number of mechanisms implemented to ensure successful knowledge management in the network is low. This is surprising, considering the increasing and high demands on the network partners in terms of their technological competence. The explanation for ASML's success, despite the limited attention it pays to knowledge management, centres around ASML's project-based approach. Technological knowledge is not shared at the network level, but pooled and integrated in the individual projects that are initiated to realize the next generation of lithography equipment. This ties in with the modular structure of the ASML products, which largely defines the network structure. Knowledge is predominantly exchanged at the level of modules, reducing the need to implement numerous knowledge management mechanisms across the entire network. On the other hand, the Power Electronics case shows that on a bilateral level attention to knowledge management makes a positive difference.

We also found that meeting the technology roadmaps poses increasing managerial challenges for both ASML and its network partners. Although the value-sourcing strategy of ASML does include the monitoring and improvement of suppliers' technological as well as managerial competence, formal knowledge exchange mechanisms directed at improving supplier technology management competence were absent.

Our case studies have shown that apart from managing time constraints and priority of projects, supplier capability is critical. The use of knowledge management solutions requires high quality partners, both technologically and managerially. When the technological and managerial skills of partners do not pass a minimum threshold, knowledge management becomes difficult. Partner selection and supplier capability development are important in meeting tomorrow's technological challenges in the fascinating nano-world of ASML.

NOTE

1. This case study is based on multiple data sources, including interviews, observations of meetings, presentations, 8 months on-site presence by one of the authors, site visits to suppliers, archival data and company documents. The Director of R&D (Harry Borggreve) and one of the Supply Chain Directors (Hans Dijkhuis) gave us access to ASML. In order to study the day-to-day practices of knowledge exchange in the supplier network, we agreed to study four technology development projects in depth, involving four different suppliers: 'Tooler', 'High Gear', 'Mechatron' and 'Power Electronics' (the names are pseudonyms). To enable learning, not only successful projects were chosen, but also some that experienced difficulties. This enabled us to contrast smoothly running projects with more challenging ones. For that reason, this set of projects is not representative for all ASML's projects. For each project, we interviewed project leaders, project employees and directly responsible managers within ASML, as well as their counterparts at the supplier, to uncover differences in interpretation of key events and dilemmas (Eling, 2007). We conducted 27 semi-structured interviews in total, each lasting between 1 and 1.5 hours. All interviews were conducted by two or more researchers to enhance reliability (Eisenhardt, 1989a). We recorded and fully transcribed all interviews. For each supplier, we drew up a description of the supplier's perspective on their relationship with ASML and the key events in their innovation project. The supplier verified the description. A full case description was developed for all four cases (Eling, 2007). All data were analysed by developing codes based on the conceptual model (see Chapter 1), ascribing codes to the transcripts of interviews, documents and archival data and developing data displays as described by Miles and Huberman (1984).

REFERENCES

ASML (2004), *Reflect & Imagine, 20 years of ASML*, Veldhoven: ASML N.V.

ASML/GWO Procurement (2004), *Procurement Strategy and Objectives 2005*, Veldhoven: ASML N.V.

ASML (2006), *Annual Report 2006*, Veldhoven: ASML N.V.

ASML/Borggreve, H. (2006), *Introduction ASML*, Veldhoven: ASML N.V.

ASML/DeYoung, C. (2007), *Presentation for Bear Stearns 18th Annual Technology Conference*, Veldhoven: ASML N.V.

Chuma, H. (2006), 'Increasing complexity and limits of organization in the microlithography industry: implications for science-based industries', *Research Policy*, **35**, 394–411.

Dijkhuis, H. (2006), 'Value Sourcing: QLTC performance in each phase of the life cycle', *Kennisbank Inkoop en Logistiek*.

Dyer, J.H. and K. Nobeoka (2000), 'Creating and managing a high-performance knowledge sharing network: the Toyota case', *Strategic Management Journal*, **21**, 345–67.

Eisenhardt, K.M. (1989a), 'Building theories from case study research', *Academy of Management Review*, **14**, 532–50.

Eisenhardt, K.M. (1989b), 'Making fast strategic decisions in high-velocity environments', *Academy of Management Journal*, **32** (3), 543–76.

Eling, P. (2007), 'Knowledge sharing: a source of value', Masters thesis, Eindhoven University of Technology.

IPO (2005), *Top 300 Organizations Granted Patents in 2005*, Washington: IPO.

Meurice, E. (2007), 'Wow' (Comments on ASML annual results over 2006), *Financieele Dagblad*, 18 January.

Miles, M.B. and A.M. Huberman (1984), *Qualitative Data Analysis*, Thousands Oaks, CA: Sage.

5. The Future Store Initiative: shopping for knowledge/knowledge for shopping[1]

Ard-Pieter de Man and Tim Graczewski

Building the retail store of the future with widely different partners requires much attention to the governance of knowledge and innovation processes. The German supermarket chain METRO did so effectively. This case highlights the importance of informal solution concepts, in combination with a clear vision, a strong lead partner and a tight deadline in bringing about the desired result. This recipe worked for the 50 companies that needed to come together to create an entirely new shopping experience.

INTRODUCTION

'The Future Store Initiative is our R&D lab', says Gerd Wolfram, METRO Group's managing director of Information Technology and leader of the Initiative. 'By creating a real-life future store METRO Group and partners are able to test and develop new technologies that form the basis of innovation in retailing.' This, in essence, describes METRO Group's Future Store Initiative, a working supermarket in which a number of new concepts and technologies for the retail industry are developed and tested in practice. Initiated by the German-based METRO Group, the world's third largest retailer, the Future Store Initiative brings together 58 companies[2] that jointly aim to drive innovation in the retail sector and to set technology standards for the industry. Among the new technologies developed in the store are customer-friendly technologies enabling automated check-out and vegetable weighing scales that recognize the products that are put on them to be weighed. One of the core technologies implemented is RFID,[3] for which METRO Group wanted to develop a non-proprietary standard for retail.

The comparison with an R&D lab is appropriate: for METRO Group, the Future Store is a testing ground for new retail concepts. They can test not only the technological feasibility of new concepts, but also the way clients react to them. The Future Store Initiative model was developed, in part, by one of the lead partners in the Future Store Initiative, micro-chip manufacturer Intel, who has used partners as a component of its R&D process in the past. By involving companies in the R&D process as partners who invest, contribute and actively share their ideas, the development and implementation of the technologies would be accelerated, while METRO Group distributed the costs and risks as well. Moreover, by making use of the competences and knowledge of dozens of companies, it was likely that more innovative solutions would be proposed. Additionally, the presence of numerous partners increases the chance that standards actually get accepted. Crucially, the store is not an experimental setting, but a real-life store with real clients. This makes it possible to measure the effects of innovation on efficiency, productivity, customer satisfaction and sales.

The reason behind the Future Store Initiative is strategic. The retail environment is subject to significant change. Some important changes are (van Weele, 2005):

- Changing consumer behaviour. Changes in consumer behaviour have a major impact on the retailer's product-market strategies. It is the retailer's job to identify these changes in time and to translate them into new product concepts and design new shelf displays and shop layouts. The following are typical of changes that confront retail organizations in European countries: ageing population, ongoing individualization. This means that retailers must constantly tailor their product assortment to ever more specific, and often smaller, target groups. This results in a wider variety of products and an increased complexity with regard to managing the incoming and outgoing goods flow.
- Concentration. Especially in retail and food manufacturing globalization of competition and concentration through mergers and acquisitions are characteristic developments. It is also expected that there will be fewer and fewer suppliers of food products in the near future and, as a result, retail companies will be dealing primarily with a few very large manufacturers. In pursuing cost reductions and operational efficiencies relentlessly, this will lead to larger integration of operational activities between the partners involved.
- International cooperation. Due to the concentration of power on the suppliers' side, many trade companies are diligently searching for possibilities with which to counterbalance this development. Internationalization is an option seen by many. It can be difficult to realize internationalization of retail organizations. In Europe, for

example, the market often turns out to be culturally determined or dependent on the country.

- Private labels. More and more retail companies have embraced private labels or company brands. Private labels support retailer identity and their (quality) image. By purchasing products, giving them a company label and taking over the promotion, the retailer will have the advantage of a higher margin. This margin can only be sustained if retailers develop highly integrated operations systems with these suppliers, which requires agreement on information standards, systems and quality and logistics procedures.
- Space management. Since shelf-space is limited, the extensive product lines offered by manufacturers force the retailer to make a selection. In this context computerized space-management systems may support the retailer. They enable the simulation of several display layouts (for a different number of facings) based on detailed cost information, to decide on the most profitable layout.
- 'Green' issues. Ecological considerations are growing in importance. This started initially with the replacement of artificial flavourings and odours by natural products. At present the emphasis is on biodegradable packing materials, PVC-less packaging and a minimum of blister packs. Today, retailers are increasingly becoming aware that they can improve their brand image by offering a wide range of green products.
- Information. Information technology is an important tool for any retailer, enabling new supply chain concepts and supporting advanced costing systems. Some developments in information technology have an immediate impact on the consumer, affecting their preferences. They are manifest in, for instance, electronic banking, barcoding and teleshopping.

These trends lead to commoditization of retail products. Together with the entry of hyper-efficient retailers into the global grocery market, they have altered how retailers compete. These developments illustrate why retail business today is such a turbulent business to be in. The future competition in this industry is not so much determined by the effectiveness and competitiveness of individual companies. It is rather determined by the effectiveness and competitiveness of the retail firm and its supply chain partners, including manufacturers, IT providers, logistics providers and transport forms.

The senior leadership at METRO recognized that to be successful over the next few years and beyond, the traditional retailing mindset of competing on price, location or selection needed to be replaced. In order to

Source: Boston Consulting Group and METRO Group.

Figure 5.1 Strategic positions of major retailers

remain competitive, innovation was thought to be a top priority. By focusing on technology and service, METRO Group believes it is possible to distinguish itself from major competitors (Figure 5.1).

The first discussions of the concept that became the Future Store began in Düsseldorf, on 11 September 2001. The meeting was attended by high-level METRO and Intel representatives. At this meeting and in subsequent conversations, the idea of a Future Store came together. This consisted of four principles.

First, the Future Store would be an operational store with real customers. If METRO was to fulfil its goal of developing an enduring advantage in customer experience that translated into greater profitability, they would need to get feedback from their customer base. A traditional R&D lab might have been more convenient and might have had lower costs, but it would also mean sacrificing the opportunity to derive lessons in a real world environment. Also, the project would be open-ended, so that new ideas could be introduced in it continuously.

Second, the Store would take a holistic view of the customer experience and store operations. They would innovate with RFID and collaborative wireless devices for the store managers, but also experiment with more prosaic retailing issues, such as store layout and lighting, the idea being that the combination of multiple innovations in one setting might lead to fundamental changes in the shopping experience.

Third, METRO was determined to be a leader in the development of technology standards around RFID that are certain to change the way retailers around the world operate. To that end, it was critical that METRO identify and recruit partners with expertise across the range of technologies and services necessary to enable a successful RFID implementation, from chip, inlay, tag and reader makers to software and services firms capable of gathering and analysing information across the supply chain.

Finally, it was agreed that this vision of a holistic and fully operational Future Store could only be created with the dedicated participation of partners. METRO recognized that it did not have the required competences and resources to create the Store they envisioned.

PARTNER SELECTION

The first question to be addressed in creating the Future Store alliance network was the type of partners required. Six types of partners are found in the network (see Figure 5.2): RFID, trade technology (partners delivering a technology specific to retail), brands (producers of consumer goods), IT technology and services, software and other services. The network of partners is cross-industry. Companies with different backgrounds and different knowledge bases need to collaborate.

A second issue to be dealt with in setting up the alliance network was that not all partners were likely to be involved with the same intensity throughout the Initiative. Some partners may be relevant for a number of the various innovation projects set up in the Future Store Initiative. Others may participate in only one. In order to strike a good balance between investments and engagement for all these partners, the Future Store Initiative used three levels of partnerships (platinum, gold, silver) reflecting the different level of participation and resources partners would commit. Three

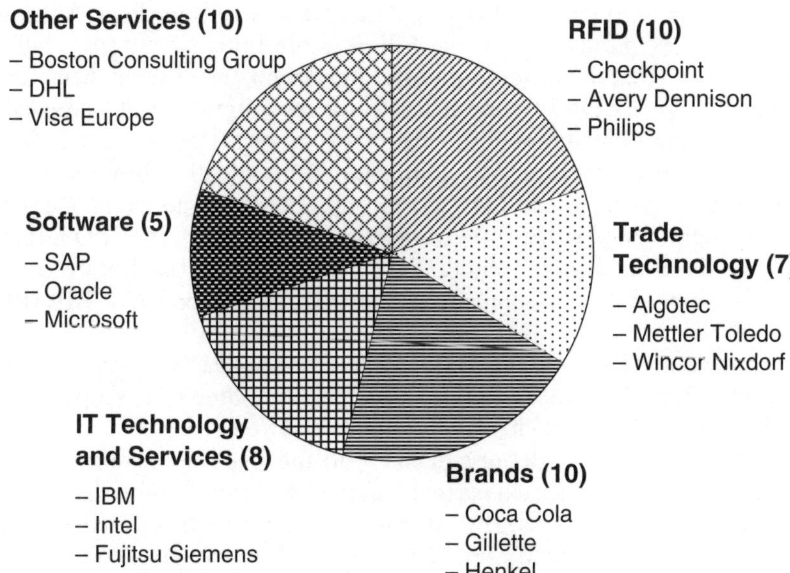

Figure 5.2 Type and number of partners in the Future Store Initiative (May 2005)

companies participated at the platinum level prior to the Future Store Initiative's launch: Intel, SAP and IBM.

Having decided on the basic three-tier structure of the alliance network, partner identification and recruitment was the next step. In order to ensure the correct partners were selected, the next principles for partner selection were adhered to. Logically, the innovative and technological competences of partners were the first partner selection criterion. Second, nearly all the original participants had long-standing personal relationships with the Initiative's leadership team. These were relationships that were forged during previous collaboration in the German retail market. Over time mutual respect and trust was built up between the persons involved. Moreover, many of the participants had similar relationships with other partners that METRO Group recruited, so the initial team resembled a web of personal relationships, all converging on the METRO Group leadership team and interconnected. In the event, there was no pre-existing personal relationship with certain types of firms, such as RFID chip manufacturers. METRO Group looked to the inner circle of partner participants to reach out to companies that they maintained a close relationship with and which had earned a certain level of trust. In the RFID example, METRO group relied on partner Philips to recruit Avery Denison, one of the world leaders in RFID technology.

Third, for most partners METRO Group is a significant client. As partners not only participated in the Future Store Initiative but also had a normal business relationship with METRO Group, this ensured their commitment. As METRO Group had a good reputation with its suppliers, companies were predisposed to support the project. However, the Future Store Initiative was separated completely from all other business deals between the partners and METRO Group. There was no guarantee that technologies tested in the store would also be bought by METRO Group for all its other stores. Neither did participation in the Future Store Initiative mean that a company would become a supplier to METRO Group.

Fourth, METRO Group recruited partners to take on very specific, predefined roles within the Future Store. Given the ambitious scope of the Future Store Initiative, it was inevitable that some partner companies would be competitors. Because of the short timeline before launch, it was also important to keep each partner focused on completing their project as quickly as possible. By clearly establishing what a partner's contribution and responsibility were METRO Group was able to mitigate internal competition within the network. The Future Store Initiative's core partner team of Intel, SAP and IBM are essentially non-competitive and were thus able to stake out their critical project areas at the beginning. Thereafter, partner companies would be presented with a specific opportunity to participate in the Future Store Initiative, such as providing the database infrastructure to the project (Oracle).

Finally, each participant company was asked to make a financial contribution to the joint development and marketing of the Future Store, in addition to the indirect costs of employee time and physical products contributed. This ensured that all partners were risk-bearing. Willingness to bear risk was the fifth element of partner selection.

To ensure collaboration, partners needed to have a clear view of the value the Future Store Initiative would deliver them. Their incentives to collaborate were:

- Strategic fit. Many partners asked to become a member of the network noted that the fit of the Future Store Initiative with the company strategy was an important reason to accept the invitation. One company noted: 'The Future Store Initiative filled the gap between our own R&D and the early learnings from (pilot) implementations. We had identified retail as a spearhead so this opportunity matched our priorities seamlessly'.
- Learning. Especially for technology companies, gaining an understanding of the effect of their technologies in a real-life situation was

very valuable. This enabled them to better understand the business implications of their technology, making it easier to explain the benefits to potential customers. After the store had been open for some time, the Future Store Initiative researched the use of different technologies implemented in the store and showed that most of them had a positive impact on sales and customer loyalty (METRO Group, 2003). In early 2005, some partners reported that more learning and data mining should take place in this area.

- Marketing and publicity. METRO Group was known for its ability to create publicity. The Future Store Initiative partners expected to obtain wide media exposure and stated that the expectation of media exposure by itself was sufficient to make the investments required. An evaluation presented at a partner meeting in 2004 showed that media exposure had indeed been extraordinary (METRO Group, 2004), with hundreds of articles being published in the worldwide press.
- Smaller companies invited into the network gained access to partners they would not have had access to under different circumstances. Small innovative companies were able to showcase their technology before some of the leading companies.

Partners would be allowed into the network at a later stage depending on the needs of the Future Store Initiative. This implied some free-riding could take place as late entrants could build on the achievements of the Future Store, without having run much risk themselves. However, most partners agreed that the way value was divided was clear and fair. The basic partner network was in place in the summer of 2002.

GOVERNANCE OF THE FUTURE STORE INITIATIVE

Figure 5.3 shows the structure of the Future Store Initiative network. In order to manage the large number of partners a network governance structure was developed. METRO Group and the three platinum partners meet regularly at the Executive Committee. The Executive Committee is responsible for admitting new partners and ending relationships, if necessary. It also reviews and approves cash outlays from the Initiative's fund (in which the cash contributions from partners are deposited), after consensus has been achieved about specific investments to be made. For the rest, partners are responsible for their own expenses and investments in the store. All partners are invited to the two to three annual meetings of the Marketing Committee. This committee reviews and evaluates progress and METRO Group shares its future plans with partners there as well. Next there are

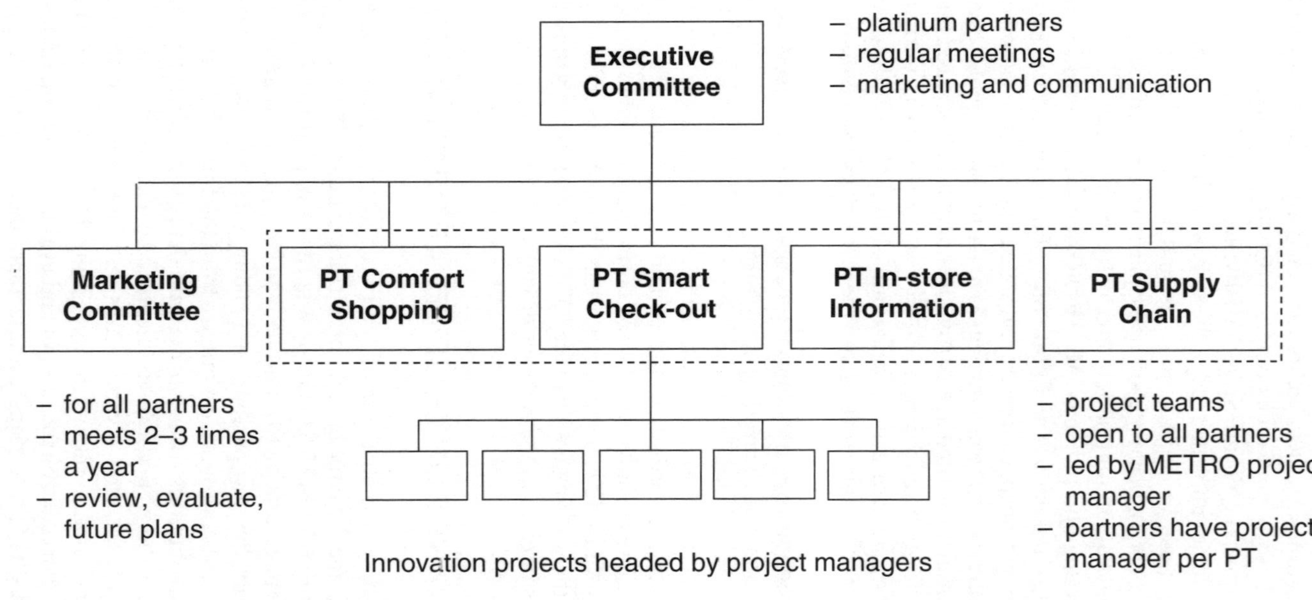

Figure 5.3 Structure of the Future Store Initiative

four project teams, each dedicated to one of the four specific areas of innovation in the Future Store: comfort shopping, smart check-out, in-store information and supply chain. Each project team is headed by a METRO Group project manager. Partners involved in these project teams have project managers who attend the meetings of the project teams. The project teams coordinate the separate innovation projects that are implemented in the store. Each of these innovation projects has a project manager as well. The different projects are set up to be run as independently as possible. This created some modularization in the network which increased the efficiency of knowledge sharing.

This structure evolved over time and was not there at the beginning. It co-evolved with the growth of the project. Clearly the role of METRO Group is more than that of first among equals. Key positions in the Future Store Initiative are occupied by METRO Group representatives and METRO Group's authority is acknowledged. However, METRO Group does not behave as if it is omnipotent. Various partners report that METRO's behaviour shows they understand the interests of the partners. They are looking for joint benefits to be realized, not just to advance METRO Group's position. METRO Group needs to balance that with the fact that it is the natural leader and has to make the occasional unpopular decision.

The structure is supported by contractual agreements between the partners. Partners sign a Memorandum of Understanding and a Non Disclosure Agreement. Both only cover high-level issues. The Memorandum describes the spirit and vision and does not specify in detail what each partner contributes and gains. Partners must commit to making resource commitments, must make a cash contribution to the Initiative's fund and must specify the individuals responsible for carrying out projects. There is no exclusivity: competitors may enter the network and partners may enter into similar relations with other companies. The Non Disclosure Agreement only relates to basic issues, like the protection of confidential information partners may share. Proprietary knowledge brought into the project remains proprietary. Lessons learned by partners are free for them to use in any way they see fit. No end date is set. The contracts are simple and straightforward and stay clear of details. This ensures that the vision, rather than the contract, is leading and that operations adapt flexibly to changing circumstances. The simplicity of the agreement does not mean there is not much at stake. On the contrary: the resource commitments the partners make tend to be substantial. Goal alignment ensures the partners will get value from their investment.

Nonetheless, the presence of competitors does create some tensions, among others when IBM was nominated to become the systems integrator for the Future Store Initiative. METRO Group dealt with this by ensuring that IBM would share the relevant information and knowledge it gathered from the Future Store Initiative with other partners in the alliance. Coopetition also has a positive function in the network: it keeps all companies alert. This helps the network avoid a common trap: when a network of long-term partners exists, the impetus for renewal may be limited.

NETWORK MANAGEMENT

The project started in September 2002 and the launch of the store was set for April 2003. This was a very ambitious schedule as at this time an existing METRO Group store had to be completely stripped and filled with technologies when it was not sure they would work. To add to the pressure, METRO Group planned a high profile launch, in which German supermodel Claudia Schiffer would open the store and use some of the new technologies. This was guaranteed to attract major media attention. If the opening of the store were to be delayed, this would involve a major loss of face for all partners involved. This acted as a powerful sanction which ensured all partners contributed sufficiently.

Together with the vision of creating the store of the future, this pressure combined to create a network identity. Almost all the people interviewed noted the special atmosphere, fun and excitement of being involved. This atmosphere built on previous relations between partners, but was intensified during the seven months of intensive collaboration. The community culture that emerged greatly facilitated progress. METRO group's behaviour as a lead partner helped as well: it focused on learning rather than dominating the alliance. Even though as a lead partner it did need to decide on issues, partners felt that METRO Group's behaviour as the dominant but benevolent partner contributed substantially to the success.

Next to this informal aspect, the overall structure, meetings and deadlines were necessary to maintain progress and coordinate the different initiatives. The project was not, however, overly structured. In fact, there was no detailed planning upfront. One manager from outside Germany commented that this was related to the German way of doing things: rather than structuring and planning upfront, there was very rigorous attention to operations and getting the details right. In this way, the Future Store Initiative was able to strike a balance between the necessity of structure and the necessity of self-organization that characterizes innovation projects.

Coordination is also facilitated by a website. Among the features of the site is a list showing the competencies of all the partners. This makes it possible for partners to rapidly find the right company and person to speak to. It increases the efficiency of knowledge sharing in the network. Otherwise, it can take some time for partners to track down the right individual, among the many companies involved.

One aspect of the network is that the partners involved are very diverse, coming from different industries. Consequently, not all partners have the same level of knowledge and quite some boundaries between companies needed to be crossed. This held a specific implication for some consumer good producers who were not knowledgeable about RFID. Even though the largest producers of consumer goods have built up some knowledge about RFID, the majority of them had not yet invested in the technology and therefore did not possess the required knowledge for them to participate in the Future Store Initiative network. For these companies, the Future Store Initiative invested in information and knowledge transfer. Written information is available to them in the form of information packages and newsletters. Also an RFID hotline was set up, which they could call with questions about RFID technology. For those companies for which this was not sufficient, a pool of RFID experts was created. These RFID experts would help these companies to implement RFID in their organization.

Even though the network functioned well, it ran into some difficulties in late 2002, early 2003. One of the issues that emerged was the fact that a system integrator did not get nominated until February 2003. At that time, IBM took on that role. As it was so late in the process, time was lost in discussions about who should do what and how to tie all technologies together. METRO Group could not fulfil that role because it is not an IT company. It is not able to decide on many technology issues that a system integrator can decide upon. A clear division of responsibilities, based on each company's competencies, solved this problem.

One challenge for a network like this is to remain vital. Companies worked towards the launch in April 2003 with great zeal, but after the opening of the store the project was to continue. Technologies needed to be developed further and new technologies to be brought into the store. The Future Store Initiative ran the risk of losing momentum after the opening. METRO Group has done three things that have ensured that the network did not stand still after the grand opening. The first is to set new challenges. One of those was to present the Initiative at some of the major retail conferences in the world. To ensure a mind-blowing and top-notch presentation, including creating a booth for trade fairs, brought new energy to the alliance. Likewise, the creation of an RFID centre for METRO Group to showcase the technology brought energy to the partners involved in the various RFID projects. A second mechanism used to maintain energy in the alliance is the introduction of new partners. By bringing new blood into the network, new ideas are generated and existing partners have a continuous incentive to contribute new ideas. Finally, the presence of competitors in the network had a similar effect. When a company saw one of its competitors actively innovating, that company felt pressure not to be left behind. To some extent, a learning race was created. Even though the Future Store Initiative has entered a phase of incremental, rather than radical, innovation, there is still sufficient renewal for partners to stay committed.

The introduction of new partners is not always welcomed by existing partners. Even though they understand that at a strategic level it is necessary, they may feel that another competitor entering the game is not in their interest. Or they may find that those who joined later are free-riders because they reap benefits from investments done by others. There is no solution to this dilemma. New partners are needed to move the network forward and they will profit from investments made by others.

As far as co-opetition is concerned, the potentially destructive aspects of co-opetition diminished over time. Important in this regard is that companies did not have to contribute the core knowledge lying behind their technologies. Most of the innovation in the Future Store consisted of tying existing technologies together, which meant that there was no need to disclose company secrets. Instead of discussing core knowledge, companies discussed the interfaces between their products. Moreover, when technical experts needed to collaborate, competition diminished even further. The technical experts were motivated by the interesting problems the Future Store Initiative created and, as one manager put it, 'loved talking about bits and bytes' and finding the best solution to a technological problem. Their focus was primarily on the fun of technology, and less on the companies they represented. Particularly at this level, tacit knowledge needed to be exchanged. The professional pride technology experts took in solving a technology problem appeared to be sufficient incentive to realize this transfer of knowledge.

DISCUSSION: KNOWLEDGE MANAGEMENT IN THE FUTURE STORE INITIATIVE NETWORK

Figure 5.4 shows the solution concepts implemented in the Future Store Initiative to overcome knowledge management challenges in the network. The first is professional pride. The fun of working on intriguing new problems was an incentive for individual technology experts to come together. When companies or individuals are motivated intrinsically, the need for complex governance structures diminishes and creativity is unleashed. A second solution to the motivation problem was creating a network identity. One factor helped to create this identity in a relatively short period: the

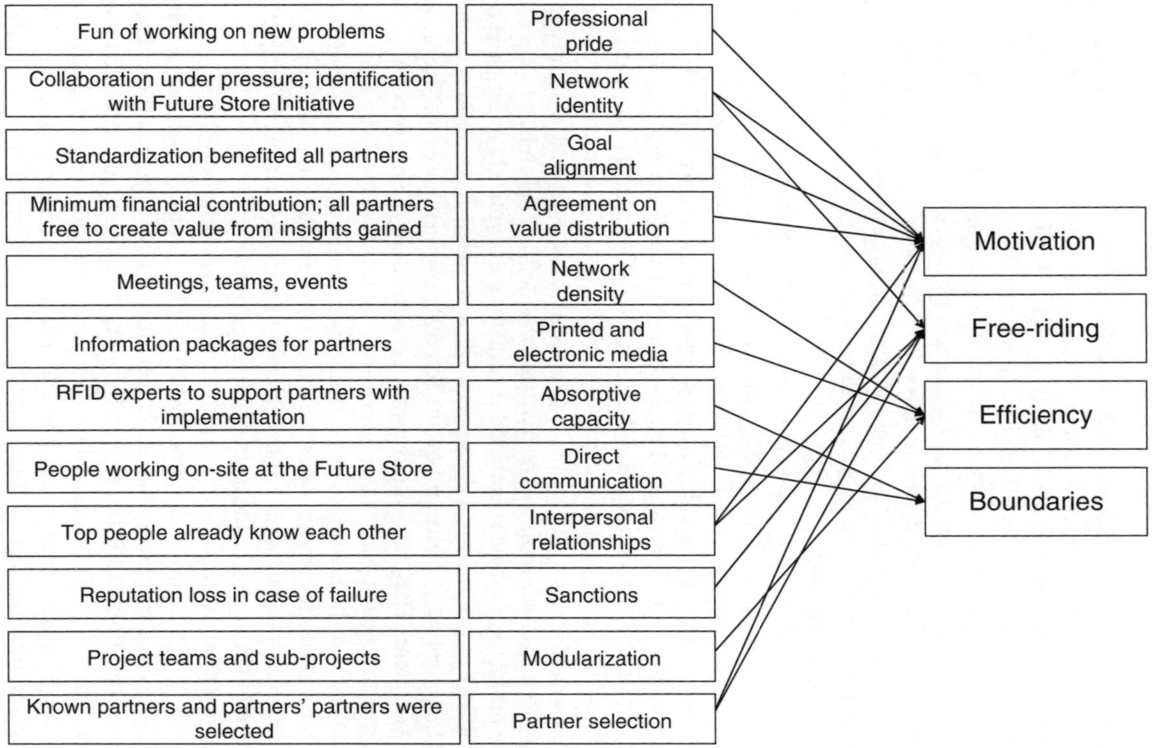

Fun of working on new problems
Professional pride
Collaboration under pressure; identification with Future Store Initiative
Network identity
Standardization benefited all partners
Goal alignment
Minimum financial contribution; all partners free to create value from insights gained
Agreement on value distribution
Meetings, teams, events
Network density
Information packages for partners
Printed and electronic media
RFID experts to support partners with implementation
Absorptive capacity
People working on-site at the Future Store
Direct communication
Top people already know each other
Interpersonal relationships
Reputation loss in case of failure
Sanctions
Project teams and sub-projects
Modularization
Known partners and partners' partners were selected
Partner selection
Motivation
Free-riding
Efficiency
Boundaries

Figure 5.4 Solution concepts applied in the Future Store Initiative

pressure partners were under created a collaborative atmosphere. The deadline contributed to the community feeling experienced by the participants. The network identity also reduced free-riding: everybody felt responsible for the entire project.

The problem of motivation was further reduced by the fact that the goals of the partners were aligned. Most important here is that by creating a standard for the retail sector, particularly for RFID, all partners would gain because it would either give them increased control over their supply chain (for consumer goods companies) or because it would allow them to sell RFID-related technology to a new market (for technology companies). Another example of goal alignment is that the value creation strategy of the Future Store Initiative also tied in with the strategies of the majority of the partners, for example because they were developing a retail strategy or a certain technology.

It was also clear how the value created by the Future Store Initiative would be divided. The knowledge protection rules of the Future Store Initiative are relatively straightforward. There is no requirement for partners to share any of the value they gain from the network with METRO Group. This in turn increased their motivation to collaborate. The Future Store Initiative has a focus on standardization. In this case the standard will automatically benefit all participants, making detailed agreements about value sharing unnecessary. The only formal issue was that a minimum quantitative contribution by the partners was defined beforehand.

The problem of efficient knowledge transfer was explicitly recognized by METRO Group. Creating a dense network was one of the solutions to this problem. Meetings, teams and events to create opportunities for people to meet were held. They helped close structural holes in the network. A more instrumental mechanism was the creation of the website listing partner companies and their areas of expertise, which reduced the time needed to search for the right competencies. This form of electronic media, combined with information packages made available to partners, ensured that partners would get access to the right knowledge quickly.

The boundary-crossing challenge occurred in the relationship with partners that had no knowledge about RFID. This problem was tackled by building up absorptive capacity in the partners. RFID experts did not teach the partners about RFID in detail. Instead, the experts implemented and delivered a well-functioning system almost as a turnkey project. Learning about RFID takes place in the process. The other forms of support (the hotline and information packages) are also aimed at bridging a substantial knowledge gap between partners.

Direct communication also helped in crossing boundaries. Persons from various companies worked on-site in the Future Store. This ensured direct contact and made immediate discussion of problems possible. Co-location on site also made it easier to create interpersonal relationships. These were important throughout the Future Store project. Even at the beginning of the project, top-level people knew each other from previous occasions. Good relationships motivate people to contribute and reduce their incentive to free-ride.

Free-riding was also tackled by sanctions. Even though the Future Store Initiative was separated from 'normal' business between the companies, the risk that a bad reputation gained in the Future Store would spill over into regular business was too great for most partners to take. Jeopardizing current or future sales by free-riding was not an option for them. In addition, the companies had to invest in the Initiative. This investment would be a deadweight loss if the companies did not collaborate in the Future Store Initiative, because the only way to obtain a return on the investment was to learn through collaboration. The risk of a high profile failure was another sanction. The Future Store Initiative was communicated widely, including all partner names. Especially when working towards the opening of the store, so much was at stake in terms of publicity that a failure to meet the deadline would not only have reflected badly on METRO Group but on all the partners involved. Not all free-riding was excluded, though. In particular, the fact that late entrants also profited from the reputation already established by the Future Store led to some concern by a number of partners. This problem was not addressed.

Modularization was applied by creating separate sub-projects and project teams working in different areas. This made the search for the right competencies easier, because it narrowed down the number of people and companies among which to search for an answer to a certain problem. Modularization of organizations is an effective means to limit coordination problems (Hoettker, 2006) and hence limits the efficiency problem. The Future Store Initiative case shows that it may be worthwhile to explore this idea in an interorganizational setting as well. In a modular organization, ideally only the interfaces between the modules need to be managed. In the Future Store Initiative, the complication was that interfacing was not that easy because of the lack of a proper system integrator until very late in the project. This made it impossible to identify the person responsible for and having the ultimate knowledge about how technical interfaces should work. Nonetheless, organizing the network in a modular way as indicated by Figure 5.3 lowered search costs within the modules.

The final solution concept applied by METRO in the Future Store was partner selection. METRO only selected known partners or partners of partners. Again, the fact that partners know each other increases their motivation to contribute and reduces free-riding behaviour.

Network Type

The Future Store Initiative is for the most part a single innovation project, with a central partner that is able to govern the network. The fact that the network is project based rather than involving multiple consecutive innovations might have created a situation in which it would be easier to free-ride. This is, however, counteracted by the fact that most partners had previous or parallel relationships with METRO. The presence of a central partner also made it easier to implement solution concepts and to maintain progress. It is difficult to see how the project could have been a success in a decentralized network. A clear leader is necessary to meet a tight deadline. Finally, the network was dispersed, but by co-locating individuals from various companies on-site, this problem was partly alleviated.

Knowledge Type

As to core and non-core knowledge, the Future Store Initiative asks companies to contribute their core products, but core knowledge is not shared. Companies connect their products without sharing core knowledge. In that process, new knowledge is created around standards and that knowledge is also non-core. Much of the knowledge contributed was explicit knowledge about technologies. Because of the co-location on-site, tacit knowledge could be exchanged as well.

SUMMARY

At first sight, this chapter shows that it is possible to create an effective knowledge-sharing network rapidly. A further look however shows that this network is rooted in previous relationships. Although it does not build directly on those historical relationships, the fact that they do exist enabled METRO to bring the right people together swiftly and get them to innovate jointly.

The network is highly informal, but it does not lose track of its purpose, because first, the purpose is clearly defined and second, a tight deadline was set. Together with a strong central partner, these two elements ensured the network was able to innovate, without extensive formal mechanisms.

NOTES

1. This case study is based on over 20 interviews, a site visit and company documents. It was sent to the respondents for review.
2. See Appendix for a complete list of the Future Store Initiative partner companies.

3. Radio Frequency Identification: a tag on an item sending out radio signals, containing information about the characteristics of that item.

REFERENCES

Hoettker, G. (2006), 'Do modular products lead to modular organizations?', *Strategic Management Journal*, **27**, 501–18.

METRO Group (2003), 'Customer acceptance of Future Store Initiative Applications', Düsseldorf, October.

METRO Group (2004) 'Future Store Initiative partnermeeting', 24 May.

van Weele, A.J. (2005), *Purchasing and Supply Chain Management*, London: Thomson.

APPENDIX 1: FUTURE STORE INITIATIVE PARTNERS AS OF MAY 2005

ADT	Mettler Toledo
AlgoTec	Microsoft
alpha	MultiQ
Avery Dennison	NCR
Bizerba	Nestlé
Boston Consulting Group	OAT Systems
Checkpoint	Online Software
CHEP	Oracle
Cisco	PAXAR
Cittadino	Philips
Coca-Cola	PIRONET NDH
DHL	Procter & Gamble
Eyckeler & Malt	SAP
FEIG	SATO
Fujitsu Siemens	Siemens Business Services
Gillette	Sonopress
Henkel	Symbol
Hewlett Packard	T-Systems
Hintzpeter & Partner	Tomra
IBM	Toshiba
Intel	Tricon
Intermec	UPM Rafsec
Johnson & Johnson	Visa Europe
Kraft Foods	WanzlService
Kurt Salmon Associates	Wincor Nixdorf
Liebherr	WMS
Logopak	X-ident
L'Oréal	X3D Technologies
Loyalty Partner	Zebra

6. Pig-breeding as a knowledge-intensive sector[1]

Ard-Pieter de Man

The production of pork has over time become a knowledge-intensive activity. Increasing demands on health, animal welfare, economic performance, innovation and internationalization are transforming the production of pork at all stages of the value chain. Breeders have had to cope with this development too. The Netherlands is one of the world's leading producers of breeding pigs and pork.

This case particularly studies knowledge management around the leading Dutch pig-breeding organization, the cooperative Pigture Group with its breeding programme TOPIGS. Pigture Group is the second largest pig-breeder in the world. First, the main developments in the pork industry are described. Next, the focus is on the role of TOPIGS in pig-breeding and the knowledge management mechanisms that are present in the TOPIGS network. Finally, the strengths and weaknesses of knowledge management in this case are analysed.

The case shows the effectiveness of using multiple solution concepts to get knowledge flowing. There is a clear difference in this case between solution concepts used for tacit knowledge and those used for explicit knowledge. Finally, the TOPIGS case shows that knowledge management in the Netherlands is effective, but that knowledge management in the international network faces some additional barriers. The Dutch knowledge management system cannot be implemented in other countries.

DEVELOPMENTS IN THE DUTCH INDUSTRY

As the second largest pig-breeder in the world, TOPIGS faces a number of contradictory challenges. First, there is continuous economic pressure to improve the financial performance of the pork industry. The Dutch pork industry has been very competitive for a considerable time (Jacobs et al., 1990). It is often remarked that there are more pigs than humans in the Netherlands. Even though the number of pigs has declined as a consequence

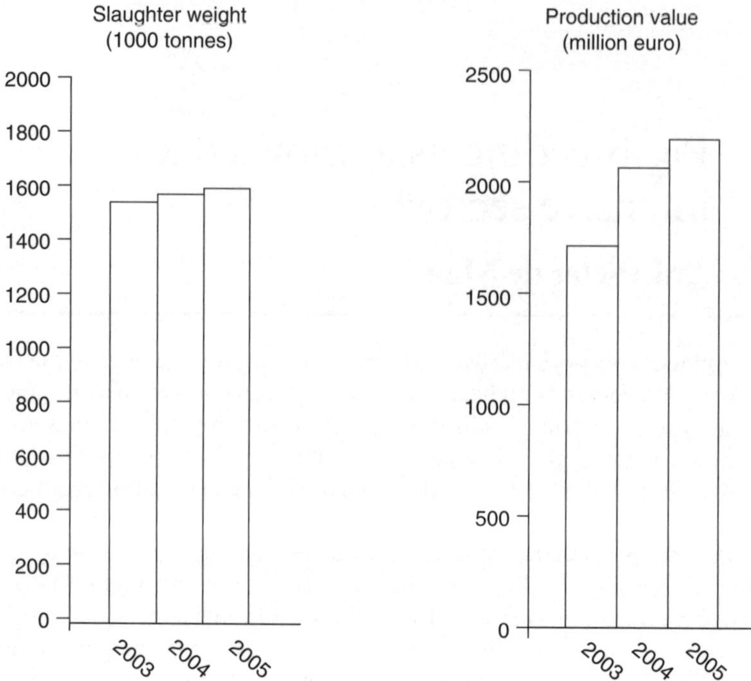

Source: PVE, 2006.

Figure 6.1 Slaughter weight and production value of pigs in the Netherlands

of environmental regulations, low prices at world market level (the sector is unsubsidized), pressure to increase animal welfare and the need to contain contagious pig diseases (after the sector was decimated during an outbreak of disease in 1997), the sector remains competitive.

The considerable and contradictory challenges of economic viability and animal welfare are met by innovation. By improving the speed of growth of pigs, making them resistant to diseases and adapting them to local market needs, TOPIGS aims to maintain its leading position as a supplier of pig genetics.

Figure 6.1 shows some key figures for the Dutch pork industry. Tonnes produced have declined since 2000, but production growth has picked up in the years 2003–5. The value of production has increased even faster. Most of the pork produced is for export: almost 1 million tonnes are exported. The most important importing countries are Germany, Italy and Greece,

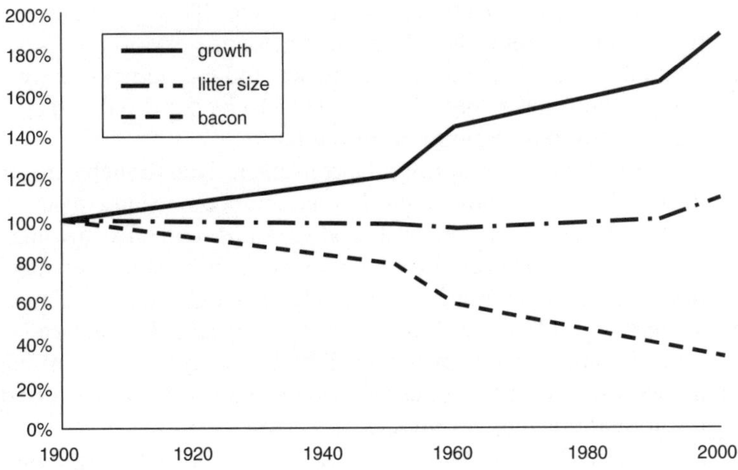

Source: Merks, 2005.

Figure 6.2 Effects of innovation in the pig sector

which together account for 60 per cent of the exports (PVE, 2006) of the Dutch pig industry.

In general, animal breeding is one of the more innovative sectors in animal production. Most agricultural sectors are scarcely innovative and have patenting growth rates below the worldwide average. Animal breeding, however, is one of the agricultural sectors that has a patent growth above the worldwide average growth rate across all sectors. Between 1995 and 2004 patent growth was 400 per cent whereas the worldwide average was 125 per cent. The Netherlands was somewhat behind. With 330 per cent patent growth, it lagged behind the worldwide average, even though this is still an impressive growth rate (de Man and Bigwood, 2006).

Figure 6.2 shows the effects of innovation in the pig sector. Over the past century continuous innovations in pig-breeding have increased the speed of growth of pigs. This is important because better growth means cost savings on food and makes it possible to send a pig to the slaughterhouse sooner. The percentage of bacon on pigs has decreased too, which is important because meat is valued more than bacon. In the last decade of the twentieth century, litter size has increased as well. The more piglets are born per sow, the more revenue for the pig farmer.

Other important developments in the business environment are:

- Health and food safety. In order to minimize the risk of diseases and to ensure a safe food supply, the pork industry is setting up total

quality systems across the entire value system. This enables the industry to find out from which farm each piece of pork originates.
- Animal welfare. There is increasing demand for animal welfare. The living conditions of pigs therefore need to be improved and already have improved in response to legislation.
- Low price, high interest from the consumer. Even though consumers demand animal welfare, so far they have not been willing to pay for it. Pork is currently a low interest product. Cause and effect are unclear: little research has been done into consumer behaviour and attempts to create consumer brands have been few in number and small in scale.
- Technology. IT systems have been implemented, specifically for tracking and tracing purposes. Biotechnology has so far had a limited impact on the industry. Genetic improvement is realized by traditional breeding techniques.
- Internationalization. Quite a few companies in the pork chain are increasingly working on an international scale.

In many ways, the sector is under pressure. At the same time, the sector is only just starting to apply marketing concepts, supply chain management, knowledge management and other management techniques. This case study will first describe the entire pork chain and next focus on the first steps of this chain, the pig-breeding aspect.

THE PORK CHAIN IN THE NETHERLANDS

Figure 6.3 depicts the main players in the Dutch pork chain. Broadly, there are three distinct phases in the chain. The first is from breeder to pig farms, the second is the slaughterhouse and the third retail/processing. Each of these three steps is relatively isolated from the others and tends to optimize its own operations, rather than the chain's. There are several suppliers to the pork chain, the most important being the feed companies. Other suppliers are equipment producers and veterinary services.

The breeder is responsible for improving the genetic make-up of the different lines and cross-breeds of pigs. Improvement of genetic material tends to be a lengthy process. Product innovation takes three to five years. At the moment, product innovation is among other things aimed at improving the colour of meat, increasing the fertility of pigs, speeding up the growth of pigs and influencing the amount of saleable bacon on a pig. The costs of R&D are increasing, forcing companies to internationalize in order to recoup their initial investments. Innovation is incremental and driven by the demands of the partners in the chain. Most knowledge required for this

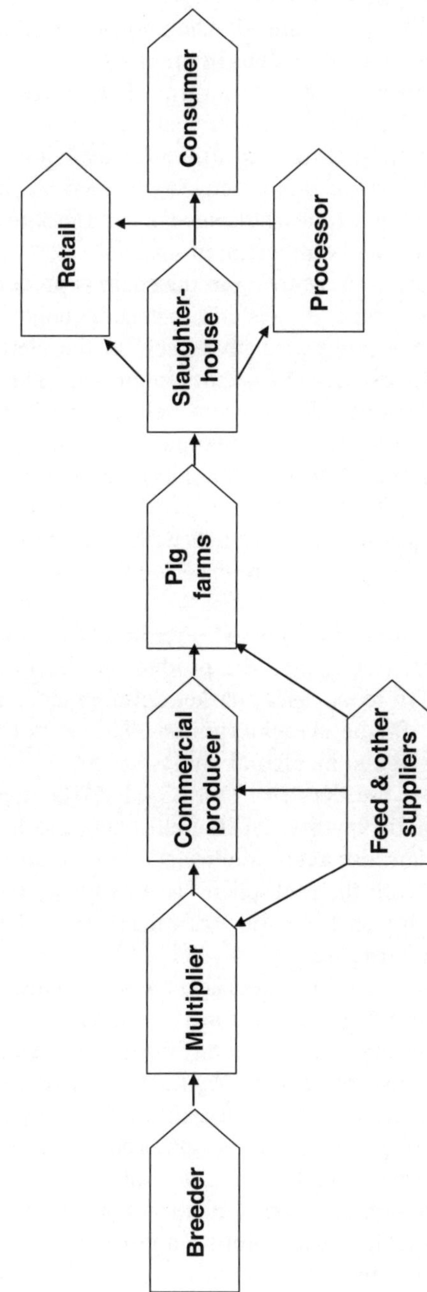

Figure 6.3 The pork chain in the Netherlands

type of innovation is explicit: measurement of pigs and knowledge about cross-breeding can easily be exchanged. The knowledge is core for breeders, but not non-core for the other steps in the chain.

Next to product innovation, a second form of innovation is related to farming itself. Knowledge about the circumstances that make pigs grow faster or be less subject to disease is continuously evolving. Much of this knowledge is tacit and developed in practice by farmers. As improving the speed of growth of pigs is at the heart of pig farming, this knowledge is core to pig farms, multipliers and commercial producers.

A third type of innovation occurring in the chain is process innovation. In particular, the application of IT systems to ensure quality and to enable tracking and tracing has progressed immensely in the Netherlands. The knowledge required to work with IT systems is mainly explicit and non-core.

Breeders' revenues mainly derive from selling semen and breeding animals. Their product is protected by two mechanisms. First, continuous innovation means that pig farmers cannot continue to breed and grow the same pig for a long time. They need to innovate and require the breeder to supply improved genetics. Second, contracts with customers ensure that no use of the genetics takes place for purposes other than use on their farm for their own production.

In general, the individual breeder is so far removed from the final market that translating market trends into the product is difficult. There is no contact with retailers. In most cases, market developments are communicated to the breeder via the slaughterhouses. This is not a formalized process, but a haphazard and incidental one.

Organizations of core breeders, like TOPIGS, help the breeder to maintain and improve genetic quality. Next, multipliers produce cross-bred sows. Often core breeders also act as multipliers. The commercial producer buys cross-bred sows from the multiplier. He uses the cross-bred sows to produce piglets which are reared by the pig farms towards slaughter weight and then sold to slaughterhouses.

The nature of the pig farms' business is changing rapidly. Their number has declined, but their average size has grown (see Table 6.1). The traditional family businesses are disappearing and family farms have become companies with different locations and hired staff. Pig farms used to sell their pigs to slaughterhouses via day trade. Increasing scale, however, is putting pressure on them to enter into longer-term contracts in order to ensure an outlet for their production. The term 'long term' is still relative: a long-term contract covers only a month, sometimes more. Differences in cost price are substantial: the cost level of the most expensive producer is 15 per cent above the average, whereas the cheapest producer produces at 15 per cent below the average. These differences appear to be caused by differences in management.

Table 6.1 Developments in pig farming in the Netherlands, 1996–2002

Year	Number of pig farms	Number of pigs per farm	Total number of pigs (× 1000)
1996	21 245	679	14 419
1998	19 345	695	13 446
2000	14 524	903	13 120
2002	12 000	983	11 392

Source: Vellinga, 2003.

Pig farms only engage in product differentiation to a limited extent. Some farms focus on organic production or try to create a regional product. So far consumers have not paid a substantial premium for these differentiated products. The Netherlands does not have products like Parma ham or Serrano ham. Almost all pig farms and pork processors follow a low-cost strategy.

The slaughterhouses are operating in a fragmented but consolidating industry. To counter the increasing power of retail in particular, slaughterhouses are merging and growing in size. Whereas internationally the largest companies in the industry only have a small market share, in the Netherlands Vion is the dominant player in the pork industry. It processes the vast majority of Dutch pigs. There is some product innovation in slaughterhouses, mainly in collaboration with or at the demand of retailers. For example, Vion has started producing 'shoarma' to satisfy increased demand for this product. Slaughterhouses pay farmers a price per kilo. Carcasses that are too heavy or too light receive a penalty. In addition, meat with a low fat ratio receives a higher price. Breeders react to these incentives by setting up breeding programmes that deliver pigs that get the highest price from the slaughterhouses at the lowest cost price.

In the Netherlands there is considerable distrust, especially between the pig farms and the slaughterhouses (Lindgreen et al., 2005). Pig farms believe slaughterhouses offer too low prices and engage too much in power play. The cause of this distrust lies in the lack of transparency in retail versus slaughterhouse prices. The information flow from slaughterhouses and retailers towards upstream members in the chain is not optimal. In short, pork is a commodity in the eye of the consumer. In the Netherlands, there are no brands in pork and the strategies of retailers are not directed at creating such brands.

Retailers enter into longer-term contracts with slaughterhouses for the procurement of meat. In relation to pork, their focus is mainly on price competition, not product differentiation. Sales promotions of pork tend to have a negative effect upstream in the chain. In order to produce pork profitably, the entire pig needs to be sold. When retailers focus their sales promotions on only one product coming from pigs, other pork meat is left over and needs to be sold at a lower price as well (Hoste et al., 2004).

A second important client group of slaughterhouses is the food industry. The food industry processes pork into other meat products. It tends to have long-term agreements with retail for the marketing of their products.

As stated before, communication across the chain is limited. It only relates to operational issues like quality management. The low trust between pig farms and slaughterhouses in combination with the short-term focus in their relationship shows that there is little communication especially between the breeder/pig farm part of the chain and the slaughterhouses and retailers. For this reason, it remains unclear whether there are other opportunities for innovation and optimization across the chain. As a consequence, each link in the chain now aims to optimize its own production process, rather than thinking about a way to improve the effectiveness of the entire chain.

The Dutch pork chain model is different from the model in other countries. In the USA, the chain is in most cases fully integrated, rather than being split across different independent companies. In other countries, slaughterhouses are farmers' cooperatives with the obligation on members to deliver pigs exclusively to the cooperative, for example in Denmark. The Dutch model has a higher level of decentralization, which on the one hand preserves the entrepreneurship of each step in the chain, but on the other hand leads to fragmentation and lack of communication.

KNOWLEDGE FLOWS AROUND TOPIGS

Knowledge in the Dutch TOPIGS Chain

Figure 6.4 shows the flow of knowledge around TOPIGS, the largest and most innovative pig-breeding organization in the Netherlands. The case focuses on the pig-breeding and pig-growing stages of the supply chain. Slaughterhouses, retailers and processors are excluded from the analysis.

During and after the 1960s the various regional Dutch breeding cooperatives merged into increasingly large-scale organizations. Especially in the 1990s concentration in the Netherlands increased substantially, because of rising investments in IT. TOPIGS came into being in 2003 when the three breeding cooperatives existing in the Netherlands at that moment merged into one. TOPIGS now accounts for 85 per cent of the market for breeding material in the Netherlands (Olijslagers, 2005). TOPIGS' aim is to develop high-value breeding material for the members of the cooperative.

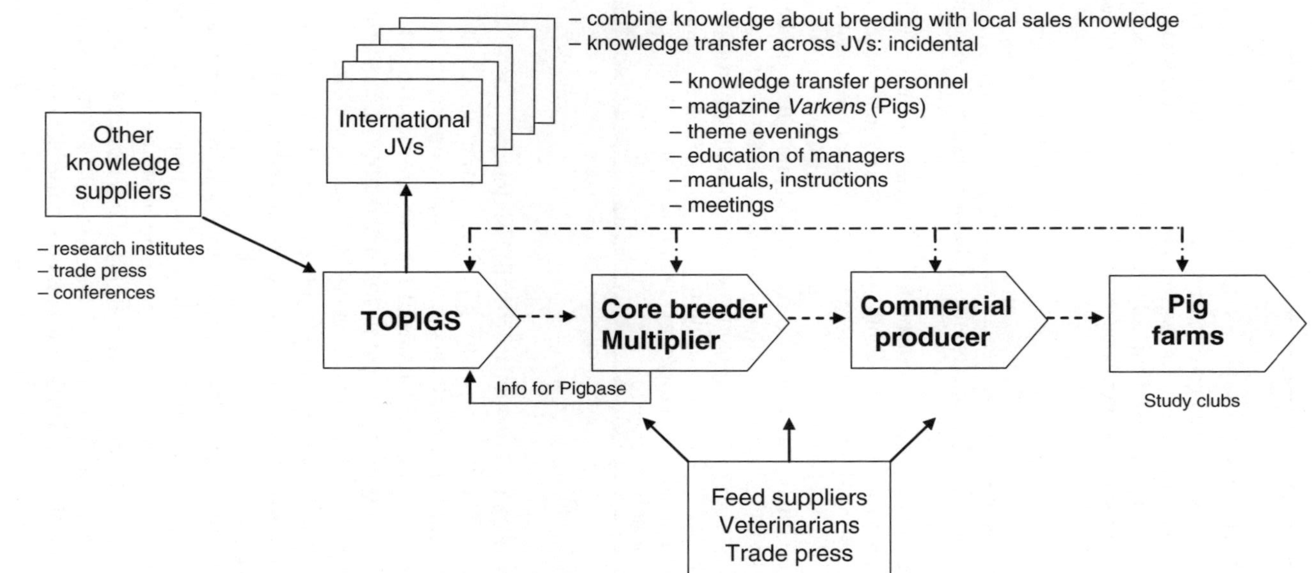

Figure 6.4 *Knowledge flows around TOPIGS*

Table 6.2 Products of TOPIGS

Sows:

- TOPIGS 20. The TOPIGS 20 is a sow with excellent mothering abilities; high fertility; good rearing capacity; a production of piglets with a high meat percentage; production of a large number of piglets per litter.
- TOPIGS 40. A sow with excellent utility characteristics; very good oestrus; vitality and sturdiness; economic piglet production; production of good fattening piglets.

Boars:

- Tempo. The Tempo boar is known for the vitality of its progeny. Especially suitable for bacon production. Its progeny has a rapid growth rate and is uniform.
- Top Pi. This boar's progeny is suitable for the German market. This boar descends from the Pietrain line of pigs, which was known for suffering from stress. TOPIGS has been able to breed this boar in such a way that it is completely stress negative. It has a good meat percentage.
- Top York. Progeny of the Top York are all-round pigs, which can be sold worldwide and are well-suited to the fresh meat market.
- Torso. The progeny of the Torso terminal boar are suitable for the fresh meat market and for bacon production.
- Tybor G. The progeny of the Tybor G are suitable for markets requiring pigs with a high meat percentage.

Source: www.topigs.com.

TOPIGS operates in 30 countries, often with local partners. The cooperative now has 3000 members, owning 77.5 per cent of the company. Core breeders and multipliers are all members of the cooperative; in the later phases in the chain a lower percentage of farmers are members of the cooperative. The remaining 22.5 per cent of the shares are owned by the slaughterhouse Vion, as a result of an earlier sale of Vion's breeding activities to TOPIGS. With production of 900 000 gilts per year, TOPIGS is one of the top three pig-breeders in the world. In the Netherlands, its market share is as high as 80 per cent.

In the Netherlands, TOPIGS collaborates with core breeders and multipliers to improve and maintain the pig lines it has, which are sold under the TOPIGS brand (see Table 6.2 for a description of the products). These breeders are responsible for the production and distribution of the breeding material based on a franchise system. The 120 to 130 franchisees are core breeders and multipliers. TOPIGS provides the basic elements for breeding, such as breeding value estimations (breeding values are numbers which indicate the expected performance of a sow or boar; they indicate whether a sow or boar has a high chance of having numerous, healthy offspring or not), product development, communication and technical support (e.g. advice on animal feed or disease prevention). TOPIGS' revenues consist of royalties and licence fees for semen and/or pigs sold by a core breeder or multiplier. The franchisees sell their products branded as TOPIGS.

Differences in sows relate among other things to the attention they need. Some pigs may be highly fertile but require continuous attention from the farm staff. Others require less attention, but may be less fertile. Shapes and sizes of pigs vary as well. Pig farms will choose one of the types of sow depending on their market.

As to knowledge flows, a number of issues are relevant. First and most important is the flow of knowledge from TOPIGS to the stages later in the chain inside the Netherlands. This takes place in various forms:

- Knowledge transfer personnel. TOPIGS sends experts to high-performing producers to learn about the reasons behind their success. This knowledge is then made available to others. Farmers are motivated to share their knowledge for two reasons. First, in the long run this system helps them to improve their product. They share knowledge as long as they get knowledge in return. Second, farmers take great pride in their work and like to talk about their successes. However, it is not always easy to make explicit why some farm managers perform better than others. Specialized personnel may help to make that knowledge explicit, but even then part of the success remains unexplained.
- TOPIGS publishes the magazine *Varkens* (Pigs). This technical magazine not only contains information about industry events and products, but also pays attention to relevant themes like optimal feeding strategies. This type of knowledge is highly relevant in furthering the production of pigs.
- Theme evenings. TOPIGS organizes meetings at which different themes are discussed. In particular, evenings that deal with the technical details of feeding, disease prevention, fertility management, improving health status or handling piglets draw good crowds.
- Education of managers. Managers of farms receive training about issues like how to organize stables, breeding, insemination management, feeding and general farm management.
- Meetings with TOPIGS experts. Core breeders in particular are in regular contact with TOPIGS. On average, there is a four-weekly meeting of TOPIGS staff and core breeders in which any aspect of the business may be discussed.

Another relevant form of knowledge transfer are manuals and instructions for working with the core IT system of TOPIGS: Pigbase. Pigbase is a database which contains data about many different aspects of pig-breeding and pig-farming. Among other things, it contains data necessary to estimate the breeding values. The basic data are delivered by the core breeders and multipliers, who gather information about the offspring of boars and sows.

Pigbase not only contains information about the animals, but also enables farmers to compare their technical results with other comparable farms inside and outside the Netherlands. It enables a commercial producer to see, for example, whether his sows produce more or fewer piglets than the sows of other farmers. Such benchmarking provides valuable information for farmers to improve their business.

Pigbase is a source of R&D for TOPIGS. The research department of TOPIGS, the Institute for Pig Genetics (IPG), carries out research into many different areas. IPG has been providing breeding programme administration, breeding value estimation and breeding and reproduction research for the breeding programmes. It also employs people dedicated to translating the research results into practice. This is an example of dealing with the crossing-boundaries problem: differences in the level of knowledge between companies are bridged through dedicated knowledge transfer personnel.

Pig farms also have their own mechanisms for sharing knowledge, apart from TOPIGS. They exchange knowledge in study clubs. Study clubs are a long-standing tradition in the Dutch agricultural sector as a whole. In study clubs, groups of farmers gather to discuss themes relevant to their particular sector. These have played a dominant role in knowledge exchange for a long time. With the restructuring of many parts of the Dutch agricultural sector, their role has become smaller, but certainly not irrelevant.

Finally, the different players in the chain learn from suppliers to the chain. Veterinarians, the animal feed industry and the trade press perform a vital function in transferring knowledge.

The overall picture is that in the Netherlands knowledge management appears to be well organized. A variety of mechanisms is in place to ensure transfer of knowledge in the chain. Attention is paid to increasing the efficiency of knowledge transfer and to crossing boundaries in firm knowledge.

International Knowledge Management in the TOPIGS Chain

A second element with regard to knowledge flows is the international operations of TOPIGS, often directed via international joint ventures. In joint ventures, TOPIGS combines its knowledge about breeding and genetics with a local partner's market knowledge. Internationalization usually starts with exporting products, but soon local production and sales follow. This is achieved by collaborating with local multipliers and commercial producers. The ultimate leadership in a joint venture lies with TOPIGS. TOPIGS has at least 50 per cent of the shares in a joint venture. There is a distribution agreement in place with each local subsidiary, stipulating the rights and obligations. All TOPIGS knowledge is available to all joint ventures except for knowledge about core breeding. This knowledge is not shared internationally.

The requirements for pigs are different across countries. Differences in climate and management mean that the optimal genetics of a pig for the production of pork differs across regions. Also slaughterhouses have different requirements about size, quality and weight of carcasses. Finally there are cultural or regional specialties. Spain and Italy require special shapes of ham to produce their local ham varieties. By working with partners, TOPIGS aims to fulfil local demand.

Knowledge management inside the countries and across countries is not as well organized as it is in the Netherlands. A farmer in a country may have a solution for a problem of a farmer in another country, but the correct information may not reach the person who needs it. Information about the performance of products in different circumstances is gathered and exchanged, but usually on an ad hoc basis. The efficiency of knowledge sharing is lower because international networks are not as dense as the Dutch network is. In general, it is not possible to transfer the Dutch system of knowledge management, not only for cultural reasons, but mainly because the knowledge requirements of, for example, farmers in large integrated farms in the USA, are quite different from the requirements of a small farm in Costa Rica. Connecting all partners in the TOPIGS network may therefore not be necessary. Nonetheless, TOPIGS managers agree there is room for improvement in international knowledge exchange.

Knowledge Management with other Knowledge Suppliers

The same is true for knowledge management with a third source of knowledge: other knowledge suppliers. These include research institutes, the feed industry and veterinarians in different countries, the trade press and conferences. The main research partners in the Netherlands are Wageningen University and Research Centre (WUR, including the Plant Research International, Animal Research Station and the departments of Breeding and Genetics, Animal Feed and Adaptation Physiology) and Utrecht University (Veterinary Faculty). Research partners outside the Netherlands include INRA (France) and the University of Bonn (Germany).

TOPIGS has expressed some unease about the quality of their knowledge management. Even though TOPIGS has been successful and has been able to innovate, there is some doubt as to whether the current focus on knowledge will be sufficient in the near future. As new challenges present themselves, markets internationalize and innovation becomes more important, the current system of knowledge management may need to be extended. TOPIGS considers the knowledge flow in the Dutch part of the chain to be effective. The process is structured and speedy. Internationally, there is room for improvement in both the speed of knowledge exchange and in ensuring the correct knowledge is obtained.

ANALYSIS OF KNOWLEDGE MANAGEMENT AROUND TOPIGS IN THE NETHERLANDS

The preceding overview of knowledge flows around TOPIGS leads to the next overall conclusions. First, there appears to be more focus on flows from TOPIGS to other companies in the chain than vice versa. There is more emphasis on sending than on creating two-way flows of knowledge among other network partners. Partly this is logical because of the fragmented industry structure; partly this means that TOPIGS has an opportunity to improve knowledge management, especially internationally.

Second, knowledge flows on a national scale receive more attention than international flows of knowledge. This is probably caused by the fact that internationalization naturally started later than national developments. Also the fact that the Dutch language is not used in other countries (except Belgium) has slowed down internationalization. A direct transfer of the Dutch system to foreign countries appears to be difficult because of the substantial differences in business systems, organization of pork production, language and culture between countries. The extent to which adaptation of knowledge management mechanisms is necessary is unknown. Even though the knowledge itself may not be different, the way in which it is transferred will probably differ across countries.

Third, motivation and efficiency are the main problems in the network. Boundary crossing is a minor problem and free-riding is minimal. Figure 6.5 shows the solution concepts identified in the case to tackle these problems.

Professional pride is an important motivator for pig-breeders and farmers. They like to share knowledge because it increases their reputation as good farmers. A network identity is present as well, even though it is not developed very strongly. Licensing under the TOPIGS brand, membership of the cooperative, the presence of study clubs and the general collaborative attitude in the industry underpin the network identity. This increases

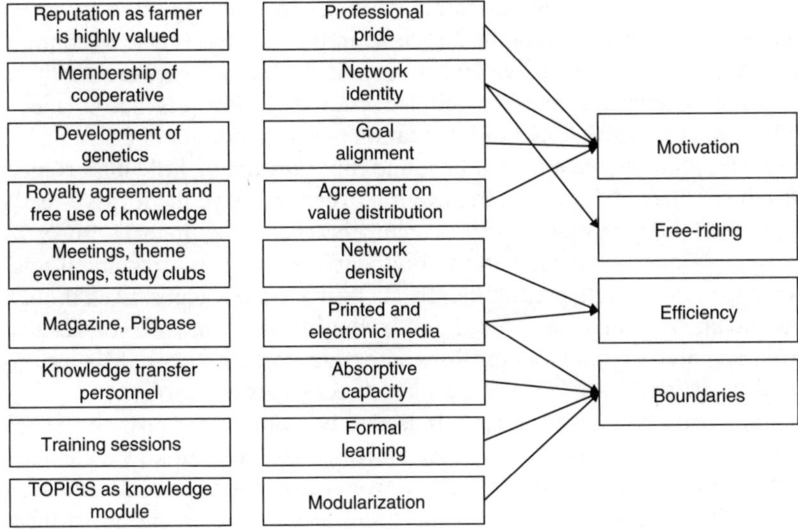

Figure 6.5 Solution concepts and knowledge-sharing problems in the Netherlands

motivation and, additionally, limits free-riding. Goal alignment is clearly present as well: all farmers realize they need to develop new genetics jointly, because they cannot do it by themselves. There is also agreement on value distribution. Royalties are paid to TOPIGS based on the number of pigs sold and most knowledge is free to be used by all in the Dutch network.

Network density in the sector is increased via regular meetings that are held to share knowledge and to meet each other. Theme evenings and study clubs increase the density as well. TOPIGS is still a first point of contact for many farmers. Network density and the role of TOPIGS as an organization connecting farmers help to increase the efficiency of knowledge sharing. Printed and electronic media further this cause as well. The magazine *Pigs*, the Pigbase database in which pig characteristics are gathered and the various manuals for using Pigbase are examples. Printed and electronic media also alleviate part of the boundary-crossing problem, because they spread knowledge and information over numerous partners.

Knowledge transfer personnel exist that transfer knowledge from one farmer to the next as well as from TOPIGS to its members. This increases the absorptive capacity in the network. Likewise, formal learning takes place via occasional training sessions. An interesting aspect of boundary crossing is TOPIGS itself. TOPIGS can be seen as a mechanism that companies use to bridge knowledge gaps. Individual farmers are too small to innovate and remain up to date about the latest advances in breeding. By setting up TOPIGS, a knowledge module has come into place that is able to conduct research, transfer knowledge and overcome boundaries between abstract, academic knowledge and the applied knowledge farmers need. Hence, TOPIGS is an example of modularization aimed at boundary crossing.

Other solution concepts can be found, but they are of little importance. Of course there is direct communication over and above the forms already mentioned. For example, TOPIGS members regularly contact TOPIGS for answers to questions. This affects boundary crossing. Interpersonal relationships exist as well, predominantly via farmers' study clubs. Even though study clubs are important for the individual farmer, they do not lead to extensive interpersonal relationships across the entire network. Much communication is still via TOPIGS and not directly between farmers.

Study clubs have also changed. It used to be common for farmers in each step of the chain to visit each other's farms. By observing how colleagues managed their farms, farmers learned from each other. Currently, no such visits take place among core breeders and in most other pig farms these visits have become much rarer. The reason for this lies in the fear of contagious diseases. In 1997, a contagious disease almost completely wiped out the Dutch pig population. Since then, strict measures have been taken to avoid the spread of disease. Ending site visits was one of those measures. Farmers now tend to meet at a 'neutral' site.

Sanctions to prevent free-riding are not really used in the network. Preventing free-riding does not at present receive much attention in the network. There may be farmers in the network that learn from others, but do not contribute their knowledge and experience to the network, but it appears that this is not an important problem. There is one other possible form of free-riding. Farmers may leave the network after they have produced sows based on genetic material from TOPIGS. This form of free-riding is possible, but it can work only temporarily. Without regular new genetic material, the quality of pigs tends to deteriorate. Farmers pursuing this imitation strategy therefore need to come back to TOPIGS to obtain new semen. There are no other formal sanctions against free-riding at the moment, apart from withholding semen to certain customers. Finally, the solution concept of partner selection is not applicable: the cooperative is open to anyone in the business. Partner selection is not a very important tool for managing knowledge and innovation in this network.

Internationalization

On an international level, knowledge sharing poses a bigger challenge. There are no structural mechanisms in place to ensure that a TOPIGS customer in one country can share his knowledge with a TOPIGS customer in other countries. International networking is limited and incidental. To some extent, this is explained by the differences in the needs of farmers in different countries and language differences, which make cross-country knowledge sharing more difficult.

International joint ventures serve to align the goals of TOPIGS and the local partners and simultaneously act as a vehicle for direct communication. In doing so, they resolve the motivation issue and the crossing-boundaries issue. The joint ventures combine local market knowledge with breeding knowledge. All international daughters and joint ventures have access to knowledge via manuals. However, not all of them pass this knowledge on to their customers. Depending on the effort made, between 10 and 90 per cent of customers have actual access to this knowledge. No other solution concepts are applied to stimulate the flow of knowledge internationally.

Network Type

The network brings forth multiple innovations. The fact that access to a continuous flow of innovations is necessary may explain the limited occurrence of free-riding. With TOPIGS as an important player the network has a certain degree of centralization, although the decentralized aspects predominate. Efficiency therefore remains a problem to be overcome. This is easier in the localized part of the network, in the Netherlands. The dispersed part of the network, spread out over numerous countries, is not yet part of an effective knowledge-sharing network.

Knowledge Type

Performance differences between pig breeders and farms persist and it is hard to pinpoint why. This is an example of tacit knowledge. Specialized staff visit the best-performing farmers and try to find out why they perform so well. Explicit knowledge sharing does not require intense interaction between individuals, but is achieved via printed and electronic media or workshops. The spread of knowledge about known pig diseases and how to prevent and treat them is an example.

The network mainly focuses on spreading core knowledge between farmers, such as knowledge about feeding and pig genetics. The only limit to the sharing of core knowledge is that TOPIGS does not share its core breeding knowledge with others. The fact that core knowledge is shared does not mean that companies hold back in contributing to the network for fear of losing their competitive advantage. The contrary is true: core knowledge is most valuable to farmers in order to meet the competitive pressures they all face. By collaborating, they can solve problems jointly without everybody reinventing the wheel. It is precisely because core knowledge is valuable that most partners are interested in sharing it. In addition, individual competitive advantages are limited and where they do exist, they are highly tacit and hence hard for others to imitate. For these reasons, the sharing of core knowledge is unlikely to harm farmers. Instead, they profit from it.

SUMMARY

In the Netherlands, a number of knowledge management mechanisms have been implemented in the pig industry and more particularly in the pig-breeding sector. Knowledge sharing within the Netherlands appears to be satisfactory at ensuring transfer of both explicit and tacit knowledge. International knowledge flows face more substantial challenges. There are gaps in knowledge management which lead to a slower and less well-structured flow of knowledge than management deems desirable. Few mechanisms exist to share and transfer knowledge and those that do exist are not effective in all circumstances. The same is true for the flow of knowledge from the other knowledge suppliers to TOPIGS.

There is a clear distinction between mechanisms used for the exchange of tacit knowledge and mechanisms used for the exchange of explicit knowledge. Tacit knowledge is exchanged via face-to-face contact and site visits by knowledge transfer personnel. Explicit knowledge is shared via magazines, IT mechanisms and meetings. The network focuses on core knowledge. Surprisingly, core knowledge is easily shared between partners. The reason is that this knowledge is most valuable in meeting joint threats.

Knowledge exchange is promoted by the fact that multiple innovations are developed in the network. The cooperative, TOPIGS, provides some centralization in pig-breeding and directs knowledge management of the chain upstream, but further downstream among pig farmers, self-organization in study clubs proves to be an effective mechanism.

The fact that knowledge flows in the Netherlands are smoother than international knowledge flows is partly caused by the fact that internationalization is relatively recent. However, international differences in types of pig farm and sector structures are the main causes that inhibit a smooth flow of knowledge.

NOTE

1. This case study is based on interviews with industry experts, TOPIGS personnel, representatives from retail and a slaughterhouse, a site visit to a pig-breeder, a study of websites, literature and previous studies of the sector. Additional input was received in a number of meetings that were part of the Transforum project IRV. The author would like to thank all participants and Transforum for their help and their contribution to this case study.

REFERENCES

de Man, A.P. and M. Bigwood (2006), 'Innovatie in landbouw terug bij af', *Economisch Statistische Berichten*, **91** (22), September, 456–8.

Hoste, R., N. Bondt and P. Ingenbleek (2004), *Visie op de varkenskolom*, The Hague, Landbouw Economisch Instituut.

Jacobs, D., P. Boekholt and W. Zegveld (1990), *De economische kracht van Nederland*, The Hague: SMO.

Lindgreen, A., R. Palmer and J. Trienekens (2005), 'Relationships within the supply chain: a case study', *Journal on Chain and Network Science*, **5**, 85–99.

Merks, J. (2005), 'De ontwikkelingen in de fokkerijtechniek', *Diergeneeskundig Memorandum*, **52** (1), 11–17.

Olijslagers, H. (2005), 'De structuur van de fokkerij in Nederland', *Diergeneeskundig Memorandum*, **52** (1), 30–33.

PVE (2006), *2005 NL Marktgegevens*, The Hague: Productschap voor Vee, Vlees en Eieren.

Vellinga, K.G. (2003), 'Relationship marketing in a Dutch business-to-business IKB pork chain', Masters thesis, Wageningen University.

7. Making horticulture networks bloom[1]

Ard-Pieter de Man and Erik van Raaij

Dutch horticulture, and especially the growth of flowers and plants, has a dominant position in world markets. The vast majority of flowers and a considerable part of the market for plants are in the hands of Dutch producers. This is remarkable because most growers of flowers and plants are small, family-owned firms. In addition, the network is decentralized: there is no central party organizing knowledge flows. How these small firms have been able to conquer world markets is the topic of this chapter. The conclusion will show that knowledge exchange and innovation have led to a unique network that has enabled family firms to dominate the international market for flowers and plants. The success in innovation and knowledge sharing is explained by the fact that several complementary and overlapping mechanisms have come into being that stimulate innovation and solve the problems of network knowledge management. Informal relationships and implicit understandings play a significant role in preventing knowledge-sharing problems in the sector. The effectiveness of these mechanisms is enhanced substantially by the fact that the network is located in a very small region.

BACKGROUND

Cut flowers and potted plants are among the most successful export products of The Netherlands. Cut flowers have been the most competitive Dutch export product for a number of years (Jacobs et al., 1990), despite the fact that the Dutch climate is not particularly conducive to the growth of all varieties of plants that are grown in The Netherlands. Porter (1990) posits that the success of the Dutch flower and plant industry can be explained through the 'cluster' concept. In The Netherlands, a cluster of organizations has emerged consisting of numerous companies that collaborate and compete in growing flowers and plants, with supporting industries like specialized transporters, consultants, and equipment manufacturers and a demanding home market in place.

This cluster is highly innovative. New techniques for growing plants, new varieties and new greenhouse technologies are only a few of the many innovations that are continuously being developed and implemented. Even though international competition is increasing from countries with more suitable climates for most plant varieties, like Colombia, Ecuador, Kenya and Israel, the Dutch horticultural sector has been able to compete successfully with these countries because of continuous innovation (Wijnands, 2006). An analysis of patenting behaviour over the period 1995–2004 shows that the patent growth rate of horticulture in The Netherlands is seven times the worldwide horticulture patent growth rate, three times the worldwide patent growth rate across all industries, and two-and-a-half times the Dutch patent growth rate across all industries (see Figure 7.1).

In addition, horticulture has become increasingly focused on international patenting. Formerly Dutch organizations filed patents in a limited number of countries. More recently, they have filed them in more states. Figure 7.2 shows the number of patents and number of countries in which organizations applied for a patent and the year of patent publication. In 1995, the number of patents was lower than in 2003, and most patents were filed in fewer than 10 countries. In 2004, most patents were filed in over 20 countries. Where previously organizations patented few technologies in few countries, they now patent more technologies in many countries. The international outlook of Dutch horticultural organizations has increased.

Horticulture takes place across Holland, but the most important and competitive part of the industry is located in a small area between the two cities of Rotterdam and The Hague. This area, known as the Westland, is almost completely covered with greenhouses in which not only plants and flowers but also fruits and vegetables are grown. The total greenhouse acreage in The Netherlands expanded from about 3300 ha in 1950 to over 10 000 ha in 2000. In earlier years, vegetables were the mainstay, growing from 2200 ha in 1950 to 5100 ha in 1965. In 1965, flowers and plants took off: they overtook the vegetable sector in 1985 and reached an area of 5900 ha in 2000 (Buurma, 2001). Total acreage has shrunk since 2000, with about 3500 ha now devoted to cut flowers (a decline of 12 per cent since the year 2000), and almost 2000 ha devoted to potted plants, up from 1750 ha since 2000 (Buurma, 2001; Berkhout and van Bruchem, 2006).

Although a small number of large players have emerged in recent years, most of the companies in the industry are family-owned small-sized enterprises. These relatively small companies have been able to compete in an increasingly global market through a long history of knowledge sharing and collaboration. Many growers are members of one or more networks. Some of those networks are temporary to solve a particular problem; some networks have existed for many years.

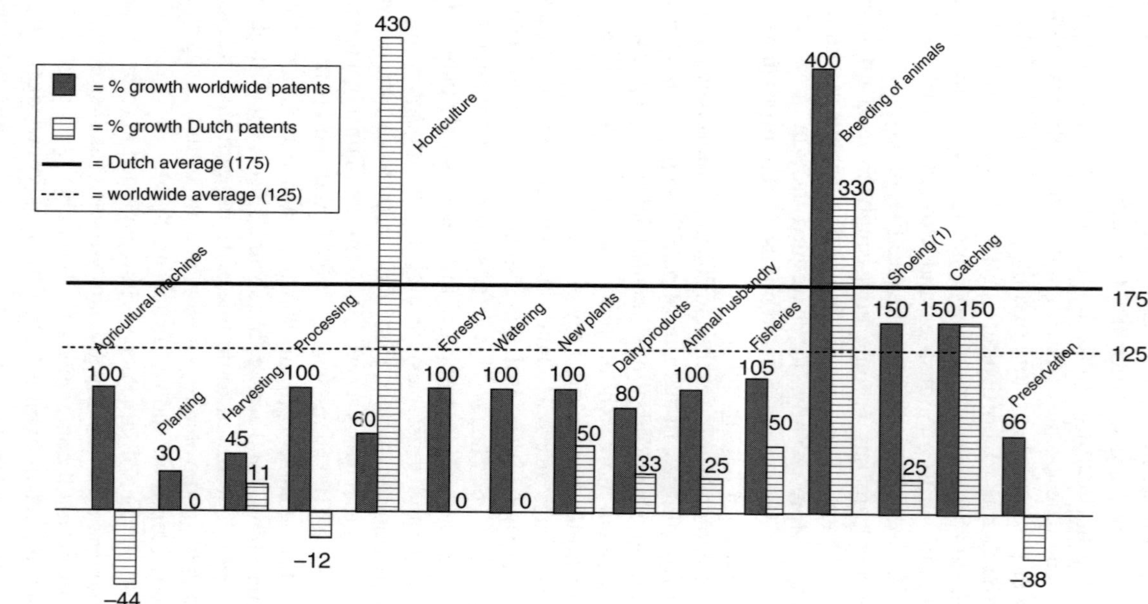

Source: de Man and Bigwood (2006).

Note: [1] Since 1999.

Figure 7.1 Patenting growth rates in agriculture, 1995–2004

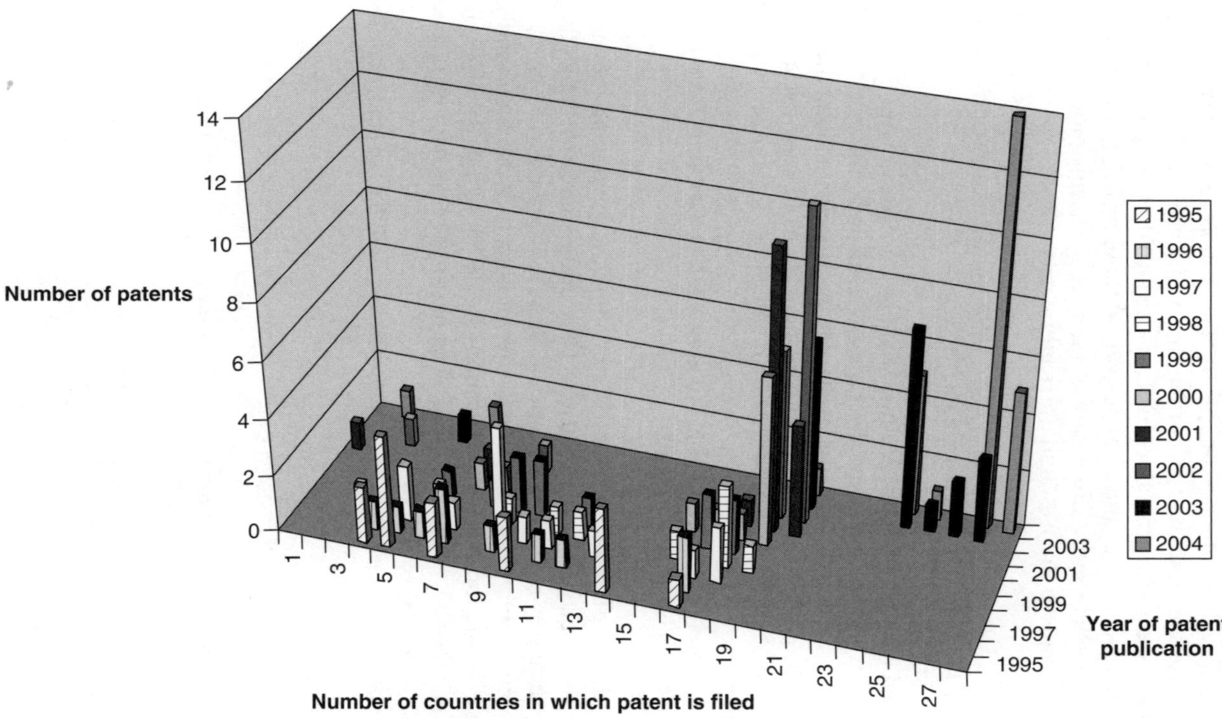

Source: de Man and Bigwood (2006).

Figure 7.2 Developments in the filing of horticultural patents

Within this broader setting of Dutch horticulture, this case study focuses specifically on flowers and potted plants. Within the general success story of Dutch horticulture, flowers and plants stand out as the most successful products. We first describe the horticulture value chain and knowledge sharing in this sector in general terms. Then, we introduce the phenomenon of growers' associations and analyse two of those associations in more detail. We conclude with a discussion of knowledge-sharing problems and solution concepts in the Westland horticulture network.

THE HORTICULTURE CHAIN

A simplified version of the horticulture chain is depicted in Figure 7.3. The chain consists of four steps: suppliers, growers, auctions, trade and retail. The focus of this case study is on knowledge management among the networks of growers. However, many of the innovations that are relevant to them are initiated by or co-produced with companies from other parts of the value chain.

There are many different suppliers to growers. The most important categories are (van Horen et al., 2000):

- Producers of seeds and slips. Seed companies are among the most powerful players in the industry. They are a source of innovation because they create new varieties of flowers and plants.
- Greenhouse builders. Greenhouse technology is developing rapidly. One of the most recent innovations is the 'closed greenhouse', in which the CO_2 that is produced when heating the greenhouse is used to further the growth of plants.
- Producers of installations. These provide installation and mainte-

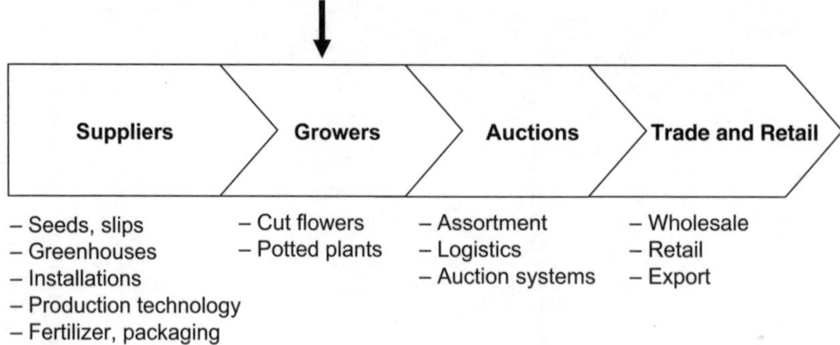

Figure 7.3 The horticulture chain

nance services for heating systems, cooling systems, water systems and electronics.
- Producers of production technologies, for example, producers of cutting and sorting robots.
- Fertilizer companies.
- Packaging materials suppliers.

Suppliers have a role in knowledge transfer, not only because they make available their own specialized knowledge, but also because they know a variety of growers. This enables them to bring growers with similar problems in touch with each other. Growers tend to have long-term relationships with their suppliers. This makes it difficult for suppliers from outside the sector to enter the horticulture market. Some of the more advanced growers are beginning to realize that learning from other sectors may help them to achieve a competitive advantage. They also look for suppliers outside their existing relationships.

The growers themselves are typically family-owned businesses that operate a number of greenhouses. The level of specialization can be extreme. Growers tend to specialize in only one type of flower or plant (e.g. only orchids) and sometimes even in one specific variety (e.g. only white orchids). The core of their business is increasing crop productivity: growing more and better flowers and plants on the same number of acres. For example, the physical yield of roses increased from 166 stems per square metre in 1980 to 226 stems per square metre in 1996, an increase of 36 per cent in 16 years. In that same period, the physical yield of chrysanthemums rose from 117 stems per square metre in 1980 to 183 stems per square metre in 1996, an increase of 56 per cent in 16 years (Buurma, 2001). By making use of the innovations from suppliers and by experimenting with lighting, temperatures, water and fertilizer, growers can achieve dramatic increases in the yield per square metre. Growers learn from each other in all these areas.

Size differences among growers are substantial. Some growers have only an acre of greenhouses, others have multiple acres, and a few growers even operate huge flower estates in one or more foreign locations. There is a consolidation trend, leading to fewer, but larger companies (van Horen et al., 2000). The number of growers of cut flowers has declined from 4400 in 1971 to 2765 in 2005. The number of growers of potted plants was 1360 in 2005 (back to the level of the early 1970s), while average size has increased from less than 0.5 ha to 1.4 ha (Berkhout and van Bruchem, 2006). The top five growers have an average size of 24 ha each (Silvis and de Bont, 2005). Production costs (such as energy costs) and increasingly high investment requirements in the latest technologies are the background for this

Table 7.1 Key figures – flower and plant auctions, 2004

	FloraHolland	VBA
Members	3803	3070
Companies bringing products to auction	7457	6000
No. of employees	3000	1945
Turnover	1.9 billion euro	1.6 billion euro

Source: Company websites.

consolidation trend (van der Meer, 2001). Increasingly, the sector is divided between large, innovative growers and smaller growers that fall behind. Growers also implement different strategies. Some serve low cost segments; others focus on exclusive or fashionable segments. Through all kinds of collaborative structures many of the growers are linked to each other. At the same time, there is a healthy dose of rivalry among them.

The next step in the horticulture chain is the auction. The Netherlands has two large flower and plant auctions: FloraHolland and VBA.[2] Both are cooperatives, established by growers. Table 7.1 shows the number of members, companies bringing their products to auction, the number of employees of the auctions, and the turnover of the auctions. In 2004, the total value of plants and flowers traded at these two auctions was 3.5 billion euros. The auctions are not only a place to sell products. They also streamline the logistics. In addition, auctions create the right assortment for wholesale and retail companies. Growers only deliver one type of flower (sometimes in one single colour), whereas a buyer typically wants a coherent assortment of different types and colours. The auctions create such assortments. At the core of the auction are the auction systems. There are a number of ways in which flowers and plants can be put to auction. The traditional method is to 'bring them before the clock', a method in which a clock shows a rising or decreasing price and traders can buy by stopping the clock at a certain price. Increasingly, however, plants and flowers are sold directly from growers to for example retail chains, thus 'going outside of the clock'. When it comes to the auctions, recent innovations include Internet access to the auction and the creation of unique product codes. The latter is far from easy. Because flowers and plants are products of nature, their size, colour and quality are never uniform. Innovations in the area of logistics include issues like predicting the supply of flowers and plants, dealing with peaks in demand (e.g. around Valentine's Day and Mother's Day) and tracking and tracing.

Trade and retail constitute the final step in the value chain. Wholesalers and retailers buy at the auctions, or directly from growers. The majority of exports of flowers and plants occur via export companies. Retailers, wholesalers and exporters are extremely fragmented industries. There are over a thousand wholesale and export companies active in The Netherlands (Berkhout and van Bruchem, 2006). The local flower shop is still the main outlet for cut flowers, while the garden centre is the main outlet for potted plants. The share of retail chains, garden centres and do-it-yourself centres is growing at the expense of small-scale flower shops (Silvis and de Bont, 2005).

Looking at the chain in its entirety, it is important to note that the level of chain integration is still limited. Most parts of the chain have only a limited view of what happens upstream and downstream in the value chain. The number of growers, for example, that know the wishes of the final consumer or even of a retailer is very small.

COMPETITION AND COLLABORATION IN THE HORTICULTURE NETWORK

Observing the horticulture industry from a distance, the hundreds of growers of plants and flowers that exist in The Netherlands operate in an interesting mix of competition and collaboration. This combination is the source of innovation. It is rooted in a long-term historical development that was particularly strong in the Westland area. Even though collaboration between growers is also found outside the Westland area, the extent of collaboration in the Westland is particularly remarkable. The most visible, recent mechanism for collaboration is the grower association. Growers' associations are mostly cooperatives set up by a group of growers with a certain specific innovative aim in mind. This phenomenon of growers' associations as a means to create and exchange knowledge in order to innovate can only be understood as part of a historical process.

Figure 7.4 shows the historical development of collaboration between growers. Collaboration between growers began in the first half of the twentieth century when the growers that had established themselves in the Westland visited each other's gardens (greenhouses are often still referred to as 'gardens') after church on Sunday to check how the neighbour's plants were growing. These visits were a kind of informal knowledge transfer. Growers then and now take tremendous pride in their products and therefore like to show their colleagues their gardens and explain how they achieved certain results. Their professional pride stimulates knowledge sharing.

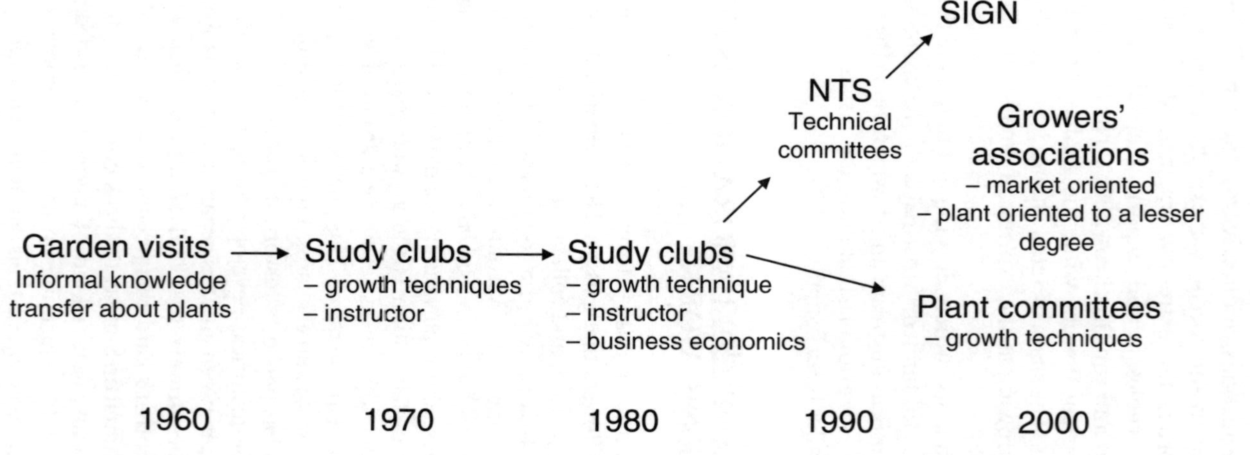

Figure 7.4 The history of knowledge exchange in the Westland network

Throughout the twentieth century, there has always been a clear need for increasing productivity. The Westland is a relatively small area that needed to provide for an ever-increasing population. The predominantly Catholic growers' families of the Westland also faced a succession problem. After the death or retirement of the elders, gardens were split among their sons, who had to make a living from smaller plots of land than their fathers owned. As the local culture was such that leaving the Westland region was out of the question, the only solution was to increase productivity dramatically. As a result, growers were continuously on the lookout for new and better ways of growing plants. For this, they needed to learn from each other and this has led to an open, knowledge-sharing culture. A grower states: 'I think most of the people are very close. I would hate it not to tell my colleagues (about a new discovery). They are also my friends; they are also my relatives'. Hence, there is a strong network identity that motivates people to share knowledge and helps to limit free-rider behaviour.

In the course of the 1960s the system of visiting each other's 'gardens' was formalized in study clubs. Within these study clubs, growers of a particular plant would get together with an instructor to discuss new growing techniques. This system was funded by the 'productschap tuinbouw' (PT), a typically Dutch sector-level organization with both public and private aspects, which growers are obliged to join and which receives support from the Ministry of Agriculture. The instructor shared knowledge gained through research with the growers. As the instructor would visit numerous study clubs, he was also able to transfer knowledge from one club to the next.

Over time, the study clubs broadened their scope to include other elements of relevance to growers. For example, growers started to share information about business aspects like the use of natural gas per acre for heating. Initially, these data were shared anonymously so growers could compare their own performance to the average. Later, names were disclosed as well and this made it possible for everyone to learn from the best performing competitor.

The study clubs remained in place, albeit under various names and with some changes in the structure. At different points in time, they were known as study clubs, NTS (Netherlands Horticulture Study groups) and SIGN (Foundation for Innovative Horticulture in The Netherlands). NTS was organized through technical committees which were highly regarded.

Nowadays new clubs are set up that still function as a study club, albeit in a modern way:

> Together with five orchid growers, we exchange knowledge about how we grow our plants. We have linked our computer systems. I can look into the core of each

> company: what level of lighting do they have? What is the temperature in their greenhouse? And we are competitors. But there are 65 orchid growers in this region. The five of us may be competitors, but we'd better try to create a product for the five of us that is better than that of the others. As a group we then get an edge over the rest.

Groups like this exist without contracts. Free-ridership is mainly prevented by the value of membership: knowledge develops so quickly that a company that leaves the group after having learned everything will not benefit much from that learning. In two years' time, its knowledge will have become obsolete. Only by remaining in the group and sharing expertise is a company sure to have access to a continuous flow of new knowledge.

The majority of the growers participated in study clubs and opened their greenhouses to their competitors. A small minority believed they were better off by keeping some of their ideas to themselves. They did not allow others to come into their greenhouses and soon found that not only were they not let into others' greenhouses, they also lost respect in the community. Some growers have actually been successful by striking out on their own and some free-riding, but the general feeling is that growers are better off exchanging knowledge. The speed of innovation has become too high to keep up with on their own.

In the course of the 1990s, a split occurred. The traditional, government-backed innovation system started to unravel. The more innovative and entrepreneurial growers were no longer happy with the successors of the study clubs, the plant committees, which were deemed too slow on the uptake with new developments. Currently, it is mainly the less innovative entrepreneurs that are members of plant committees, which occupy themselves for the most part in discussing growth techniques. These committees are still supported by the PT. The top entrepreneurs avoid the plant committees and are setting up their own growers' associations, which may also focus on growth techniques, but in addition focus on innovation, sales and marketing. Previously, the weaker companies learned from the stronger ones and simultaneously held them back from improving faster. Currently, the more advanced companies have become more businesslike by demanding mutual learning: they want to gain as much knowledge from other growers in the association as they put in themselves.

Overall, the industry network in horticulture consists of a large number of growers who exchange knowledge via different structures. One of the most eye-catching is the growers' association. Because of their increasing relevance, two growers' associations are now studied in more detail.

GROWERS' ASSOCIATIONS

There are about 50 different growers' associations active in The Netherlands. Some have only a handful of members, some have dozens. Some focus on the development of a new technology, others aim to bring products to market, still others cover both areas (and more). They may focus on growing or selling carnations or chrysanthemums, orchids, roses.

Besides these growers' associations that have modernized the study club idea and make an important contribution to knowledge sharing and innovation, other growers' associations have moved beyond that and look beyond plant or flower varieties. They focus on marketing, sales and branding or they are set up to deal with a specific business issue. Below, two examples of growers' associations with this type of goal are analysed. Decorum Plants is a market-oriented association; Plantform is issue-oriented.

Decorum Plants

Decorum Plants is a growers' association aimed at creating a quality brand for potted plants and strengthening the market orientation of the associated growers. Historically, the auction was responsible for marketing plants and flowers, and growers would not spend any resources on branding or marketing. With the growth in size and the rise of retail chains as outlets for plants and flowers, growers are becoming increasingly interested in market demand and client feedback. The larger the size of companies and the higher their investments, the more companies feel the need to ensure sales are stable.

Within Decorum, 45 growers of different types of potted plants have begun investing in setting up a brand focusing on the better quality plant. The initial aim is to create brand recognition with traders and next to leverage that brand in retail and eventually with the final customer. Tests are being held with retailers to find out how best to create brand awareness in the eyes of the customer.

Growers are member of Decorum based on their product quality and their willingness to invest in Decorum activities. A willingness to collaborate is relevant as well. The initial group consisted of 18 companies; currently 45 growers are members. New members sign a contract stating that they will remain a member for at least a year. This is a relatively short period, because Decorum does not believe forced collaboration will work. Companies should remain members because they want to be, not because the contract forces them to stay in the association. The contract does define penalties for quality: when a grower does not produce an adequate quality, he is not allowed to sell his plants under the Decorum brand.

The large majority of the growers are based in the Westland region. Only a handful are located elsewhere in The Netherlands. Knowledge sharing within the network occurs naturally, motivated by a passion for continuous improvement and safeguarded by implicit agreements and informal sanctions. A Decorum grower states:

> Here, people are used to collaborating . . . Abroad, companies tend to protect their knowledge. The closer you get to this region, the less people protect their new stuff. Here it's like when you have something new you immediately want to share it with others: see what I have got! Because we see that when you share knowledge, you also get knowledge in return . . . 80% of the ideas I use in my greenhouse, I learned from others. If I would close my greenhouse to others, I would not be allowed into their greenhouses and hence would miss out on 80% of the innovations . . . I do take the names of the people who come to see the innovations in my greenhouse. Then I know who to call when I want information from them. There are these characters who tell you that you can not visit their greenhouse in return. I cross those off my list; they can no longer come and learn from me.

This quote shows the growers understand how value is created and distributed in the network. An informal sanction like crossing a name off a list is applied to punish free-riding.

The 45 growers do not sell their entire output under the Decorum brand. The quality of plants, being a product of nature, differs and hence sometimes only a part of the production can be sold under the Decorum label. As a result, not all growers perceive Decorum as an important outlet. When only 10 per cent of revenues are generated via Decorum, growers are less amenable to follow Decorum guidelines than when 70 per cent of revenues are generated via Decorum. For this reason, a target was introduced in 2005 stating that at least 50 per cent of the production of each Decorum member should be of Decorum quality and that within two years that 50 per cent should be sold via Decorum. Such a strict criterion may result in a number of members leaving. However, Decorum believes the remaining ones are more committed to developing a brand and investing in marketing innovations.

Because the associated growers sell different types of plants, it is not easy for them to check each other's quality. An orchid grower is not necessarily knowledgeable about a plant like the ficus. In order to be able to cross such expertise-related boundaries, Decorum has hired its own quality inspector. In addition, feedback from exporting companies about plant quality is important to maintain the quality image of Decorum. Complaints are registered in a database, as are other remarks, points of improvement and questions about products. Members of Decorum are increasingly feeling the pressure from each other to perform well; they discuss the quality of each other's plants, and when complaints are received, these are discussed with the particular grower.

Decorum plants were initially delivered on an exclusive basis to particular traders and export companies. This was necessary because without exclusivity it was difficult to get a commitment from traders and export companies to create market opportunities for Decorum. Decorum may be in competition with existing traders because Decorum has started to approach retailers directly, which traditionally was the role of the trader. Decorum is also beginning to hire sales people. The power base is clearly shifting. After five years, Decorum has stopped doing business exclusively with a limited set of traders and has moved to a broader, yet still selective, base of traders.

Another process innovation being introduced is to give clients access to a website that presents all Decorum products. Export companies have not always offered the full range of Decorum products to final customers. By giving clients direct access to a site showing the entire product portfolio, this filter is removed.

Knowledge about markets and marketing is gathered by collaborating with a specialized consultancy firm and the Flower Bureau Holland, an organization that tracks market developments worldwide. Most of the knowledge, however, is created through learning by doing.

Decorum members meet every four to six weeks. As the group is relatively large, not all members have the same interests or the same knowledge base. Trying to keep everybody on board and keeping visions aligned is therefore a continuous struggle. Company visits occur on a six-weekly basis, to learn about members but also to get to know each other in an informal atmosphere. 'Going to a company every six weeks has been a good step for building commitment.' In short, goal alignment and good interpersonal relationships underpin the success of Decorum.

Plantform

Plantform is a growers' association aimed at developing Enterprise Resource Planning (ERP) systems dedicated to horticulture. Twenty-five growers of potted plants have jointly set up this growers' association. As they grow in size, growers also feel an increased need to get a firmer grip on their production processes. Most growers do not know the cost price of their plants and their production planning is intuitive. Moreover, some have reached the limits of increasing production by traditional means and now need to delve much deeper into the data to see how they can further improve their yields.

Existing ERP systems do not take into account a number of horticulture-specific issues. An important issue is that ERP systems like those of SAP, Navision and Baan cannot cope with the fact that products change over time. In horticulture, however, a plant at the beginning of a quarter is very different from a plant at the end of that quarter. Plants grow or deteriorate. Another issue is that most ERP systems require a customer to trigger an order. For an important part of the horticultural sector, there are orders without customers or prices being known, as many flowers and plants are still sold via auction.

The growers' association Plantform has its roots in a first meeting, attended by a number of growers gathered by a local consultancy firm, VanderZandeFlorpartners. This meeting was needed to find out whether indeed the absence of a specialized ERP system was a problem and whether it was seen as a competitive issue. For a number of growers, especially the larger ones and those working at multiple locations, it was clear that they needed better software support to run their businesses. At the same time, this issue was found to be non-competitive: the growers did not perceive ownership of an ERP system as a thing that would give them a competitive advantage over other growers. Joint development of a system was therefore an option.

It was decided to set up a growers' association that would develop the specifications for an ERP system that could subsequently be built by a software company. Members of the growers' association pay a membership fee to the association. Further funding was obtained in the form of a subsidy from the PT. This funding is used to hire specialized consultants to help the association. Even though most growers have experience with IT systems, they are not specialists in this area. Two IT consultants were hired, one of whom knew both the agricultural world and the IT world. As such, this consultant was able to bridge the divide and cross the boundaries between these very different areas of expertise. It was the task of the consultants to help define the blueprint of an ERP system. They were introduced to the association by the consultant who initiated the first meeting.

Four members of the association were selected whose processes would be described in detail. The flow charts describing the business processes were defined in such detail that an ERP system could be built from them. The companies selected were quite different in order to ensure that the flow charts had some general validity. However, they were similar in that all four were advanced and innovative companies. One difference between the companies was for example the time needed to grow plants. Some plants grow in six weeks; others need over a year. Yet at the process level, they may be similar. For example, all plants need a 'growth shock' at some point, speeding up their growth. So, by working with the specialized consultants, Plantform was able to define the desired flow charts forming a blueprint for an ERP system. The IT consultants also organized workshops about IT and management, to bring the knowledge level of the growers up to the required level. Most learning, however, was done by doing, by working through the processes.

With the blueprint in place, the association selected two software companies to build ERP systems for two of the association's members. The reason for asking two companies to build the software was to spread risk and ensure competition among suppliers. If one of the software companies fails to create a good system, the other may still bring a good system to market. If both are successful, there will be two suppliers of adequate ERP systems for the horticultural industry. One supplier modifies the Navision software; the other builds a dedicated ERP system from scratch.

Both IT firms collaborate with one grower to develop a demo version of the software. These growers are selected based on an organization scan that was developed to determine their IT readiness. The pilot growers run the risk that the software demo developed in their company is not successful. If one of the IT companies fails to deliver good software, the pilot grower working with that company will receive the software developed by the other IT company from Plantform free of charge. This lowers their risk.

The software companies have access to the blueprint, but the blueprint is owned by the growers' association. The software companies license the blueprint from the association. The suppliers receive a trademark, signalling that their software is approved by Plantform. For each system they sell, they pay a fee to Plantform. In addition, association members receive a discount when they want to buy ERP software from either one of the suppliers. The association does not aim to be profitable, but it does hope to recover its initial investments. The most important objective is to bring decent ERP software for horticulture onto the market. Hence there is explicit agreement on how value is distributed.

In order to prevent free-riding by growers not making the investments now and joining Plantform at a later date to buy software cheaply, the associations stopped letting in new members by early 2006. Everyone who has joined so far and has made an investment will profit later. Still some free-ridership cannot be excluded: existing members may stop investing and leave the association, hoping that others will pick up the bill for development. This lowers their individual risk in the short run, even though in the longer run they may have to pay more for the software. Each grower makes his own calculations.

So far no grower has left for this reason. Initially, 30 growers were involved. Five growers left because they closed down their businesses or because they were too small to warrant the investment. The remaining growers tend to be bigger and more innovative. There is some overlap between the membership of Decorum and the membership of Plantform. The fact that people are part of different groups increases network density and makes knowledge sharing more efficient.

> Members of Plantform have usually been involved in other growers associations as well. I keep meeting the same guys, who are active in other functions or groups as well. I wonder why that is . . . Perhaps others may copy us and still do alright. But I believe you get further by being involved yourself. You really live through the project.

Not all 25 members are actively involved in the association. There is a technical working group consisting of some core members who do most of the work. The others are mainly needed to create scale and to get a sizeable group to pay for the research. The less active members follow developments from a distance. Every couple of months all members are updated on progress. This proved to be too long between meetings and hence the board of the association also decided to send out newsletters to update growers on progress. A deep long-term relationship is not really necessary for Plantform, because it is issue driven. There is no need to integrate companies. It is a project that needs to be done. 'I think this is a type of study club, except we don't focus on issues related to plant growth but on IT. We learn a lot with each other.' Nonetheless, keeping all growers in the association requires constant attention and energy. Some members remain sceptical and their scepticism needs to be allayed.

KNOWLEDGE MANAGEMENT IN THE DUTCH HORTICULTURE SECTOR

Knowledge sharing in the horticulture sector is generally not problematic. The sector has a long history of extensive knowledge sharing, founded on shared cooperative norms and supported, for many years, by a government-backed system of study clubs. The government has reduced its supporting role, however, and knowledge sharing is increasingly dependent on grower-initiated associations and commercial intermediaries.

A number of trends are slowly changing the sector. Potted plants is a growth sector, while cut flowers and fruit and vegetables are shrinking. Growth in potted plants is achieved by a decreasing number of growers with increasing acreage and ever-increasing yields. Greenhouses are becoming more and more high-tech, investment levels are increasing, and growers are becoming more professional and business-like. Knowledge sharing may become more of a business decision than a historical-cultural automatism.

The first of the four common knowledge-sharing problems is how to motivate network partners to share knowledge (see Figure 7.5). Our analysis of the two case examples of knowledge sharing shows five solution types that are used to tackle this problem. The professional pride of growers works as an intrinsic motivator to share knowledge. There is a

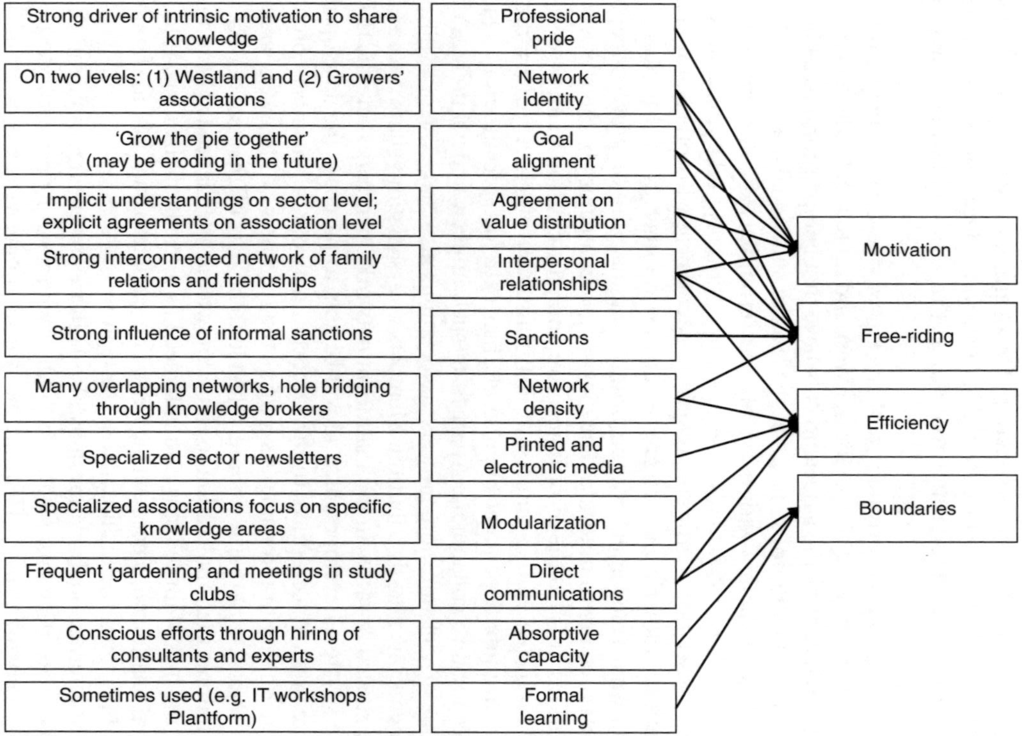

Strong driver of intrinsic motivation to share knowledge — Professional pride
On two levels: (1) Westland and (2) Growers' associations — Network identity
'Grow the pie together' (may be eroding in the future) — Goal alignment
Implicit understandings on sector level; explicit agreements on association level — Agreement on value distribution
Strong interconnected network of family relations and friendships — Interpersonal relationships
Strong influence of informal sanctions — Sanctions
Many overlapping networks, hole bridging through knowledge brokers — Network density
Specialized sector newsletters — Printed and electronic media
Specialized associations focus on specific knowledge areas — Modularization
Frequent 'gardening' and meetings in study clubs — Direct communications
Conscious efforts through hiring of consultants and experts — Absorptive capacity
Sometimes used (e.g. IT workshops Plantform) — Formal learning

Motivation
Free-riding
Efficiency
Boundaries

Figure 7.5 Knowledge-sharing problems and solutions in the horticulture sector

natural tendency within the sector to show others what you have achieved. A second solution type that is used to solve the motivation problem is building a network identity. For historical reasons, such an identity exists. Growers in the Westland generally have a sense of belonging to this specific region. Growers' associations also invest in building a network identity at the level of the association. Decorum, for instance, requires its members to at least fly a Decorum flag or show the Decorum brand name on their trucks. These identities at the level of the association are managed identities.

Growers are also motivated to share knowledge because they have a shared goal of growing the pie for the Westland on the global horticulture market. Members of the associations believe that competition takes place at network level and not so much at the level of individual companies: the Westland is competing with other regions (group-based competition, see Gomes-Casseres, 1994). This type of competition also takes place at the level of associations: growers' associations compete with other growers' associations, rather than one grower against another. It is also clear to growers what value collaboration brings. The majority of growers feel a constant pressure to innovate. The most active companies in the growers' associations are also the most innovative and participation in an association thus increases the chances of learning from others. Furthermore, growers are interdependent because of their extreme specialization. This requires them to collaborate. Apart from such implicit understandings of the value of collaboration, growers' associations also make use of explicit agreements on value distribution. Members of associations share risks and receive special rewards. In the Plantform network, members share the risk of failed system development, and will be able to purchase the developed software at a reduced price. In the Decorum network, all members profit from the quality brand name. As long as the members of a growers' association understand that it is more valuable to be part of the network than to go it alone, their motivation to share knowledge is enhanced. The motivation to share knowledge is also enhanced as a result of the many interpersonal relationships between growers. These relationships include family ties and personal friendships across the region.

These interpersonal relationships also help to prevent free-riding in the network. This mechanism works in tandem with a strong network identity and high network density. There are many overlapping networks of growers' associations, shared links with intermediary organizations, such as consulting firms and auctions, family and friendship ties. This means that everyone knows everyone else directly or through a limited number of connections. Anyone who tries to be a free-rider in a group with such high network density would quickly find himself ostracized by the entire group, his reputation ruined. A grower who is not willing to share his knowledge is excluded from the network. He is no longer allowed to visit the greenhouses of others.

Apart from such informal sanctions to prevent free-riding, formal sanctions, agreements on value distribution, and aligned goals help to address the free-riding risk in growers' associations. In the specific case of Plantform, there are clear rules to assure membership has added value: free-riding by late entrants to the network is prevented by setting an end-date for companies to enter the network free of charge. After that date, new members need to pay a fee to become a member.

Network density and interpersonal relationships also help to tackle the efficiency problem. Search costs in the network are lowered by the many points of contact that exist in the network. Overlapping structures like friendship and family networks, growers' associations, project groups, members of cooperatives and study clubs substantially increase the likelihood that growers get access to the knowledge they need. In addition, an extensive trade press makes new initiatives known throughout the horticultural sector. Intermediaries play a role here too. Specialized consultants help form new growers' associations, for example, and suppliers also bring their clients, the growers, into contact with each other. In the Decorum case, intermediaries helped growers find knowledge about marketing and quality management, while in the Plantform case, they helped to connect growers to software developers.

Efficiency is also helped through modularization of the network. Subgroups within the network focus on specific topics (knowledge modules). Plantform is an example in point. Everyone who wants to know something about horticulture and ERP systems knows Plantform is the place to go to look for information.

Crossing boundaries is the final challenge for knowledge sharing within networks. We have found evidence of boundaries that had to be crossed between horticulture and other professional expertise (e.g. marketing, management, information technology), and boundaries within horticulture (e.g. between different varieties of potted plants). Bringing people together in study clubs and growers' associations is one way of addressing this issue. The sector also makes efforts to create absorptive capacity through specialized consultants and incidental training. Specialized consultants are for instance used as knowledge interpreters. For example, Plantform hired an IT consultant who had specialized in working in the agricultural industry. His industry knowledge, and perhaps more importantly his ability to speak their language, enabled him to bridge the gap between IT and horticulture. Another example is the specialist hired by Decorum to judge the quality of plants. This specialist is able to compare a variety of plants on quality: a capability the average grower does not possess.

Our analysis of knowledge sharing in the potted plants sector provides us with additional insights into the influence of network type on knowledge-sharing problems and solutions. The growers' associations can be characterized as decentralized, localized, and multiple innovation networks. Decentralized networks appear to have particular efficiency problems as they lack a central player who can act as a knowledge broker. Decentralized networks may therefore have more need for solution types like overlapping structures (closure) and knowledge interpreters (absorptive capacity). Furthermore, decentralized networks have to rely more on informal sanctions against free-riding in the absence of a central player with the authority to apply formal sanctions. Overlapping structures, a strong network identity and a clear value proposition are important mechanisms to counter free-riding in a decentralized network. The other two network characteristics appear to be supportive of knowledge sharing. Localized networks can be expected to have fewer efficiency problems than dispersed networks, and it may be easier to build a strong network identity in a localized network. It appears this localized aspect of horticulture in the Westland stimulates the effectiveness of many solution concepts. Direct communication is made easier because of short travel distances. Interpersonal relationships are easier to maintain. Sanctions are felt more intensely when they are exercised by the neighbour you see every day than when exercised by somebody you hardly ever meet. Professional pride is more visible. In addition, a multiple innovation network offers a longer time frame for building a network identity, and it changes the value perception of network members in the sense that they are more willing to make more long-term investments.

This case study also sheds some light on the relationship between knowledge type, problems and solution types. When core knowledge (in this case, horticultural knowledge) has to be shared, boundary crossing is less of a problem, as all growers can be expected to be specialists in this area. For non-core knowledge, it is more difficult to set up a growers' association and to keep everyone committed. The sharing of explicit knowledge can be facilitated by relatively simple solutions such as databases, websites and newsletters. The sector has many specialized newsletters, enabling efficient sharing of explicit knowledge. The sharing of tacit knowledge, however, is associated with problems in efficiency (how to find the person with the required tacit knowledge) and crossing boundaries. Historically, the sector has tackled this problem with the habit of 'gardening', the regular visits to each other's gardens on Sunday afternoons. Furthermore, when tacit knowledge has to be shared, the many overlapping structures in the sector and the existence of knowledge interpreters help to create the much-needed network closure and absorptive capacity.

The future may hold a threat to knowledge sharing, however. Historically, growers were small family-owned businesses, too small to play any role on their own vis-à-vis other market parties, such as suppliers, the auction or trade and retail. No single grower was large enough to be a threat to the community of growers, which made cooperation and collaboration between growers a natural way of life. 'Chinese walls' existed between the links in the value chain, prohibiting growers from speaking directly to retailers. These knowledge-sharing boundaries are now being crossed, as discussed in the case description. The current trend of acquisition and consolidation has led to the emergence of large, sometimes multinational, players who are able to strike out on their own and make exclusive deals with suppliers and with customers. Should the old feeling of interdependence be replaced by a feeling of independence, knowledge sharing may decline in favour of increased knowledge protection.

In addition, the focus on the Westland area may lead to groupthink. Among tomato growers, this led to severe problems in the 1990s when consumers turned away from tomatoes that had become tasteless because of the spread of industrial growing methods. As information and knowledge from outside the network did not enter it and growers were very focused on the Westland, they no longer delivered the right product. For flowers and plants, this has not yet happened and there are some initiatives to link to knowledge centres outside the region. Individual growers appear to recognize the problem as well:

> For a new idea around packaging, I am now working with people from outside horticulture. In a network like ours it is easy to speak to each other but you don't get access to new knowledge. If you really want to innovate you have to look at a problem differently. Otherwise you are stuck. When I talk to somebody in horticulture about packaging, they all tell me the same thing.

For a vital network, it appears to be important to set up links with knowledge sources outside the sector.

CONCLUSION

Our analysis shows that in the horticultural sector in the Netherlands, in particular in the Westland area, there is a natural tendency amongst growers to cooperate and to share knowledge. Historically, this was limited to knowledge about growing plants and improving quality and yield, but this has evolved into many different types of partly overlapping knowledge-sharing networks, addressing not only the primary process of growing plants, but also secondary processes such as marketing and IT. Knowledge sharing is generally a success in this industry, with very few reported problems of free-riding or lack of motivation to share knowledge. Due to its long tradition of knowledge sharing, the sector has developed a multitude of solutions in order to prevent or correct problems in knowledge sharing. The regional concentration of the sector has greatly enhanced the effectiveness of these solutions.

NOTES

1. This case description is based on nine interviews, company visits, company websites and earlier research reports. The interviewees have reviewed the case study on factual accuracy. The authors are very grateful to VanderZandeFlorpartners for their extensive help.
2. At the time of writing. The two auctions merged in 2007.

REFERENCES

Berkhout, P. and C. van Bruchem (eds) (2006), *Landbouw-Economisch Bericht 2006*, Report 06.01, The Hague: LEI.

Buurma, J.S. (2001), *Dutch Agricultural Development and its Importance to China*, Report 6.01.11, The Hague: LEI.

de Man, A.P. and M. Bigwood (2006), *Innovation in the Dutch Agri-food Industry: An Exploratory Study of Patents and Scientific Publications*, June, Eindhoven: Technische Universiteit Eindhoven.

Gomes-Casseres, B. (1994), 'Group versus group: how alliance networks compete', *Harvard Business Review*, July/August, 62–74.

Jacobs, D., P. Boekholt and W. Zegveld (1990), *De Economische Kracht van Nederland*, The Hague: SMO.

Porter, M.E. (1990), *The Competitive Advantage of Nations*, London: Macmillan.

Silvis, H. and K. de Bont (eds) (2005), *Perspectieven voor de Agrarische Sector in Nederland*, The Hague: Ministerie van Landbouw, Natuur, en Voedselkwaliteit.

van der Meer, R. (2001), 'Sterke stijging investeringen glastuinbouwbedrijven', *Agri-Monitor,* April, The Hague: LEI.

van Horen, L.G.J., J.T.W. Alleblas, J. Bremmer and O. Hietbrink (2000), *Sierteelt en Beleid in Ontwikkeling*, Report 1.00.10, The Hague: LEI.

Wijnands, J. (2006), 'Nederland blijft grootste exporteur snijbloemen', *Agri-Monitor*, June, The Hague: WUR/LEI.

8. The fibres that hold an innovation network:[1] an analysis of knowledge-sharing in the Glare network

Elco van Burg, Erik van Raaij and Hans Berends

During the 1950s, failure of aircrafts due to material fatigue was becoming a nightmare. In 1954, two De Havilland Comets crashed. Investigation of the wreckage of the first Comet established metal fatigue as the cause. Aluminium, the metal commonly used for the skin of aircrafts, is fairly susceptible to fatigue. Fatigue cracks can cause weaknesses in the aircraft structure, which can result in accidents. Aircraft need to be inspected frequently for fatigue cracks, corrosion and impact damage. These inspections and repairs, if needed, are very costly because the aircraft cannot be operated at that time. The failure of aircrafts, due to metal fatigue, encouraged aircraft manufacturers to improve their structures. Strengthening the structure by adding more aluminium leads to heavier aircraft, however, which results in higher fuel costs.

In a search for solutions to fatigue, corrosion, and impact damage, aircraft manufacturers and research labs started to look for new materials. Different directions were promising. In the 1950s and 1960s, composites emerged as a new class of materials: modern fibres such as carbon, aramid and glass embedded in plastics. This class of materials is almost insusceptible to fatigue and is relatively light. However, composites are brittle and have less favourable impact properties than aluminium. The possibilities of improving the aluminium alloy itself, the second option, were only limited. The third direction was explored by the Dutch aircraft manufacturer Fokker, the Dutch aerospace laboratory NLR and the Delft University of Technology (TU Delft). They examined the combination of the good properties of aluminium with those of composites. Together with industrial partners like Alcoa, Akzo and 3M, they developed the sandwich material Glare. This material is built up from layers of aluminium and fibres (see Box 8.1). A part of the research was funded by the Dutch government, through NIVR, the Dutch agency for aerospace programmes. After more

BOX 8.1 GLARE®

Glare is an aircraft material built up from thin layers of aluminium bonded together with adhesive containing embedded glass fibres (prepreg). Its major application is in the fuselage of Airbus superjumbo A380. The material has several advantages, compared to the 2024-T3 aluminium alloy (Vermeeren, 2003; Vogelesang, 2003). First, the material has remarkably reduced and slower crack growth, about 10 to 100 times slower than in aluminium alloys. As a consequence, inspection of the structure for fatigue is not really necessary during the operational life of the aircraft. Second, the residual strength of Glare after multiple site damage is significantly higher. Third, the impact resistance is higher because of the high strain rate strengthening phenomenon in the glass fibres and the relatively high failure strain of the fibres. Fourth, the weight of the material is approximately 10 per cent lower than aluminium. Fifth, the flame resistance is extremely good. All in all, this means that aircraft can be designed with less material, and less need for inspection, thus saving costs.

The relatively high production cost of the laminates is the main disadvantage. These high costs are primarily caused by the complex and labour-intensive production process.

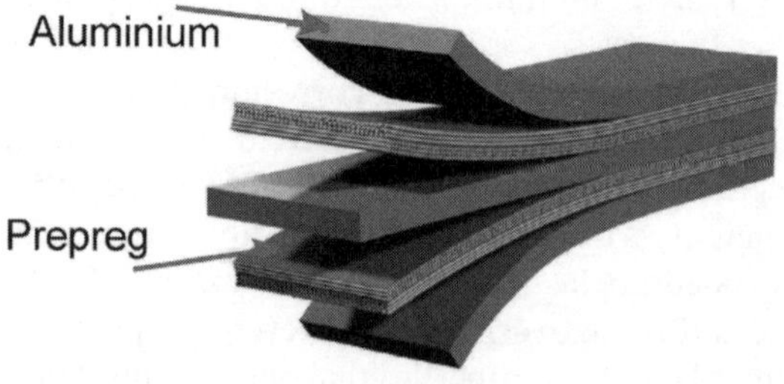

Source: Picture: TU Delft.

than 30 years of development and testing, Glare was eventually applied to the Airbus A380 mega-liner, as the first large-scale application of a fibre-metal laminate to an aircraft fuselage (the body of the aircraft).

The Glare network can be characterized as a network with continuous collaboration centred on a single innovation. The level of involvement of the individual partners constantly changed over time, as did the composition of the network. But Fokker, TU Delft and NLR always stayed together. The goal of this collaboration was to develop fibre-metal laminates, first Arall and later Glare, and to get these applied to aircraft. This innovation is explorative in its nature, as it is a new aircraft material and involves new concepts of manufacturing, designing and applying these materials.

In the network, TU Delft had a central role as the initiator of the research and the knowledge centre. Later on, the role of the knowledge centre was taken over by a joint venture of Akzo and Alcoa, named Structural Laminates Company (SLC), succeeded by the Fibre Metal Laminates Centre of Competence (FMLC). Airbus and Stork Fokker AESP had a more central role in managing the network when the application of Glare to the Airbus 380 materialized. Despite the presence of three core network partners (TU Delft, Fokker, NLR), there was no central authority that could exert power over all the other network members.

We find that in a decentralized network like this, the motivation problem is the main challenge. The knowledge that has to be shared in this network is mostly tacit, and is often core knowledge for the network partners. A striking conclusion is that the free-riding problem is not found, probably because the continuity of the collaboration bounded opportunistic behaviour by network members.

Seven solutions are found that enable knowledge-sharing in this network. These are, in order of importance: interpersonal relationships, agreements on value distribution, direct communication, network density, absorptive capacity, printed and electronic media and goal alignment. Interpersonal relationships were very important to motivate partners. These relationships created a network identity, thus improving commitment and motivation, and probably preventing any free-riding. Second, agreements were important to create commitment to engage in development. Finally, direct communication was important in establishing interpersonal relationships and as an opportunity to share knowledge. The solution concepts are, however, not without risks. Relationships are vulnerable because relationships can be harmed by personal tensions, and personnel change could sever interpersonal ties between organizations. Formal rules and agreements can exclude certain parties from knowledge-sharing, thus possibly cutting off innovation opportunities.

In the remainder of this chapter we will first describe the historical development of the Glare network. Subsequently, we analyse knowledge-sharing in this network. We present an overview of the knowledge-sharing problems and discuss the solution concepts that were applied. Finally, we conclude this analysis by discussing interesting findings.

THE HISTORY OF THE GLARE NETWORK

Period I: Early History (1971–1981)

The philosophy of Glare and its predecessor Arall rests upon two techniques: bonding and laminating. The first idea stems from the Dutch and British aircraft manufacturers Fokker and De Havilland. These companies used to build aircrafts by bonding the wooden parts. This idea was subsequently applied to metal, and Fokker applied their first bonded metal wing structure in the Fokker F-27 in 1955. The second technique, laminating materials, also stems from the manufacture of wooden aircrafts. Fokker introduced the first laminated wing structure in 1916. Laminating multiple layers of plywood provided an opportunity to use different fibre orientations, arranging them in such a way that the directional strength of the material was optimized. This technique is also applied in Glare, where the fibres run in different directions.

In the first two decades after the Second World War, Fokker started looking for ways to improve the fatigue properties of metal structures. This kind of research was carried out in cooperation with NLR and also with TU Delft. The industrial needs of Fokker drove the research. Special research projects were funded by the NIVR and qualified testing was done by NLR. Fokker, TU Delft and NLR formed a close triangle in development, research and education (Figure 8.1).

This research at Fokker resulted in the bonded metal structure of the F-27. Fatigue tests indicated that the fatigue properties were good. In 1971, Fokker and TU Delft started studying reinforcements of bonded aluminium structures with fibres, an idea they had seen at NASA during a visit to the US. But this research did not show promising results, so the idea was

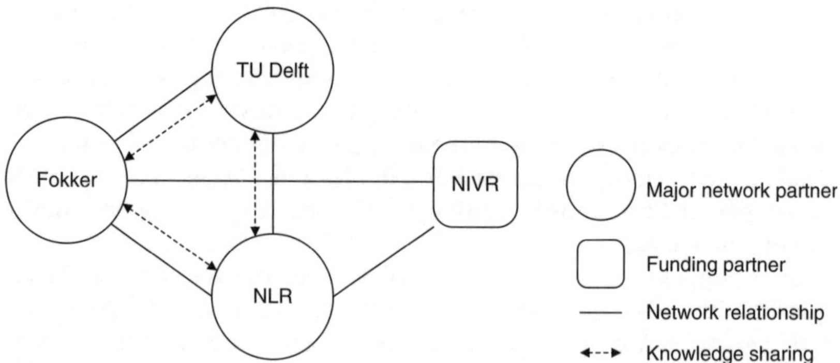

Figure 8.1 Early history of the network (1971–1981)

officially abandoned by Fokker's R&D management. Some people at Fokker, like Paul Bijlmer, still believed in the possibilities. He tried to continue the research contrary to the management's decision, but was forced to stop. At the individual level, however, some Fokker employees continued their cooperation with the people at TU Delft.

Researchers at TU Delft were convinced that fibre-metal laminates could have better fatigue properties than aluminium alloys. These researchers included the group around Professor Schijve (who was the former head of the Structures and Materials Department at NLR) and Vogelesang (who later became Schijve's successor as a professor in Delft). This group initiated a research programme on laminated sheet materials, which resulted in a new kind of material, called Fibre-Metal Laminates (FMLs).

One of the first projects was carried out by a graduate student, Roel Marissen, who finished his thesis in 1980. Using the framework he developed in his thesis, the research group was able to optimize the aluminium sheet thickness, the types of fibre and the fibre volume fraction. This resulted in thinner aluminium sheets, and for the fibre, aramid was chosen. Tests on this improved laminate showed that the material had excellent fatigue performance. The key to this is the 'crack bridging' mechanism of the fibres. Fibres remain intact under fatigue loading, whereas the aluminium cracks. The research at TU Delft thus resulted in a new material, which they called 'Arall' (Aramid Reinforced Aluminium Laminates) (de Vries, 2001: 2; Vlot, 2001: 43).

Period II: Network around Arall (1981–1991)

Inspired by the promising results for Arall, TU Delft continued its research on fibre-metal laminates and looked for industry collaboration and funding. Because the management of Fokker was not interested in fibre-metal laminates at that time and because specific material knowledge was needed, TU Delft looked for other industrial partners. Industry involvement was especially needed for the supply and knowledge of strong fibres and thin aluminium sheets. Vogelesang got the Dutch chemical company Akzo interested in providing aramid fibres. The first step Akzo took was to acquire the rights of the Arall patents that were filed in January 1981 by TU Delft with Vogelesang and Marissen as inventors. Akzo, in return, supported the research in Delft with a grant of 100 000 guilders a year, by providing equipment and materials, and by giving access to their lab.

By the end of 1981, a second industrial partner had become involved. Through existing contacts at TU Delft, the American aluminium producer Alcoa became interested in the new material. Alcoa was willing to supply the thin aluminium sheets needed for Arall, although manufacturing these thin sheets was difficult and required a lot of work. But Alcoa was concerned that composites would replace aluminium in the future, and with Arall they could both supply their aluminium *and* play a role in the market for composite materials. Alcoa received a five-year exclusive licence to produce Arall, and launched the first commercial version of Arall in 1983. The third company to become involved was 3M, which supplied the 'prepreg' for bonding the aluminium sheets and the fibres. Unlike Alcoa and Akzo, 3M was not a development partner, but just a supplier of the adhesive.

Despite the lack of interest in FMLs, Fokker was still an obvious industrial partner in the development because of the long relationship between TU Delft, Fokker and NLR. Therefore, the different parties tried to get Fokker involved. First, NIVR asked Fokker to play a more active role in Arall applications. In 1984, this request resulted in an Arall working group with representatives from TU Delft, Fokker, NLR and NIVR. A wing panel for the existing Fokker F-27 could be developed and tested. First studies on the application of Arall on an F-27 wing had already been carried out by two students of Jan Willem Gunnink at TU Delft. This marked the first involvement of Gunnink in the development of FMLs. It was remarkable, certainly at that time, that Delft had designed the wing panels and had even made the production drawings according to Fokker specifications, so that Fokker could easily produce the panels. Delft also designed all kinds of detailed test specimens and tested them. So Fokker could test the larger size panels including the full-scale panel. The development of this wing was funded by NIVR, the first time TU Delft received direct funding from NIVR. This sparked a new era in which the role of TU Delft moved from basic research towards development and testing, directly funded by the government.

Tests on the full-scale F-27 panel again showed the excellent properties of Arall for fatigue and damage tolerance. As a result, TU Delft tried to convince Fokker to use Arall in one of their aircrafts. In 1984, however, Fokker decided not to use Arall in its new F-50. According to Daan Krook (former member of the board of directors of Fokker), Fokker would develop the F-50 with a 'minimum change configuration' from the existing F-27. Therefore, a major change like applying Arall instead of aluminium was out of the question. The good results of the F-27 wing project nevertheless prompted Fokker to ask NLR to get more involved in the project, which the people at TU Delft felt was an attempt to by-pass their involvement (Vlot, 2001: 71). TU Delft was upset by this behaviour of Fokker and told Fokker that it would continue with Akzo, Alcoa and 3M as primary partners. So the relationship between TU Delft and Fokker became strained. Individual relationships between people at Fokker and TU Delft were stronger than the official dispute, and people on both sides continued to be involved in the project and remained on speaking terms and cooperative, because they personally believed in the material and in the need for cooperation. But Arall was never applied to a commercial F-27, mainly because it was too expensive to qualify as the new material for an existing aircraft.

Roel Marissen, one of the inventors of Arall, moved to the German aerospace research institute DFVLR (later called DLR). This created links between DFVLR and Alcoa, NLR and TU Delft. However, DFVLR never had a real role in the development of Arall because Marissen was working in other directions than the people at TU Delft. The industrial partners in the Arall network limited knowledge-sharing between people at TU Delft and Marissen at DFVLR because they were concerned about leaking core knowledge in the direction of their German competitors.

The skies looked bright for Arall, but soon some clouds would show up. In 1987, Alcoa opened an Arall plant in Pittsburg (PA). Knowledge about the material properties of Arall originated from TU Delft and was integrated with the production knowledge of Alcoa. Shortly after the opening of the Arall production facility, an Arall conference was held in Seven Springs (PA). At this conference, the 'jury of the international aviation community' was present and the TU Delft community presented excellent results for Arall at the conference. Off-stage, however, Geert Roebroeks, a Ph.D. student from TU Delft, had discovered some disappointing Arall properties and the group at TU Delft had already started working on a solution with glass fibres as an alternative to aramid. Marissen, who was still working on Arall in Germany, had also found that aramid fibres around a crack would break under the cyclic loading conditions that occur in fuselages. Marissen was upset about the fact that his role in the development of Arall was not acknowledged by the people from TU Delft. He therefore decided to mention the detrimental properties in his presentation in order to thwart, as he saw it, the development of Arall. The publication of some disappointing results and the attempts of the people at TU Delft to develop an alternative material harmed the image of Arall to some extent. The aviation community, however, became convinced that the principle of the material was promising, which created space for the acceptance of an improved material (Vlot, 2001: 78).

The new variant of the material, with glass fibres, did not have the detrimental properties of Arall, and TU Delft concentrated on further development of this material, which they called Glare (GLass Aluminium REinforced). A patent on this new material was filed by Akzo in October 1987 and was finally accepted in 1991. At the same time, Alcoa had introduced its first commercial Arall products and had managed to get a first application of Arall in the cargo door of the McDonnell Douglas C-17

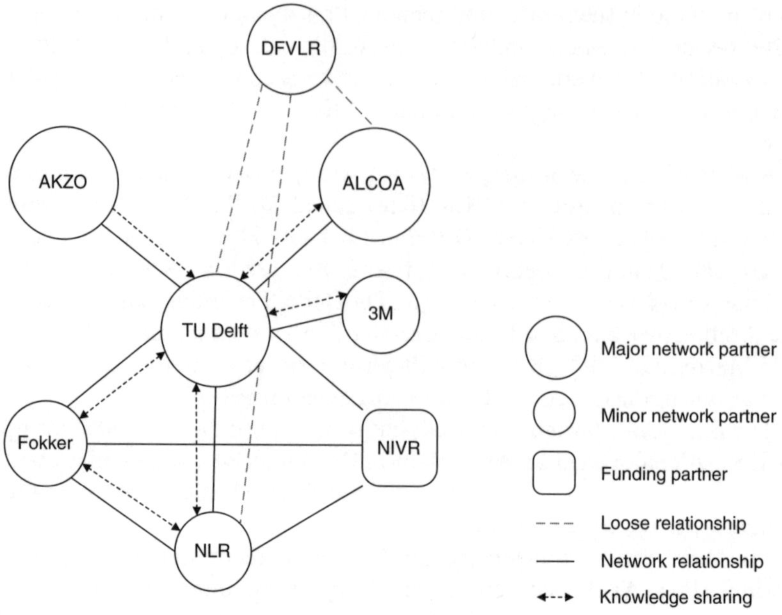

Figure 8.2 Network around Arall (1981–1991)

military transport aircraft in 1988. The complete network at this period is shown in Figure 8.2.

Period III: Network around Glare (1991–2001)

While Alcoa had its first commercial Arall application, the relationship between Alcoa and Akzo deteriorated. The exclusive production rights that Akzo had licensed to Alcoa were expiring. Akzo was losing interest, but thanks to Daan Krook's lobbying with the Akzo management, they continued to be involved, and started a Glare business. Akzo wanted to set up a joint venture with Alcoa for both Glare and Arall because this would possibly give Akzo opportunities to sell fibres to the aerospace market. But Alcoa was not willing to have this joint venture, and the relationship became strained. Furthermore, a Dutch lobby at the international aerospace community for Glare, consisting of people from Akzo and TU Delft, harmed the commercial position of Arall. Alcoa finally decided to go along with Akzo and Glare. This resulted in a joint venture, Structural Laminates Company (SLC), in 1991, which owned the patents. Akzo owned one-third and Alcoa two-thirds of this joint venture. The partnership company SLC, located in the US, was responsible for the commercialization of Glare and Arall. On the Dutch side, the subsidiary of SLC, Structural Laminates BV (SLBV), was located in Delft and was supposed to do research and technical marketing.

Although there was a promising new material, there was still a long way to go. The goal was to get FMLs on a new aircraft type. The first challenge was to test and qualify the material. Another challenge was to achieve the acceptance of the aviation industry. A major disadvantage for the aviation industry was the high costs of Glare, which were at that time up to 10 times higher than aluminium. Production was labour intensive and difficult. A major breakthrough came in 1993 when the concept of splicing was developed. With splices, Glare panels can be wider than the size of the metal sheets they are made of. These wider panels significantly reduce the installation costs of Glare.

Various aircraft construction companies developed an interest in the material. First, in 1988, people at MBB (which later became a part of Airbus Germany) read an article about Arall by Vogelesang and considered it to be a promising material. These people were responsible for testing a segment (called a 'barrel') of the Airbus A330 and A340. They were able to test new materials too, and they asked TU Delft to produce a Glare test panel for the barrel. With funding from Akzo, TU Delft could get Fokker to produce the panels. The tests were performed in 1990 and the results were good. The people at Airbus Germany (the current name) continued testing Glare for different applications during the 1990s.

A second company with an interest in Glare was Boeing. In 1990, Glare was selected for a cargo floor in the Boeing 777 because of its excellent impact properties. In 1993, Rob van Oost from SLC was sent to Boeing to study the application of Glare on the successor of the 747 Jumbo Jet. Because the requirements of this new plane frequently changed, he finally studied application in the already existing Boeing 777. Although the results looked promising, Boeing decided not to use Glare for the primary structure of the 777.

While industry interest grew, Alcoa was frustrating the people from SLC who tried to sell Glare to the aircraft industry. During the 1990s, the policy of Alcoa regarding Glare had changed. First, Arall was not a commercial success, and therefore their Arall plant was operating at a loss. Second, Glare was more and more seen as a competitor for their aluminium, because it was targeted at the same fuselage market. Strategically, they wanted to prevent the application of Glare and therefore they obstructed the commercialization of Glare through SLC, sometimes by preventing SLC people from talking to decision-makers at aircraft construction companies, at other times by giving inadequate or inaccurate information. The reason why Boeing decided not to use Glare, in spite of good test results, was in part a result of Alcoa's behaviour. Bill Evancho (at that time, head of SLC) believed that the salespeople from Alcoa convinced Boeing not to use Glare. In 1993, this finally resulted in a moratorium on Glare studies, set by the management of Boeing.

While this closed the door to Boeing, interest from other sides grew. The third organization that became interested was the US Air Force. A US Air Force officer had heard about Arall and started his Ph.D. study on Glare at TU Delft in the early 1990s. On his return, he convinced the US Air Force to use Glare for fuselage repairs of the C-5A Galaxy transporter (Vlot, 2001: 130, 131; Scholtens, 1995). Besides this programme, the US Air Force also evaluated Arall for a rudder, for flaps and for dorsal covers.

A fourth company with an interest was Bombardier Aerospace. In 1996, they decided to use Glare for a part of the Learjet 45 business jet. The fifth company was Garuda Airlines (Indonesia) who used Glare for a panel of an Airbus A330 (Vlot, 2001: 138). And subsequently, in April 1999, an experimental Glare fuselage panel was installed on a German Luftwaffe A310. Furthermore, US Airways used Glare in a cargo bay floor, and Galaxy Scientific Corporation used Glare in an explosion-hardened container.

Also Aérospatiale (later Airbus France) became involved. In 1994, Buwe van Wimersma was sent to Toulouse by SLC. He studied the application of Glare to the A330. Later, in 1997 and 1998, he and his colleague Gise Wit became members of the Large Aircraft Division led by Jens Hinrichsen. They prepared information about Glare to convince him to apply it. This eventually resulted in the choice of Glare for the fuselage of the A3XX which later became the A380.

The group at TU Delft needed extra funding for the increasing number of tests and experiments. The Dutch government saw the need for a strong push to Airbus, helped by the lobbying efforts of Krook, Gunnink and Vogelesang. They funded half the costs of the A310 panel and also allocated in total about 30 million euros to the Glare project in the period 1997 to 2003, which was coordinated by the NIVR. This funding was used to start the Glare Technology Program (GTP, later Glare Research Programme, GRP), in which TU Delft, SLC (later SLI and FMLC), NLR, Airbus and Stork Fokker AESP were involved. Later, a significant part of the money was also used to get Glare tested in the mega-liner barrel test, a huge fuselage section similar to the A380. This test began in 2001 and the panels are still being studied today. These tests were performed at Airbus Germany, but NLR engineers were involved in these tests as well. Through this involvement, they learned about Airbus's test methods and results.

Alcoa considered Airbus's growing interest in Glare as a threat to their core business, the production of aluminium. They convinced Akzo to shut down the production facility of SLC, formally because of low customer

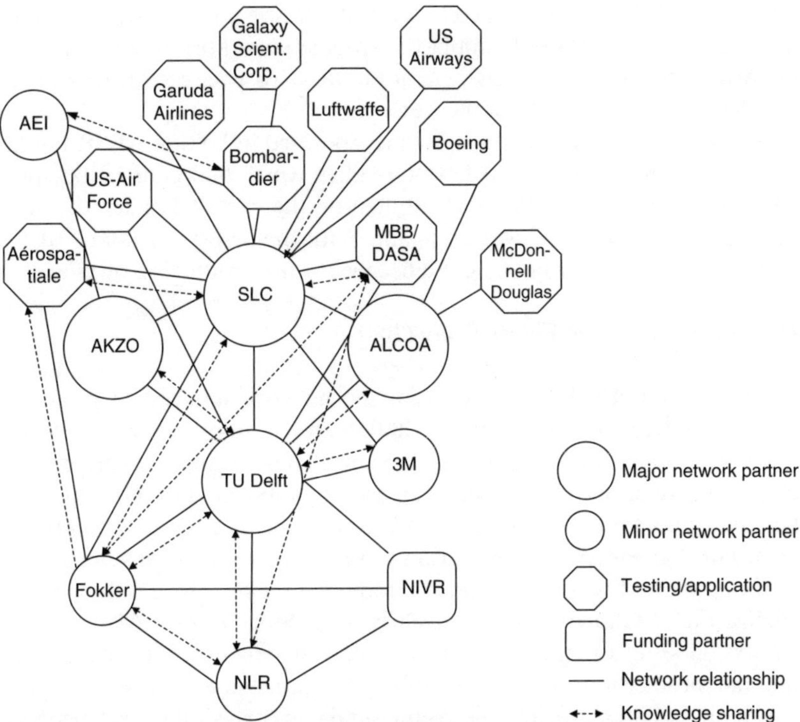

Figure 8.3 Network around Glare (1991–2001)

interest. Alcoa stopped supplying thin aluminium sheets and the production of Arall and Glare was stopped in 1997. As a result, McDonnell Douglas and Boeing needed aluminium replacements for respectively the cargo door of the C-17 and the cargo floor of the Boeing 777. The commercial activities of SLC were stopped as well. Alcoa just kept SLC alive to keep control over the patent rights. A licence for secondary applications was given to Aviation Equipment, Inc. (AEI). They were successful in the application of Glare to hardened containers and aircraft cargo bay floors. They also provided Glare for the Learjet 45 and supported Bombardier in their fibre-metal laminates R&D programme. The entire network for the period 1991–2001 is depicted in Figure 8.3.

Alcoa eventually withdrew and the joint venture SLC was broken up. At first, Akzo continued its Glare activities. With the help of Daan Krook (who was a board member of SLC), Akzo acquired licences for Glare in Europe. Akzo restructured SLBV to Structural Laminates Industries (SLI). But shortly after that, Akzo reconsidered the fit of SLI with the core business of Akzo. They decided to sell SLI because they could not produce the material, they did not supply the specific glass fibre that was used in Glare and their core activities were not in the aerospace sector. As a result, in 1998, Akzo sold SLI to Stork Aerospace.

At Stork Aerospace, SLI became incorporated in Fokker AESP. Fokker AESP consisted of what was left of Fokker, which had gone bankrupt in 1996. So, after years of low commitment on the part of Fokker, the 'new' Fokker became heavily involved again. With the incorporation of SLI in Fokker AESP, Fokker finally got a licence for the production of Glare.

Period IV: Airbus and Future Glare (2001–)

As Alcoa and Akzo withdrew from the network, interest from Airbus (which resulted from a merger in 2001 between aerospace companies in Germany, Spain, England and France) grew. They became convinced of the excellent properties of Glare after an exciting lobbying period. In particular, the opportunity for weight reduction persuaded them. In 2001, the Heads of Agreement for application of Glare in the A380 was signed with Stork Fokker AESP, who would be producing the material. But the industrialization of Glare was still at an early stage. Stork Fokker AESP quickly started building a manufacturing plant, industrializing Glare and qualifying the production process according to aerospace norms. The plant was built in Papendrecht, The Netherlands, and was officially opened in November 2003, although production had already begun in 2002. Airbus also wanted to acquire the knowledge and capability of manufacturing Glare and opened a plant in Nordenham, Germany, to manufacture five of the 27 Glare panels. The knowledge about Glare properties required for these production facilities was mainly obtained from people from the former SLC, now working at FMLC and Stork Fokker AESP.

To get the material ready for the manufacture of the first A380, the parties worked closely together. The design of Glare parts and development of the design principles occurred in close cooperation between Stork Fokker AESP and Airbus. These companies also jointly developed production and improved the material further. This resulted in a new generation of Glare, with improved strength, called HSS Glare. For the qualification of the material, NLR, Stork Fokker AESP, FMLC, TU Delft and Airbus worked closely together to demonstrate the quality of the material and to perform all tests. TU Delft, with its very enthusiastic group of students and employees, performed tests that showed which fields needed more testing or even further improvement and which fields had been tested satisfactorily. The qualification testing was subsequently done by NLR, according to the norms in aerospace.

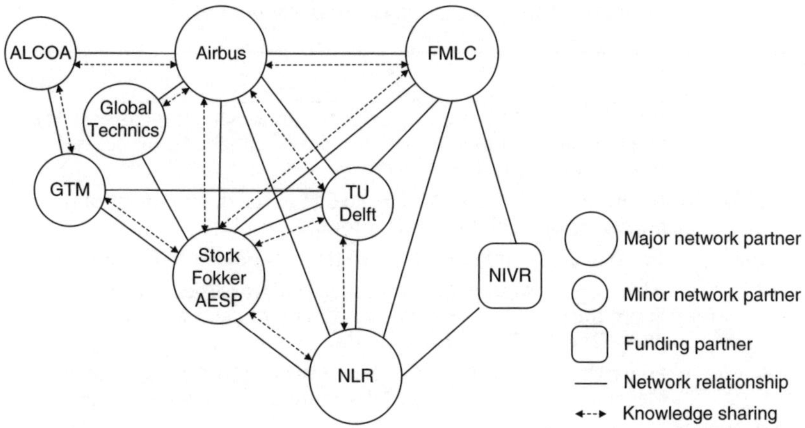

Figure 8.4 Network Airbus and Glare (2001–)

To continue research on the material and to provide knowledge about Glare to the network partners, a Glare centre of competence was established. This centre, Fibre Metal Laminates Centre of Competence (FMLC), was founded by TU Delft, NLR and Stork Fokker AESP in 2001. This centre also had the task of exploring different applications of Glare. Another task was to distribute the funding from the NIVR and the government. But because Airbus became fully involved in the development of Glare, the necessity for external funding decreased. In 2003, also due to policy changes by the Dutch government, funding was reduced to a minimum. The managing director of FMLC was Jan Willem Gunnink. But, by the end of 2004, following a dispute over policy, Gunnink left FMLC and started a new company named GTM. Almost all the employees from FMLC joined this new company. GTM is currently, among other projects, developing new materials and structures, which include improvements to aluminium structures. One of their clients is Alcoa, which again has expressed interest in the development of FMLs and is also cooperating with Airbus on developments around Glare and laminated aircraft materials.

Besides GTM, another small new company appeared, GlobalTechnics (see Figure 8.4 for the network as of 2001). Gise Wit, Adel Khoudja and a third partner founded this enterprise. They provide knowledge and experience of Glare to the network and perform calculations on Glare. Their main clients are Stork Fokker AESP, Airbus, and Airbus partners.

Table 8.1 lists the main events in the development of Glare. Thirty years may seem like a long time for such an innovation to come to fruition. One reason for the long development path is the fact that extensive material

Table 8.1 Main events in 30 years of Glare development

Year	Event
ca. 1978	Professor Boud Vogelesang develops fibre-metal laminates (FML) at TU Delft, building on two decades of collaboration between Fokker, TU Delft and NLR.
ca. 1981	Involvement of Akzo, Alcoa and 3M in the development of an aramid fibre reinforced FML product: Arall.
ca. 1984	Jan Willem Gunnink leads Arall tests on Fokker F-27 wing panel.
1987	Alcoa opens Arall plant; Arall material properties questioned at Seven Springs conference; Akzo files first patent for a new, glass-fibre-reinforced FML product: Glare.
1990	Glare tested at Boeing; first Glare tests at MBB (later: Airbus Germany); further tests at MBB continued through the 1990s.
1990–1999	Various small-scale applications of Glare at Bombardier, US Air Force, German Luftwaffe and others.
1991	Glare patent accepted; Alcoa-Akzo joint venture (SLC) for Arall and Glare established.
1993	Technological breakthrough ('splicing') enables more efficient production of Glare.
1994	Buwe van Wimersma (from SLC) studies Glare application at Aérospatiale (later: Airbus France).
1996	Bankruptcy of Fokker; Stork Fokker AESP established.
1997	Buwe van Wimersma and Gise Wit (both from SLC) seconded to Airbus to study application of Glare to the Airbus A3XX mega-liner.
1997	Glare Technology Project (GTP) established, funded in part by the Dutch government. Partners include TU Delft, SLC, NLR, Airbus, Stork Fokker AESP.
1998	Alcoa withdraws from SLC; Akzo restructures SLC into SLI, which is eventually sold to Stork Fokker AESP.
2001	Start of the mega-liner barrel tests at Airbus Germany.
2001	Heads of Agreement signed between Airbus and Stork Fokker to produce Glare for the A380 mega-liner fuselage. Stork Fokker and Dutch government invest in Glare production capability.
2001	TU Delft, Stork Fokker and NLR establish fibre-metal laminate centre of competence (FMLC).
2002	Glare production started in Papendrecht and Nordenham.
2003	Airbus takes full control of Glare developments related to the A380 and thereby limits the role of other partners like FMLC and TU Delft.
2004	Two new start-ups established for further development of Glare: GTM, by Jan Willem Gunnink, and GlobalTechnics, by Gise Wit and two partners.
2005	First Airbus A380 prototype takes off with a 350 m^2 Glare fuselage section.

qualifications are necessary before a new material can be applied to any aircraft structure. A second reason is that aerospace manufacturers will generally only make an investment in a new material when they design a completely new type of aircraft. This has severely limited the number of windows of opportunity for Glare. With only a limited number of sufficiently large aerospace manufacturers in the world, the developers of Glare had to make sure that the right people at such companies were convinced of the superior properties of Glare just as plans for a new aircraft type were being developed.

KNOWLEDGE-SHARING PROBLEMS IN THE GLARE NETWORK

The development of fibre-metal laminates, eventually leading to the production and application of Glare, started as a loose cooperation between Fokker, NLR and TU Delft. Over time, the network expanded and the level of involvement of partners changed. Problems and tensions between partners came and went. Over the years, the partners in the network had to create, share, and integrate knowledge related to material properties, materials testing, aerospace requirements, design knowledge and production knowledge. Some of this knowledge could be codified and shared 'on paper'; other knowledge was of the tacit kind. All this knowledge-sharing took place without a core network player orchestrating the process or a *grand design* for knowledge-sharing. Yet, in spite of various knowledge-sharing problems between network partners, and the lack of explicit knowledge management to solve these problems, the goal was eventually achieved: the first Airbus A380 super-jumbo took to the air in April, 2005 with 350 m^2 section of Glare panels in its fuselage. What is the story behind this success?

To unravel this story, we will first discuss the four general knowledge-sharing problems and subsequently pay attention to the solutions, as they appeared in this case study. In the Glare network, the main knowledge-sharing problems were those related to efficiency and motivation. These problems were tackled through interpersonal relationships, agreements on value distribution and sanctions. These solution concepts are the most salient and provide an explanation of the successful knowledge-sharing in spite of the lack of a grand design of knowledge management.

Motivation

The motivation of partners to share knowledge is very important. In the Glare case, motivation was not a problem generally. Various individuals acted as passionate inspirers, motivating others to stay involved and share knowledge. Professional pride and a passion for fibre-metal laminates facilitated knowledge-sharing in the network. But, at times, competition, conflict, and personal pride would negatively influence motivation. The relationship between TU Delft and Fokker was not always without problems, for instance. They repeatedly argued about who invented Arall. Fokker would give presentations about Arall without naming TU Delft as the inventor. There would also be competitive strife about who should receive funding from NIVR; the industrial partner Fokker, or the academic partner TU Delft. This caused recurring conflicts between Fokker and TU Delft, although these were sometimes more moral than formal conflicts (Vlot, 2001: 72, 73). Such conflicts decreased the motivation of the partners to cooperate with each other. After the bankruptcy of Fokker in 1996, the problem largely disappeared because the people involved in the initial conflict were no longer working at TU Delft or Fokker.

Issues caused by personal pride and personal 'battles for competence' were the second driver behind the motivation problem. This problem first appeared in the relationship between NLR employees and people from TU Delft. The very enthusiastic Vogelesang came to NLR with his new material and NLR performed tests on the material. But the people at NLR were sceptical and have more or less remained so ever since. This caused difficulties in the relationship. The tensions between Marissen and the people from TU Delft were also about personal pride. And in the last phase of the development, knowledge-sharing between Fokker AESP and Airbus Nordenham was less optimal because people saw it as a 'battle for competence', thus creating a situation where it would be a weakness to ask the other for help.

Finally, the competitive strategies of firms in the network also hindered the motivation to share knowledge. In the early years of Glare, Alcoa obstructed contacts between SLC and Boeing because they started to see Glare as a competitor to their aluminium. They were no longer motivated to turn Glare into a success. More recently, the motivation to share knowledge between Airbus-Fokker and other interested parties has been hindered by Airbus's concerns over knowledge leaking to Boeing.

Boundaries

In the Glare network, people from different organizations and from different backgrounds had to work together and share knowledge. Crossing the boundaries between different practices, cultures and organizations was sometimes difficult. In this case study, the two most influential boundaries that had to be crossed were boundaries between cultures (both national and corporate) and between professional backgrounds.

The boundaries between cultures appeared for example in the relationship between TU Delft and NLR. This caused discussions about the demarcation of tasks. According to Vogelesang, this can also be interpreted as a tension between a professional research organization (NLR) and an educational institute without a qualified testing lab (TU Delft). Boundaries between national cultures were present between Alcoa and the Dutch partners, and between Airbus France and the Dutch partners together with Airbus Germany.

Knowledge-sharing was at times hampered because of boundaries between people with different backgrounds. Even when people had the same profession, for example researchers, it was hard to understand each other's results, because of the differences between the research areas and interests. For example, in the 1990s, when Fokker AESP and Airbus were asked to provide guidance on the developments at TU Delft, they lacked the appropriate knowledge to do this.

Efficiency

As the development of Arall and Glare progressed, the stock of knowledge accumulated, and more and more individuals became involved. This exacerbated the challenge of creating and sharing knowledge in an efficient way. The efficiency problem has two main causes: lack of industry leadership in development, and frequent change of personnel.

The first challenge was related particularly to the efficiency of *creating* knowledge. The developments at TU Delft did not always fit the needs of industry. More 'guidance' from industry was needed. But the industrial partners lacked the appropriate insight to see the way ahead or did not understand the priority of providing guidance. As a result, sometimes research was undertaken which was not very useful for the further development of FMLs. Gise Wit, who was involved in the cooperation of Airbus, TU Delft and Fokker, said: 'A lot of reports were very useful, but also a number ended up in the garbage can'. After a while, some individuals at Airbus were appointed to guide the research, but they often lacked appropriate knowledge and time to provide efficient guidance. Therefore, SLBV, later on SLI and in the last phase FMLC, took the lead in directing activities.

Second, the efficiency of knowledge-sharing was harmed by regular change of personnel in the network. At TU Delft, a lot of research in the lab was carried out by graduates. These former students usually worked very enthusiastically in the lab for about two years and then moved to a job elsewhere. When they did not end up working for one of the network partners, the knowledge they acquired often disappeared from the network. According to Gise Wit, at that time working for Fokker: 'The knowledge rests with a limited number of people, because the others leave the network quickly. Of course, it rests with the permanent employees, like Ad Vlot and Geert Roebroeks. But Ad Vlot died, Boud Vogelesang left. . . . So, I think that the knowledge also seeped away to some extent.' On the other hand, graduates heading out to other companies within the network helped to disperse knowledge, thus improving efficiency.

Knowledge-sharing efficiency was not helped either by the frequent change in those attending GRP meetings. Some network partners did not acknowledge the important role of the GRP meetings for knowledge exchange and sent whoever was available to these meetings, thus forgoing the opportunity to build long-term relationships between team members.

The efficiency problem was never fully eliminated. Regular meetings and strong interpersonal relationships somewhat reduced this problem. In particular, the research programmes increased the efficiency of knowledge-sharing, because these established some sort of central coordination. Nevertheless, 10 (out of 17) respondents named the efficiency problem (also talking about the last phases), because it was a central issue in knowledge-sharing in the whole development trajectory.

Free-riding

In the Glare network, no clear instances of the free-riding problem were found. Sometimes, the danger of free-riding raised its head, as in 1986 when Fokker started negotiations with NLR to get them more involved in the development, while the centre of development was still at TU Delft. Fokker even questioned whether there was still a role for TU Delft. At TU Delft, they felt, however, that Fokker had 'hijacked' the Arall project without having put much effort into it before. Because Delft did not want to support this new direction, the attempt failed. Thus, the free-rider problem was tackled in a natural way. All respondents, looking back at the whole development trajectory, said that no partner profited more than their fair share considering their contributions. Some partners profited more than others, but they also took more risks and spent more effort and money on the Glare development. Because all partners were willing to cooperate for a long time, the free-riding problem did not occur. Within this long time frame, partners did not show any significant opportunistic behaviour. Another explanation for the prevention and reduction of the free-riding problem is the strong network identity among the core of the individuals involved. Such a network identity motivated them to share knowledge, and created commitment (shared norms and beliefs) and trust, which prevented free-riding.

SOLUTIONS TO KNOWLEDGE-SHARING IN THE GLARE NETWORK

In the absence of conscious knowledge management in the Glare network, several solution concepts were applied more or less unconsciously that enabled and improved knowledge-sharing. An overview and illustration of the findings is presented in Table 8.2. Each solution concept is discussed in the following text, in order to provide more insight into their effectiveness in the Glare case. This discussion concludes with a graphical representation of the relationships between solution concepts and problems.

The Effectiveness of Interpersonal Relationships

The concept of interpersonal relationships is a solution that explains the success story of Glare to a large extent. Where organizations often considered their own aims and goals instead of the common good, the interpersonal contacts provided a strong informal network committed to the development of FMLs. This 'Glare community' was also a basis for trust. The informal network was an important enabler for knowledge-sharing in the network of organizations. When organizations practically withdrew from the network, individual engineers continued to be involved, carried on the development and shared their knowledge. Although organizations restricted knowledge-sharing, the engineers continued to share their knowledge, because of shared beliefs and passion for the material. These interpersonal contacts were created at conferences like the Arall conference, meetings within the aerospace field (Brite Euram programme, GRP, etc.), and last but not least through TU Delft graduates heading out into companies all over the world. Over time, the interpersonal network grew because more people became involved and more graduates swarmed out.

The solution concept of interpersonal relationships is, however, fairly vulnerable. When relationships break up because of conflicts or personnel change, the channel for knowledge-sharing between organizations disappears. For example, a conflict that occurred in the 1980s damaged the relationship between people at Fokker and people from TU Delft for a long time, creating Chinese walls between these groups and influencing knowledge-sharing. In the words of Adel Khoudja: 'In the past, there was a conflict between TU Delft and Fokker. I was part of Fokker. Much later, you could still not easily come back in the TU Delft group'.

Table 8.2 Overview and illustration of solution concepts

Solution concept	Subcategories	Examples
Interpersonal relationships		Adel Khoudja (Fokker, GlobalTechnics) had good relationships with people at Airbus and with Gise Wit and Geert Roebroeks. Jan Willem Gunnink had good relationships with Jens Hinrichsen, Bill Evancho, Daan Krook and Boud Vogelesang.
Agreements on value distribution	Agreements, knowledge protection rules, knowledge-sharing rules, property rules	TU Delft with Akzo, Alcoa and 3M; SLC; GRP; Barrel test; Airbus with Fokker AESP; MOU of Airbus.
Direct communication	Co-location, conferences, frequent communication, meetings, site visits, social events, team working, training	GRP teams who worked on assigned Glare-related developments. The Large Aircraft Division at Airbus in Toulouse (co-located) where SLC people and Fokker (AESP) people were involved. Arall conferences (Seven Springs, 1987 and TU Delft, 1988) and Glare conferences with presentations for researchers, aircraft manufacturers and aviation companies. Frequently held GRP meetings. NLR engineers who visited the barrel test. People from TU Delft visiting Airbus's production facilities and design teams. Milestone events for the people involved in GRP. Design trainings held at Airbus.
Network density	Knowledge brokers	FMLC functioned as a formal knowledge institute, brokering knowledge of involved partners. There were contacts at Airbus, who were responsible for bringing the right people in contact with each other. The spin-offs, GTM and GlobalTechnics, can broker knowledge within and outside the (core) network.

Absorptive Capacity	Personnel transfer, graduating students	Buwe van Wimersma was transferred from SLC to Aérospatiale, in 1994 to study the application of Glare on the A330 and in 1997 to participate in the Large Aircraft division (for the A380). In 1993, Rob van Oost from SLC was sent to Boeing to study the application of Glare on the successor of the 747 Jumbo Jet, Tjerk de Vries, a Ph.D. student working on Glare from TU Delft went to Airbus; in addition, many graduates from TU Delft went to aerospace companies.
Printed and electronic media	Information systems, reports, publications	Common e-mail systems; data-links for the design of the Glare parts of the A380 between Fokker AESP and Airbus; 200 test reports with results for 'basic Glare'; a stress manual for Glare, written by people at GlobalTechnics and used within Airbus. dissertations from TU Delft; graduation reports from TU Delft; journal articles from researchers at TU Delft.
Goal alignment	Shared goals, demarcation, guidance of industry	Shared goal: application of Glare on the A380 of the Demarcation responsibilities and work fields between NLR and TU Delft. Priority setting of Airbus and Fokker for TU Delft.

Agreements on Value Distribution: Protection and Creation of Commitment

Another important solution concept that can shed some light on the dynamics of the development of Glare concerns the rules and agreements in the Glare network. Over time, several formal agreements were made. These rules and agreements had the positive effect that they created commitment to sharing knowledge, but on the other hand knowledge-sharing with excluded parties became more limited. For example, TU Delft made agreements about intellectual property and funding with Akzo, Alcoa and 3M. These agreements solidified the commitments of Akzo, Alcoa, and 3M to the development of FMLs. But these agreements also had an opposite effect: they restricted knowledge-sharing with partners in the periphery of the core network, like Marissen working for DFVLR in Germany.

The positive effect of agreements is also illustrated by the agreed joint venture of Akzo and Alcoa: SLC. This agreement proved to be effective in support of knowledge-sharing when Alcoa wanted to get rid of Glare. Because Alcoa had an agreement with Akzo, ending the involvement would have had legal consequences. Therefore, Alcoa was urged to find a better way out, which created the chance to keep Glare in The Netherlands. Otherwise, Alcoa would probably have put the Glare patents and knowledge on a shelf, thus restricting further development and knowledge-sharing.

Direct Communication

Meetings were an effective means of direct communication between representatives of network partners. Different kinds of meetings existed: site visits, training sessions, discussion meetings, (co-located) team working, conferences and social events. Each had their own effectiveness, frequency and attendees. Site visits were effective and efficient because they enabled rich interaction (live), provided the complete context (e.g. production facilities, test set-up) and also enabled knowledge-sharing in a protected situation. For example, with the barrel test, visiting engineers from NLR had a chance to see the whole test and set-up. If they had not visited the test, this knowledge would not have been shared.

Meetings were a standard way of knowledge-sharing throughout the development trajectory. In the 1980s and at the beginning of the 1990s, there was no formal network-wide consultative structure. From the inception of the research programmes (GTP, GRP), frequent meetings were held with the different parties and at different levels. These meetings were effective in reducing conflicts through trust-building, in dealing with motivation issues by creating commitment, and in increasing knowledge-sharing efficiency through providing a rich knowledge channel. Not all parties were as motivated to attend these meeting and contribute, which in some cases led to frequently changing representatives in the meetings. This was not conducive to knowledge-sharing. A context-specific kind of meeting was the (academic) conference. Such conferences were effective at sharing knowledge, creating interest in prospective partners, sharing beliefs, building new relationships and creating a network identity.

Network Density

Knowledge brokers were an effective solution, especially for creating network density and thus tackling the efficiency and boundaries problems. Two types can be distinguished: the formal, institutionalized knowledge broker; and the informal knowledge broker. The first type is represented by the research group at TU Delft, later SLC and FMLC. In the cooperation with Airbus, there were also formal knowledge brokers: contacts that brought people from Fokker AESP and Airbus together.

The second type, the informal knowledge broker, is represented by informal contacts (interpersonal relationships) and 'spin-offs'. These 'spin-offs' were especially efficient at overcoming the knowledge protection issue. GTM, which consists of people who worked at FMLC and SLC, is now more able to share knowledge with different clients and less tied to protective measures of other partners.

Absorptive Capacity

Through the exchange of people between network partners absorptive capacity was created in the network. Boundaries are bridged and people become more motivated because of shared passions. It also provides a means for context-rich personal interaction, thus enabling efficient knowledge-sharing. Two instances of personnel exchange are found, the 'normal' exchange of people between organizations for a certain time period, like van Wimersma and Wit, who were stationed at Airbus France for a period of time. A second form of personnel transfer is the 'swarming out' of graduating students from the structures group at TU Delft. They acquired knowledge in the curriculum, often wrote a thesis on FMLs and sometimes stayed one or two years at the faculty to perform testing. When they subsequently moved to an employer in the aerospace industry, they brought with them their knowledge, contacts and enthusiasm. This created motivation and channels to find and share knowledge more efficiently.

Besides the efficient knowledge-sharing and the motivation effect, personnel exchange was also effective at crossing knowledge protection barriers (similar in effect to site visits) and dispersing knowledge, thus establishing more common knowledge, creating absorptive capacity.

Printed and Electronic Media

Codified knowledge can be transferred through reports and information systems. This creates knowledge-sharing opportunities, thus providing a solution to the efficiency problem. Reports consisted mainly of test reports, handbooks and publications. The effectiveness of reports and publications depended on the context. Because publications contained more information than the parties actually needed, the knowledge was sometimes not used very effectively. Knowledge-sharing via reports and publications was especially efficient when the receiving party had a question that was answered in the report.

With the development of information technology, information systems were more often used to share information and codified knowledge. In the last phase, when Airbus was heavily involved, special data links were used for engineering and design, besides regular systems such as e-mail. But, in general, the use of special information systems was very limited.

Goal Alignment

This solution concept can be split into three: decisions about the demarcation of the work area, shared goals and focus of the industry. First, demarcation was useful to create clear understandings of each other's tasks, thus reducing possible competition conflicts. At one time, there were tensions between NLR and TU Delft about doing materials tests and building a test lab at Delft. They dealt with this issue by making arrangements about the demarcation of tasks.

Second, the common goal of the Glare project and especially of the research programmes was to get the material applied to an aircraft. This common goal was beneficial and attractive to all partners and thus provided the basis for motivation. This common goal ensured that the different individual goals of the partners never dominated, which would probably have resulted in the end of the cooperation. However, the knowledge-sharing was to some extent restricted by the different goals. Partners were not always willing to cooperate entirely, because they had different interests or priorities. This caused inefficiency, delayed the development process and reduced the motivation of other partners.

Third, at an industry level a more efficient allocation of research funding could have been achieved by a greater focus. Focus only emerged when Airbus became fully involved. From then on research was carried out which was more closely adapted to the needs of a specific partner, Airbus.

Relationships between Solution Concepts and Problems

We will complement the overview of problems and solution concepts with Figure 8.5 which summarizes the insights and relationships discussed. This figure is built upon the interview data. We carefully analysed the frequency with which solution concepts, problems and relationships between them were mentioned.

DISCUSSION AND CONCLUSIONS

Our analysis provides a number of interesting insights. First, it is striking that free-riding appeared not to be a problem in the Glare network. Although it is a decentralized network, without a central orchestrator, none of the parties displayed free-riding behaviour. The long-term scope of the network may have prevented free-riding. At particular moments, a situation of free-riding seems to appear, but this is quickly corrected by other partners. And considering the whole time span, more or less opportunistic behaviour by a partner at one point in time is balanced by a lot of collaboration at another time. Second, this study showed interesting evidence of the importance of informal mechanisms in a decentralized network, but also demonstrated the vulnerability of these informal means (e.g. to personnel change and disagreements). Another important finding was the effectiveness of agreements on value distribution. On the one hand, this solution concept constitutes trust and commitment, thus enabling knowledge-sharing. On the other hand, agreements on value distribution can also limit knowledge-sharing and reduce absorptive capacity. Hence, some solution concepts may have drawbacks. Furthermore, the Glare case also made clear that more solutions are not always better. Some solutions are more applicable in some networks than in others.

Regarding knowledge types, the case analysis shows that it is harder to share core and tacit knowledge than non-core and explicit knowledge. For example, the knowledge regarding specific Glare properties was difficult to share. Sharing core knowledge increased the motivation problem, because (industrial) partners wanted to protect this knowledge. But also at an individual level, people were sometimes not willing to share their core knowledge because of personal pride. The protection problem was reduced by creating more commitment by formal agreements. Informally, interpersonal relationships, meetings, and site visits were very important to sharing

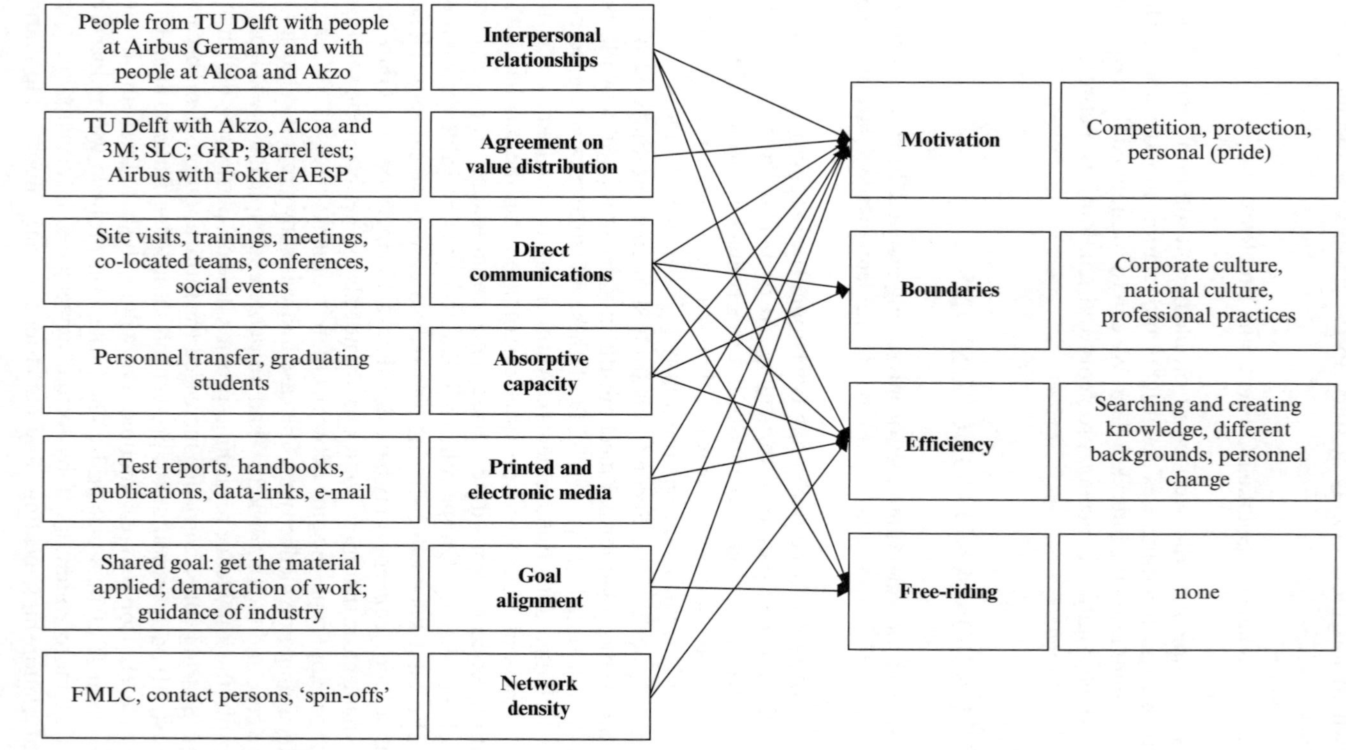

Figure 8.5 Solution concepts in relation to knowledge-sharing problems

core knowledge. The latter three solutions have the advantage that they also provide an opportunity for sharing tacit knowledge. Sharing this (highly) tacit knowledge requires absorptive capacity. But in the Glare case, a common knowledge base was often absent and Glare's development was slowed down by protective measures.

Considering network types, the Glare network could be characterized as a decentralized, continuous, international network focused on a single innovation. In a decentralized network, few central solutions can be applied, and commitment to knowledge-sharing cannot be enforced. Thus, informal and decentralized solutions, like interpersonal relationships and direct communications, were extremely important for knowledge-sharing. Fortunately, because the cooperation spanned a long time period, a bigger structure could emerge from local solutions. Central teams like the GRP teams were founded, which was possible because there was funding, support and commitment. Also the function of the knowledge centre could become more formalized in the founding of FMLC by three network partners (NLR, TU Delft, Stork Fokker AESP). These new entities at the core of the network never fulfilled the role of network orchestrator, however, and could not exert any power over the other network partners.

Explorative innovation is surrounded by uncertainty, as the Glare story clearly shows. There was uncertainty in the application of the material, uncertainty regarding the involvement of network partners and often it was uncertain whether the material would ever be successful. The indefinite time frame and the unknown obstacles in the development path were the reasons why industrial partners lost motivation when clear progress and application opportunities were lacking. That Glare, however, became successful is largely a result of the perseverance of a limited group of 'believers' combined with the appearance of an application opportunity in which the advantages of Glare were recognized.

Was it necessary that this process took 30 years? Perhaps not, but things always look simpler in hindsight. The development and application of Glare was bounded by many constraints that could not easily be changed, like funding possibilities, application possibilities and the time needed for the acceptance of a fundamentally new material in a community already divided by the battle between the aluminium engineers and the composite engineers. Moreover, in the aircraft industry, introductions of completely new large aircraft are few and far between. The Airbus A380 was the first aircraft where Glare could be applied on a large scale. There were a number of other possibilities, but for various reasons Glare was not adopted in those designs. Two of our respondents discussed this issue and said: 'We are talking about a situation where facts and relationships have to come together. If we did not have a good relationship with Airbus, Glare would have never been applied on this plane.' 'But maybe on the Boeing 787 instead . . .' 'Or neither. It depends on a good product and on having good relationships. If one of these is lacking, nothing happens.'

The continuity of the network bounded opportunistic behaviour by parties. There were always one or more network partners who saw the long-term benefits of continued cooperation and knowledge-sharing. Even when certain parties temporarily withdrew (Fokker) or permanently left the network (Akzo), other parties saw room for continuity. The fact that the network was dispersed across national borders and continents did not make knowledge-sharing easier, but good personal relationships and frequent meetings between a core group of individuals kept all major network partners involved and 'in the loop'.

It is precisely this passion for fibre-metal laminates shared by a select number of individuals that has eventually landed Glare on the Airbus A380. Knowledge-sharing and cooperation in the network have been a struggle at times, but by the conscious and, more often, subconscious application of various solution concepts, the knowledge-sharing problems of motivation, free-riding, efficiency and boundaries were overcome. Eventually, 30 years of passionate work on an essentially Dutch invention connected with a window of opportunity in the fiercely competitive battle between the two aerospace giants in the world.

SUMMARY

This case study describes the development of the new aircraft material Glare in an international network. After 30 years of development, this new material was finally applied on a large scale, on the Airbus A380. Regarding knowledge-sharing, it becomes clear that motivation may be an important challenge in a decentralized network where knowledge is shared with high tacitness and coreness. It is striking that the free-riding dilemma was not found, probably because the continuity of collaboration bounded opportunistic behaviour by network members. In the Glare case, knowledge-sharing was managed by a number of means, most of which were applied more or less unconsciously. The three most important solutions were: (1) interpersonal relationships, which were very important in motivating partners; (2) rules and agreements, which were important in creating commitment to engage in development; and (3) meetings, which were important in establishing interpersonal relationships and which served as opportunities to share knowledge.

NOTE

1. For this case study, two data sources were used: interviews and documentation. The interviews sought to uncover multiple understandings of the same phenomena. Eighteen interviews were conducted; interviewees were selected such that all the main network players were represented. These semi-structured interviews lasted 1.5 hours on average. All interviews were recorded and fully transcribed. Subsequently, the transcription was checked with the interviewee. Complementary documentation consists, first, of the book *Glare: History of the Development of a New Aircraft Material*, written by Ad Vlot (2001). More information about the development of Glare is found in *Around Glare: A New Aircraft Material in Context*, edited by Coen Vermeeren (2002). A third source of information is the 19th Plantema Memorial Lecture by Boud Vogelesang (2003). Furthermore, different kinds of additional documentation were collected: dissertations, newspaper articles, public interviews, project documentation and patent databases. These sources were used to prepare for the interviews and as a means of interpreting, checking and enriching interview findings.

REFERENCES

de Vries, T.J. (2001), *Blunt and Sharp Notch Behaviour of Glare Laminates*, Dissertation, Delft: Delft University of Technology.

Scholtens, B. (1995), 'Delftse pleisters voor kapotte vleugels', *de Volkskrant*, 2 December.

Vermeeren, C. (ed.) (2002), *Around Glare: A New Aircraft Material in Context*, Dordrecht: Kluwer Academic Publishers.

Vermeeren, C.A.J.R. (2003), 'An historic overview of the development of Fibre Metal Laminates', *Applied Composite Materials*, **10**, 189–205.

Vlot, A. (2001), *Glare: History of the Development of a New Aircraft Material*, Dordrecht: Kluwer Academic Publishers.

Vogelesang, B. (2003), 'Fibre metal laminates: the development of a new family of hybrid materials', 19th Plantema Memorial Lecture, ICAF, Switzerland.

9. Best practices: key lessons from the cases

Irene Lammers, Hans Berends, Ard-Pieter de Man and Arjan van Weele

INTRODUCTION

This chapter presents the cross-cases conclusions on knowledge sharing in innovative networks. The analysis is based on the five in-depth case studies in this book: METRO Future Store Initiative, Dutch horticulture, pig-breeding, the Glare network and the supplier network of ASML. The main observations are:

- In innovation networks, knowledge processes like finding, accessing and sharing knowledge are important enablers for innovation;
- Knowledge sharing is sometimes problematic. The four key problems are: problems with motivation, efficiency, free-riding and boundary crossing;
- In all five networks, managerial strategies are applied to address these four knowledge-sharing problems, be it implicitly or explicitly;
- Companies use 13 solution concepts to address knowledge-sharing problems. The solution concepts vary in the kind of knowledge-sharing problem(s) they address;
- In different networks, different solution concepts are effective;
- Decentralized, dispersed networks that aim at developing multiple innovations face more knowledge management challenges than centralized, local networks developing only one innovation;
- Surprisingly, core knowledge is associated with fewer management problems than expected. Tacit knowledge is harder to manage than explicit knowledge.

The structure of this chapter follows the themes of knowledge management in networks discussed in Chapter 1. The themes will be discussed in the order presented in Figure 9.1. Some additional insights will be discussed

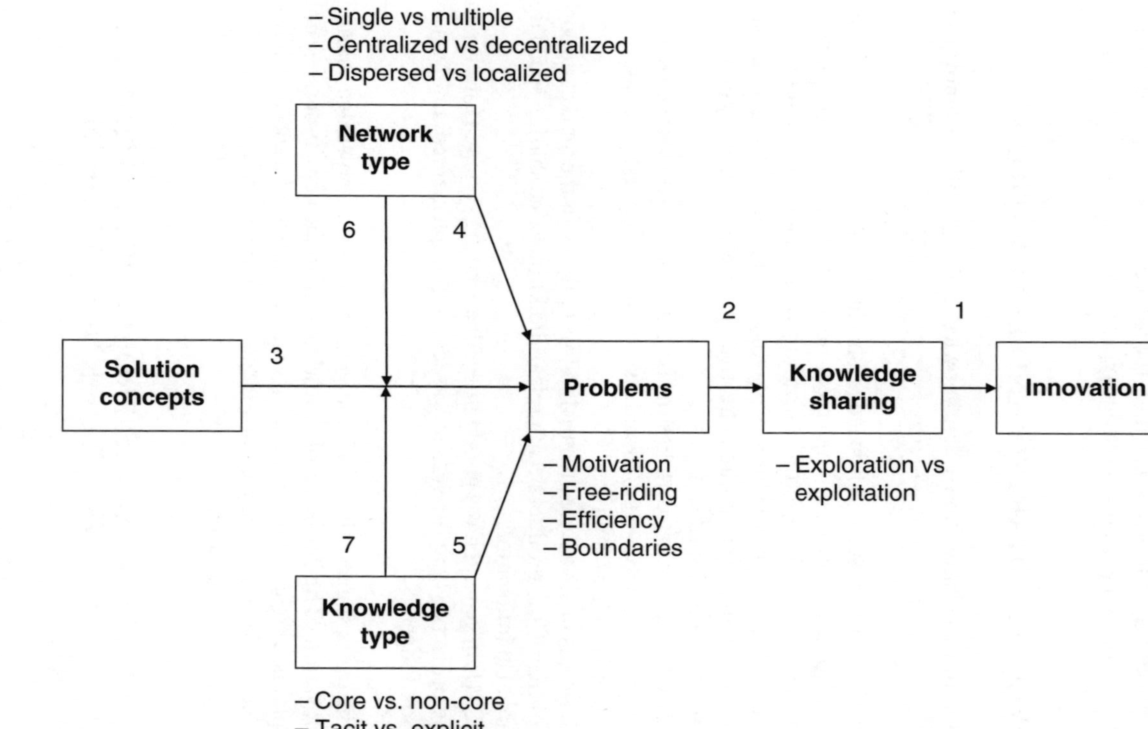

Figure 9.1 *Themes around knowledge management in innovation networks*

at the end of this chapter. The themes are: knowledge sharing and innovation (1); knowledge-sharing problems and the effective transfer of knowledge (2); solution concepts to alleviate knowledge-sharing problems (3); network type and knowledge-sharing problems (4); knowledge type and knowledge-sharing problems (5) and the effectiveness of solutions for different network types and knowledge types (6, 7).

KNOWLEDGE SHARING AND INNOVATION

The different cases have shown that knowledge sharing affects innovation positively:

- In the Future Store, knowledge sharing went smoothly and this enabled this network to implement numerous innovations rapidly;
- In the pig-breeding sector innovation went well in the Netherlands, where effective knowledge sharing takes place. International innovation is still in its infancy and effective knowledge-sharing systems are still being developed;
- The horticulture network has the best-developed knowledge-sharing system of the cases studied and also shows the highest patent growth rate in Dutch agriculture;
- Glare has taken a long time to develop. Only when the market opportunities of the product became clear did knowledge sharing speed up and also innovation;
- ASML in general has a good knowledge-sharing system. However, in the projects where the system was less well implemented, innovation took longer.

Hence the cases suggest there is a connection between knowledge sharing and innovation. The presence of knowledge management processes not only explains whether innovation occurs but also affects the speed of innovation. Networks with effective knowledge management processes are able to innovate more and faster.

KNOWLEDGE-SHARING PROBLEMS LIMITING THE EFFECTIVE TRANSFER OF KNOWLEDGE IN NETWORKS

Dyer and Nobeoka (2000) identified three key problems associated with knowledge sharing: motivation, free-riding and efficiency of knowledge transfer. The replication of the three knowledge management problems identified in the Toyota case by Dyer and Nobeoka (2000) is an important finding of this study. Next to the three knowledge management problems identified by them, a fourth problem was found: crossing boundaries. Boundary-crossing refers to the difficulty of for example transferring knowledge across companies with different knowledge bases and across cultural barriers. A brief search of the literature shows that theory has identified this problem as well. Carlile (2002) has referred to syntactic, semantic and pragmatic boundaries, and Orlikowski (2002) identified boundaries created by time, geography, culture, history, technology and politics. The concept of absorptive capacity (Cohen and Levinthal, 1990) is related to boundary-crossing as well: firms that do not have a basic level of expertise in a particular area will not be able to absorb new knowledge in that area. This is a barrier to the exchange of knowledge between companies. In the METRO Future Store case, there was a clear example of lack of absorptive capacity: some of the companies that needed to work with RFID had no knowledge about it and were initially unable to deal with it. Figure 9.2 shows the various challenges networks need to overcome before effective knowledge transfer can take place.

In all the cases studied, these four problems were identified. The framework in Figure 9.2 therefore appears to be a valid description of the problems occurring in knowledge-sharing networks. The case studies also show that these problems can be overcome by implementing solution concepts, as the next section will show.

SOLUTION CONCEPTS TO ALLEVIATE THE KNOWLEDGE-SHARING PROBLEMS

Although knowledge-sharing problems did exist in the five networks studied, every network implemented effective strategies to address these problems. Specific strategies to address knowledge-sharing problems may be unique in their actual appearance, but each strategy is based on a limited set of mechanisms that influence the occurrence of certain problems. We have named these mechanisms solution concepts (see Chapter 3). In the five networks, 13 solution concepts were at work. Each solution concept addresses a subset of the knowledge-sharing problems discussed earlier. The Appendix gives a detailed description of the solution concepts, including examples from the cases.

The solution concepts help networks to overcome the four barriers to knowledge sharing. Not all solution concepts help to overcome each barrier to knowledge sharing. Companies apply different solution concepts

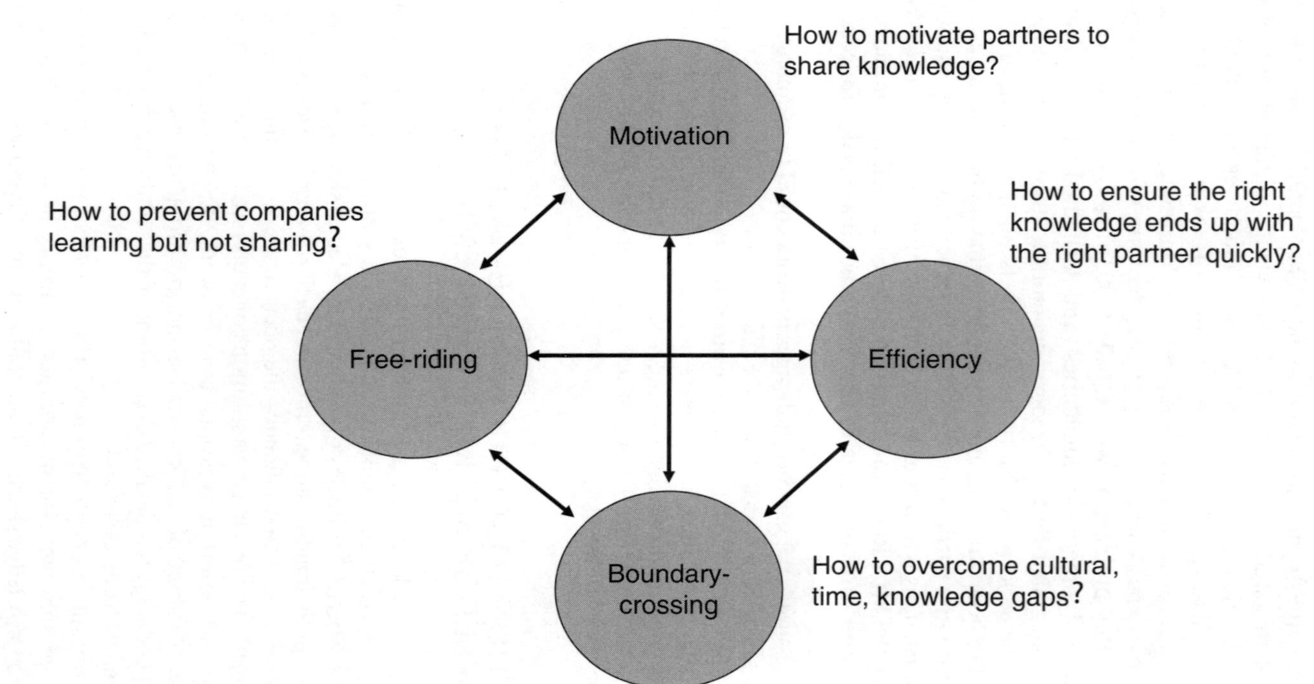
How to motivate partners to share knowledge?
Motivation
How to prevent companies learning but not sharing?
Free-riding
How to ensure the right knowledge ends up with the right partner quickly?
Efficiency
Boundary-crossing
How to overcome cultural, time, knowledge gaps?

Figure 9.2 Problems with knowledge sharing in networks

Table 9.1 Solution concepts and their impact on knowledge-sharing problems

Solution concepts	Motivation problem	Free-riding problem	Efficiency problem	Boundary-crossing problem
1. Professional pride	√			
2. Network identity	√	√		
3. Goal alignment	√	√		
4. Agreement on Value distribution	√	√		
5. Network density	√	√	√	√
6. Printed and electronic media			√	
7. Absorptive capacity				√
8. Formal learning			√	
9. Direct communication	√	√	√	√
10. Interpersonal relationships	√	√	√	√
11. Sanctions	√	√		
12. Modularization	√	√	√	
13. Partner selection	√	√	√	

to deal with different knowledge-sharing problems. Table 9.1 shows the main relationships identified in the cases.

Some solution concepts appear to be very powerful in that they help solve multiple problems. Network density, for example, addresses all four knowledge-sharing problems. When everybody knows everybody else this is apparently a strong impetus for knowledge sharing. People are motivated to help their partners, free-riding is difficult because word will get around quickly, efficiency is less of an issue because knowledge can reach a company via multiple pathways and finally, in dense networks, companies know each other, thereby limiting the boundary-crossing problem. Direct communication and interpersonal relationships positively affect all four problems too. Professional pride, on the other hand, only helps to solve the motivation problem.

Most solution concepts address the motivation problem. Four out of the 13 solution concepts alleviate the problem of boundary crossing. Whether this means that this problem is less important or whether companies underestimate this problem and therefore devote less attention to it, cannot be concluded on the baies of our analysis.

NETWORK TYPE AND KNOWLEDGE-SHARING PROBLEMS

The cases show that knowledge-sharing problems differ per network type. Chapter 1 has given an overview of the cases and how they relate to network types. The first characteristic involves the scope of the collaboration. We have distinguished between networks created to achieve a single well-defined goal (single innovation networks) and networks aimed at achieving a broad spectrum of process and/or product improvements (multiple innovation networks). The second characteristic involves the power distribution in the network. In central networks, one (or more) central players exist who are able to exercise direct control over other network partners, for instance by deciding who can join the network, or what the rules of engagement in the network are. In decentralized networks, the power in the network is distributed more or less equally among network partners. A third characteristic involves the geographic dimension of the network. Is the network local, in the sense that the majority of the network partners are situated within the same region, country or area? Or is the network dispersed; in other words, do network partners come from different countries, maybe even continents?

The four knowledge-sharing problems were traced in the different cases and linked to the network characteristics. Table 9.2 provides an overview of the analysis. As can be seen from this table, the network characteristics have a clear impact on the occurrence of knowledge-sharing problems.

In the cases with a *single innovation*, this proved to be a powerful condition to prevent most knowledge-sharing problems from occurring. A single innovation network clarifies to the partners what knowledge should be shared and why. In addition, it makes it easier to identify the benefits of collaboration. Therefore, the motivation problem and free-riding behaviour did not occur in these networks. The Glare case showed, however, that when the goal of a network partner isn't aligned with the overall goal of the project, conflicts and motivational problems do arise. In the case studies, a single goal was also associated with a clear division of tasks between network partners. This facilitated the search and transfer of knowledge within the network. A single goal was not a remedy, however, for the occurrence of communication problems due to boundary crossing. The problems some partners had with implementing RFID in the METRO Future Store Initiative illustrate this.

In networks with *multiple innovations*, there was a need to keep a close watch on the motivation of network partners and on free-riding behaviour, as both problems occurred regularly. For instance, horticulturalists monitored whether visitors to their greenhouses opened up their own greenhouses

Table 9.2 The impact of network characteristics on the occurrence of knowledge-sharing problems in networks

Network characteristics		Motivation	Free-riding behaviour	Efficiency	Boundary crossing
Goal	Single Innovation				√
	Multiple Innovation	√	√		
Power distribution	Central				
	Decentralized	√	√	√	
Geography	Dispersed			√	√
	Local				

to visitors as well. The broad goals of these networks caused network partners to constantly re-evaluate the cost–benefit balance of their efforts. We did not find communication problems due to boundary crossing in the broad goal networks, possibly because the broad goal networks we studied also tended to be local and limited to one sector. In such circumstances, boundary problems are less likely to occur.

In the *decentralized networks* we studied, almost all knowledge-sharing problems mentioned in the literature occurred. In the Glare network, competitive behaviour impacted the motivation to share knowledge in the network. Also in the pig-breeding and horticulture cases, network partners might have been tempted to display free-riding behaviour. This was countered by several measures. As was expected, in decentralized networks, it also appeared to be difficult to find or access the knowledge of partners efficiently.

Central networks display a strikingly different picture. In a centrally organized network, knowledge-sharing problems do occur, but compared to decentralized networks their impact is limited. The central player in the network is able to prevent free-riding behaviour and lack of motivation to share through the ability to select partners, to organize goal alignment and apply sanctions against misbehaving partners within the network. It is probably also easier for central players to gather and organize the information needed to create an overview of the capabilities and knowledge within the network, and to mediate in helping network partners to access each other's knowledge.

As might be expected, in dispersed networks communication problems are important. In these networks, we also found evidence of problems over the efficiency of finding and accessing knowledge. Problems with free-riding behaviour or a lack of motivation to share were absent, maybe because in the dispersed networks we studied, there were high benefits in return in the long run.

It is remarkable that the cases did not bring substantial knowledge-sharing problems in *local networks* to the fore. We ascribe this to the increased possibilities for developing a network identity, having face-to-face meetings and the absence of cultural, time or language barriers. In networks grounded in local communities, network partners have a shared socio-cultural background and meet each other frequently. Displaying free-riding behaviour in such networks might lead to the shunning of network partners and might impact working relations for decades. Hence the incentive is to collaborate.

In short: decentralized, dispersed networks working on multiple innovations face more challenges to effective knowledge sharing than centralized, localized networks focusing on a single innovation.

KNOWLEDGE TYPE AND KNOWLEDGE-SHARING PROBLEMS

The cases in this book not only differ in terms of the characteristics of the networks at hand, but also in terms of the type of knowledge that is shared. *Tacit knowledge* is knowledge that cannot be codified, and resides for instance in routines, skills and competences. *Explicit knowledge* is the type of knowledge that can be expressed in codified symbols, language or anything else (see Chapter 2). Another distinction is between core knowledge and non-core knowledge. *Core knowledge* refers to knowledge that is important for a firm's core competence, which is the basis for the sustainable competitive advantage of a firm (Prahalad and Hamel, 1990). *Non-core knowledge* is less important. For example, although employees in most companies know how to use word-processing software, in only very few companies will this knowledge be a source of competitive advantage.

Table 9.3 provides examples of the types of knowledge that were shared in the networks. It is evident that knowledge sharing in these networks was not limited to one type of knowledge. Each case provides examples of both tacit and explicit knowledge and both core and non-core knowledge. The pig-breeding network, for example, has electronic conduits for explicit data on pigs to be recorded in Pigbase. But also tacit knowledge on breeding and nurturing is shared through intensive site visits. Knowledge types may also change over time. For example, basic knowledge on the material properties of Glare was really core to TU Delft and SLI in the formative years of the product, but became more common knowledge later on in its development. The multifaceted and dynamic nature of knowledge has implications for

Table 9.3 Examples of knowledge shared in the five networks

ASML	*Explicit:* Procedures and policies of ASML, project plans, new product designs, production plans. *Tacit:* Technological expertise to make new product designs. Cultural knowledge of how to get things done within ASML. *Core:* Technological expertise to make new product designs. Technological expertise to develop new products. Technological/industrial expertise to organize production process for series production. *Non-core:* Managerial and procedural knowledge products, like product documentation and supplier profiles.
METRO Future Store Initiative	*Explicit:* Features of software and hardware in use. RFID in retail standards. *Tacit:* Tacit knowledge associated with knowledge bases of partners (not shared), Technological knowledge to connect technologies. *Core:* Knowledge bases of partners (not shared). *Non-core:* RFID in retail standards (non-core for the partners).
Pig-breeding	*Explicit:* Pig diseases, and how to prevent and cure them. Breeding techniques. *Tacit:* Keeping and nurturing pigs. There are significant performance differences between pig-breeders, but it is unclear why. *Core:* Feeding pigs. Pig genetics. *Non-core:* [no example available]
Horticulture	*Explicit:* Knowledge on light intensity per various stages of growth. Yields associated with certain approaches. *Tacit:* The ability to recognize plant diseases. Organizing natural pest control in a greenhouse. *Core:* Knowledge related to potted plants and cut flowers, e.g. fertilizer, use of light, how to give a plant a growth shock. *Non-core:* Knowledge related to managing a greenhouse company, e.g. human resource management, IT, marketing.
Glare	*Explicit:* Knowledge of material properties of Glare. *Tacit:* Ability to design Glare parts. Production capabilities of Fokker. *Core:* Knowledge on design of fibre-metal laminates (FMLC). Production Capabilities (Fokker). *Non-core:* Properties of Glare (in the last phase).

Table 9.4 Impact of type of knowledge shared on the occurrence of knowledge-sharing problems

Knowledge-sharing problems / knowledge characteristics	Motivation	Free-riding behaviour	Efficiency	Boundary crossing
Core knowledge	Mixed results			
Non-core Knowledge			√	
Explicit knowledge	Mixed results	√		√
Tacit knowledge	√		√	√

the management of knowledge sharing in networks, because different types of knowledge benefit from different types of solutions.

Table 9.4 presents an overview of the relations found between knowledge characteristics and type of knowledge-sharing problems. Contrary to expectations, a focus on core knowledge was an enabler of rather than a constraint on successful knowledge sharing. Given that core knowledge is defined by its value for the competitive advantage of an organization, we had expected that network partners would be particularly hesitant to share core knowledge. The case studies, however, show that the involvement of core knowledge may be a prerequisite for effective knowledge networks.

In the pig-breeding case, for example, much of the knowledge that was shared concerned the core business of the parties involved. This held both for explicit knowledge fed into databases and the tacit knowledge that differentiated superior from mediocre breeders. It was because this knowledge was relevant to their core activities that breeders were interested in participating in the network. The same pattern emerged in the horticulture and METRO Future Store Initiative cases. The different parties were motivated to engage in the network precisely because it concerned the core of their activities. This was valuable to them; non-core knowledge was seen as less valuable.

Of course, organizations are likely to be more cautious when their own core knowledge is involved. In the case of Glare, we found defensive behaviour in order to prevent the leakage of valuable knowledge. In the METRO Future Store Initiative case, companies were involved because of their core knowledge, but did not have to share that core knowledge, due to the modular structure of the network activities. Yet, in other cases, companies also unrestrictedly shared their core knowledge. In the pig-breeding case, companies took pride in being presented as a role model for others. In the horticulture case, the unconditional sharing of core knowledge motivated other partners to show the same behaviour in sharing core and non-core knowledge. One difference is that the partners in the pig-breeding and horticulture cases considered each other far less as direct competitors than did certain organizations in the Glare network. But although the sharing of core knowledge may often be done more cautiously than the sharing of non-core knowledge, the relevance of the network to one's core activities is a necessary condition for being motivated to join in the first place. The transfer of non-core knowledge faces an efficiency problem. This is probably due to the fact that it does not receive much attention and is harder to identify than core knowledge.

The case studies support the view that explicit knowledge is easier to share than tacit knowledge. In the case of *explicit knowledge*, problems with a motivation to share only occurred when intellectual property rights came into sight. The degree of explicitness usually made it easy to find, access and share knowledge, which was observed for example in the horticulture and pig-breeding cases. One problem associated with explicit knowledge is free-riding behaviour. It is very easy, for example, to take the manual of another network partner home. Another potential problem is the interpretation of explicit knowledge. Explicit knowledge can only be shared when there is a shared context that enables interpretation. In the Glare case, this shared background was present due to the fact that many technicians from different companies received their education at the Aerospace Engineering department of TU Delft.

Tacit knowledge presents a different picture. Sharing tacit knowledge takes time and is hard work, thus increasing the likelihood that network partners are not very motivated to share this knowledge. It is also hard to find the tacit knowledge partners need, due to its hidden nature. Members of the pig-breeding network, for example, visited each other's farms to trace the origins of superior performance. Often the sources of performance differences could not be identified, suggesting that these differences had a strong tacit nature. Tacit knowledge is a good way of preventing the occurrence of free-riding behaviour, however, as the mere act of trying to access tacit knowledge demands much effort from both partners. In short, the explicit/tacit dimension affects knowledge sharing most. Tacit knowledge is more difficult to share.

THE EFFECTIVENESS OF SOLUTIONS FOR DIFFERENT NETWORK TYPES AND KNOWLEDGE TYPES

Not all solutions are used in each network type or with each knowledge type. An analysis of the mechanisms used in different network types to cope with different problems shows however that overall there are few differences in the effectiveness of solution mechanisms across network types and knowledge types. The main findings are:

- Solution concepts are as effective in single innovation networks as in multiple innovation networks. Even though multiple innovation networks face more problems, the application of solution concepts is effective in these networks as well.
- Decentralized networks make more use of network density, direct communication and interpersonal relationships to stimulate knowledge sharing. In the absence of a central partner who is able to guide and direct knowledge sharing, it is logical that these mechanisms are especially relevant here. They replace the central partner.
- Local networks focus more on network identity than dispersed networks. This finding ties in with other research that identifies regions as important hotbeds of innovation (e.g. Best, 1990; Porter, 1990). The regional identity reinforces the network identity and leads companies to look for collaboration with regional partners.
- More solution concepts aim at core knowledge than at non-core knowledge. A possible explanation is that core knowledge is seen as more important and hence gets more managerial attention. Whether this is completely justified can be debated. In the horticulture network, for example, the spread of non-core knowledge about management best practices contributed substantially to the innovativeness of the network. Companies may therefore underestimate the importance of non-core knowledge for creating an effective knowledge-sharing network.

These findings show that for managing knowledge networks attention must be paid to implementing the right mechanisms for the specific network at hand. At the same time, the fact that the differences are limited implies that most solution concepts have a positive effect on knowledge sharing regardless of the situation in which they are applied.

DISCUSSION

Solving knowledge-sharing problems requires a set of managerial mechanisms and tools applied simultaneously. The case studies have shown that there are a number of such micro-level mechanisms. Some mechanisms like personal relationships, direct communication and building a network identity can be traced in all or a majority of the cases. Others, like the use of

RFID experts by METRO, were found in only one case. Hence, there appear to be some mechanisms that are widely applicable, but these mechanisms will always be applied alongside idiosyncratic mechanisms that fit a specific case.

The fact that multiple mechanisms are used in the cases implies that a major investment needs to be made in order to get knowledge management in networks up and running. It appears to be far from easy to stimulate knowledge flows and the demand on management time is high. In areas where these mechanisms have not been implemented, such as in the international network of pig-breeding, important gaps in knowledge flows were found.

Not all micro-level mechanisms were consciously used to improve the flow of knowledge. Whereas the website in the Future Store was set up to stimulate the flow of knowledge, the primary objective of the tight deadlines was to maintain speed. That they contributed to building the community was an unexpected result. In future case studies, it may be helpful to distinguish between mechanisms directed at knowledge management and contextual mechanisms that are not consciously introduced to affect knowledge management, but contribute to it because of unintended consequences.

This is in line with the observation that in none of the case studies was a grand design of knowledge management implemented. Knowledge management in networks in most cases was not explicitly on the managerial agenda, even though it was implicitly recognized as an important issue. For this reason, one conclusion is that it is not necessary to develop a grand design for knowledge management. The horticulture case shows that, without such a design, knowledge may still flow. Another conclusion may be that with a grand design the effectiveness of knowledge flows may improve considerably. This may be concluded from the performance of the METRO Future Store Initiative case. In particular, the fact that in the Future Store innovation was realized rapidly may imply that focused attention on knowledge management speeds up the process of innovation in networks considerably. An interesting question for further research might be to study the conditions that make a grand design necessary and the conditions under which such a design is not required.

The conclusions are based on only five cases. However, the research methodology has been geared at achieving a high level of generalizability. First, the research builds on and extends prior research. Our case studies have been conducted with a clear theoretical framework as a starting point, building on existing theory. Second, all cases were studied using a similar method, ensuring consistency in data-gathering and analysis. Third, the variety of cases gives some understanding of the degree of generalizability of the findings. For example, the fact that all four problems with knowledge sharing in innovative networks have been recognized in all five cases, despite the fact that the cases relate to entirely different sectors, may imply that the findings arc robust.

To conclude, it seems there is a good understanding of problems in network knowledge management, that there is a basic understanding of solution types companies may employ to solve these problems, but that the way the solution types are translated into practice is relatively idiosyncratic. However, we did find evidence that a relationship exists between the characteristics of a network and the knowledge management approach that is adopted. This will be elaborated in the next section.

EXPLORATIVE AND EXPLOITATIVE NETWORKS

The case studies show that different knowledge management processes are used depending on the network type. A distinction that may summarize this is that between explorative and exploitative networks. A description of these two types of networks is provided below in Table 9.5. We suggest that a misfit between network context and solution concepts will make it more difficult to get knowledge exchange going.

The demarcation between explorative networks and exploitative networks is based on March (1991). Explorative networks relate to situations where partners are challenged to develop fundamental new solutions to business problems. In these cases, the challenge is often clear (for instance, a new material needs to be developed), but the technologies that are to be used to produce the final solutions need to be explored. Since technology options may change over time, the network boundaries are blurred. Apart from a core group of experts, new experts may enter and leave the scene. Bringing new experts on board is risky, since every new individual must engage with and prove himself to the core group. Personal reputation therefore is an important qualification variable. Over time, the role of experts within a network may change as insights may change over time. Persons who initially had a core role in the network may lose their position as technology choices become clearer. The motivation of individuals to participate in the network lies predominantly in getting access to new knowledge, interacting with peers at the same intellectual level, and gaining personal status derived from membership of the network. Hence informal solution concepts are more applicable in this situation than formal ones. Glare and some parts of the ASML network are examples of this category of network.

Exploitative network contexts relate to situations where partners collaborate to realize a predefined goal or project and have learning goals that are

Table 9.5 Knowledge management in different contexts

	Explorative networks	Exploitative networks
Context	– fundamental research and applied technology development – heuristic, iterative processes with network partners	– applied research and applied technological development – project management, more concrete collaboration processes
Knowledge processes	situated around limited number of highly reputed individuals/peers/carriers of specific knowledge	knowledge processes situated within several companies and institutions
Solution concepts	less manageable, hence emphasis on informal concepts: professional pride, direct communication, partner selection	more manageable, hence emphasis on formal concepts: formal learning, printed and electronic media, agreement on value distribution
Motivation	knowledge creation, building personal reputation, status	optimization of existing knowledge, exchange best practices, new business revenues
Example	Glare, ASML	METRO Future Store Initiative, Pig-breeding

incremental to existing knowledge (for instance, the METRO Future Store Initiative). Technologies that are to be applied are known and require only marginal development; however, the mix of technologies and when and how to apply them is a matter of debate. Against this context, it is easier to find a party that has a core role in defining and managing the network context. This core partner may control access to the network by using some explicit and implicit selection criteria when inviting partners to join the network. Next, this core partner may define rules and guidelines for the behaviour of network partners. Given the more concrete objectives and defined technology content, project management rules may be used to manage the relationships between network partners. Compared to explorative network contexts, this type of collaboration therefore can be more business-like and concrete. Network partners can be more easily judged on their actual contributions to the network. Since many representatives of the network partners possess the relevant technological knowledge, personal reputation plays a less important role than institutional reputation. The solution concepts applied in explorative networks therefore are more formal and more focused on seizing new business opportunities and profits. The METRO Future Store Initiative and pig-breeding cases serve as examples of this type of network.

Horticulture combines the two types of networks. There is exchange of best practices through the traditional means of visiting each other's greenhouses. This is in line with an exploitative network. For more advanced knowledge, the growers' associations are used, which enables exploration of new technologies and business concepts.

SUMMARY

This study shows that there are four core problems managers need to address when setting up effective knowledge sharing in networks: the motivation problem, the free-riding problem, the efficiency problem and the boundary-crossing problem. They have 13 different mechanisms to cope with these problems. Even though some of these mechanisms are more applicable and effective in some networks than in others, in general implementing more of these mechanisms improves knowledge sharing. Creating an effective knowledge-sharing network requires a major investment in diverse, overlapping solution concepts. Decentralized, dispersed networks that aim at developing multiple innovations face more knowledge management challenges than centralized, local networks developing only one innovation. In networks, core knowledge may require protection, but the value of exchanging core knowledge also provides an incentive to share it. Contrary to expectations, core knowledge is for this reason sometimes shared more easily than non-core knowledge. Finally, tacit knowledge is harder to manage than explicit knowledge.

REFERENCES

Best, M.H. (1990), *The New Competition*, Cambridge: Polity Press.

Carlile, P.R. (2002), 'A pragmatic view of knowledge and boundaries: boundary objects in new product development', *Organization Science*, **13** (4), 442–55.

Chuma, H. (2006), 'Increasing complexity and limits of organization in the microlithography industry: implications for science-based industries', *Research Policy*, **35**, 394–411.

Cohen, W.M. and D.A. Levinthal (1990), 'Absorptive capacity: a new perspective on learning an innovation', *Administrative Science Quarterly*, **35** (1), 128–53.

Dyer, J.H. and K. Nobeoka (2000), 'Creating and managing a high-performance knowledge-sharing network: the Toyota case', *Strategic Management Journal*, **21**, 345–67.

March, J.G. (1991), 'Exploration and Exploitation in Organizational Learning', *Organization Science*, **2** (1), 71–87.
Orlikowski, W.J. (2002) 'Knowing in practice: enacting a collective capability in distributed organizing', *Organization Science*, **13** (3), 249–73.
Porter, M.E. (1990), *The Competitive Advantage of Nations*, London: Macmillan.
Prahalad, C.K. and G. Hamel (1990), 'The core competence of the corporation', *Harvard Business Review*, May–June, 79–91.

APPENDIX: DETAILED DESCRIPTION OF SOLUTION MECHANISMS

Professional pride provides an intrinsic motivation to share knowledge. In many cases, people share knowledge out of sheer passion for their own profession or the product they are contributing to. For instance, the unique high-tech character of ASML made technicians within the network, both within as well as outside ASML, eager to share their expertise and bring forward solutions to new technological problems. Also the pig-breeders, the horticulturalists and the participants in the Glare network shared knowledge of their own volition. Professional pride is a mechanism that prevents knowledge-sharing problems arising from a lack of motivation.

Another reason to share knowledge is the feeling of belonging to a community. Some networks have been able to develop a *network identity*. The network identity is usually supported by social events, some shared symbols (like a name or logo for the network) and/or some shared norms and values. For instance, in the case of the horticulturalists, the network identity of being part of 'the Westland' has strong historical roots, as most of the companies are family-owned small and medium-sized enterprises (SMEs) and they are all located in the same area. They tend to share their knowledge, as they are aware that they are unable to innovate on their own. A network identity creates feelings of loyalty among network partners and therefore prevents motivation and free-riding problems.

A strong mechanism that enhances knowledge-sharing behaviour is *goal alignment*. When it is in the strategic interest of all business partners involved to collaborate, all knowledge, including core knowledge if necessary, is shared freely. This solution concept is applied throughout all five cases. For instance, 'Creating a future store' proved to be a powerful vision guiding the activities of the partners of the METRO Future Store Initiative. It also made the process of setting a standard possible, as all partners understood the benefits of doing so. Goal alignment makes knowledge sharing in the direct interest of the partners involved, making it unlikely that motivation and free-riding problems will occur.

Although it is important to have a shared goal, it is no less important that there is clear *agreement on value distribution*. Whether it is through explicit agreements on intellectual property or implicit understandings of the value distribution, for each partner the benefits of collaboration should exceed the costs. In the case of Glare, there were a number of deals that facilitated the agreement on value distribution. For instance, TU Delft provided the patent of Arall to Akzo, which in turn supported research at TU Delft with a grant. Like goal alignment, transparency over the value distribution of the collaboration makes it unlikely that motivation and free-riding problems will occur, as there will be no uncertainty about whether collaboration is in the best interests of each partner individually.

Another mechanism facilitating knowledge sharing in a network is *network density*, by which we mean the number of relations in a network. The more network members know and meet other network members, the fewer knowledge-sharing problems occur. Although the density of networks played a role in all cases, it was most remarkable in the horticulture case. Growers maintained many social ties: not only were the family businesses operating in the same region (which made it likely that they met each other outside work), most were members of one or more grower associations and visited each other's greenhouses. 'I keep meeting the same guys', one of the interviewees said. The density of this network explained the absence of all four knowledge-sharing problems. The number of relations provided ample opportunities for social control, making the motivation problem and the free-riding problem unlikely to occur. For most network partners, it was clear where useful knowledge resides, making efficient knowledge access possible. Lastly, cultural or language barriers did not exist, so boundary-crossing problems were absent as well. A dense social network therefore appears to be an efficient mechanism to prevent knowledge-sharing problems from occurring.

One solution concept frequently emphasized in the knowledge management literature is the use of *printed and/or electronic media* to facilitate knowledge exchange. In our five cases, we did find exchanges in written information, whether via specific journals, newsletters, databases, websites, reports or books. Pig-breeders, for instance, exchanged information via the magazine *Pigs*, and through 'Pigbase', a database in which pig characteristics are gathered. The use of printed and/or electronic media is probably an effective mechanism to address efficiency problems within knowledge-sharing processes. Printed and electronic media enhance the exchange of explicit knowledge in the networks, and have benefits in crossing over boundaries of time and space.

Knowledge can only be exchanged when there is a certain overlap in the knowledge of the knowledge-sharing partners. Without this overlap, partners will have problems understanding each other. Cohen and Levinthal (1990) refer to the ability to understand the knowledge of a partner as *absorptive capacity*. Absorptive capacity may be enhanced by specialized consultants, experts or temporary exchange of personnel. In the horticulture case, specialized consultants acted as knowledge brokers mediating between the world of growers and the world of information technology, to facilitate the development of an ERP system. In the METRO Future Store

Initiative, an RFID hotline and RFID expert pools were present to help companies with RFID implementation. Absorptive capacity, therefore, is a solution concept that is particularly suited to addressing boundary-crossing problems between partners coming from different cultural, language or knowledge bases.

In some cases, the creation of *formal learning* opportunities is a useful mechanism to facilitate knowledge exchange. Formal learning creates opportunities for enduring and close face-to-face contact that enables the transfer of local and tacit knowledge. In the Glare case, there are some examples of individuals who were sent out to learn about a specific topic: one person was transferred from SLC to Aérospatiale in 1994 to study the application of Glare on the A330 and another was sent in 1993 by SLC to Boeing to study the application of Glare on the successor to the 747 Jumbo Jet. ASML sometimes gives formal instructions to suppliers, for instance safety training to handle a certain laser. As formal learning is an effective way to transfer specific and specialist knowledge, this is a useful mechanism to address efficiency problems in knowledge sharing.

Learning not only takes place through formal learning. It is also part of the frequent interactions between people. In all cases, the possibilities of *direct communication*, whether organized by meetings, co-location or site visits, were highly appreciated as a means to exchange knowledge and to prevent knowledge-sharing problems from occurring. Telephone calls, email exchanges and video conferences were mentioned as useful modes of communication after the establishment of a working relationship via face-to-face contact. For instance, an engineer of ASML and his counterpart in a partner firm paid about 10 one-day visits to each other when redesigning a part. Besides that, they had frequent contact via email and telephone. This allowed them to work together on solving the technical problems at hand. Although these engineers worked in two different organizations and might have encountered several knowledge-sharing problems, they did not. Motivation problems and free-riding problems did not occur. To conclude, it is hard to overestimate the importance of direct communication, as it is an effective mechanism to prevent knowledge-sharing problems from occurring.

The *interpersonal relationships* between the people involved also played a role in the extent to which knowledge was shared. The METRO Future Store Initiative builds on the already existing personal relationships. In the horticulture case, many family ties and friendships feature in the network, providing a trusting climate where knowledge flows easily. At the other extreme, in the ASML case, relations between suppliers and ASML employees are mainly business. Interpersonal relationships provide the psychological bonds between individuals in the network and create loyalty, trust and joy in the collaboration process. They address potential problems of motivation and free-riding and make it less likely that boundaries pose lasting problems for knowledge sharing. Interpersonal relations enhance the knowledge that partners have of each other and therefore are beneficial for finding and accessing relevant knowledge within the network.

The *possibility of sanctions* is also a mechanism to prevent knowledge-sharing problems from occurring. Sanctions take various forms. In the case of the METRO Future Store Initiative, the sanction would be the loss of face if the store failed to meet the deadline. Also, future business loss could be seen as a sanction here. The METRO group is a major client for most partners, so free-riding or underperformance could be punished by taking business away. In the horticulture case, the threat of shunning a partner who does not conform to the rules guiding knowledge exchange was an informal sanction that was felt. ASML mainly uses the threat of taking business away from partners as its sanction. Especially when business is withdrawn completely, it has the effect of reputation damage, as having ASML as a customer is important for the suppliers' image. It is not the actual use of sanctions, but the possibility that sanctions may be applied that prevents motivation problems and free-riding from occurring.

Specialization within a network, or *modularization*, is another strategy that is being pursued by network partners. Modularization enhances the effectiveness of knowledge exchange within a network, as it concentrates on knowledge exchange within certain areas. For instance, in the pig-breeding network the module IPG exists, which concentrates on improving pig genetics in the breeders' network. The success of the ASML products has been ascribed to its explicit strategy of modularization (Chuma, 2006). ASML's supplier network is organized around the modules in the lithography systems. So-called 'product account teams' from ASML steer the development of a module by more than one supplier. Knowledge exchange within the network is mainly organized within these modules. As knowledge exchange within these modules is highly effective and goal oriented, modularization is an effective solution concept to decrease motivation, free-riding and efficiency problems.

The last mechanism influencing knowledge sharing in networks is *partner selection*. In the METRO Future Store Initiative, new partners were carefully selected, based on their knowledge base, their reputation and the existence of personal contacts. ASML is highly dependent for its future development on the technological expertise, development and reliability of the processes of its suppliers. It is very careful in its selection of new suppliers and uses a system of supplier evaluation forms to underpin partner selection. This careful selection of partners probably saves the network from the occurrence of many knowledge-sharing problems. Partners will be motivated to share knowledge and not to display free-riding behaviour as there will be clear reasons why each partner participates in the network. The process of partner selection also produces transparency in the knowledge bases of network partners. This might also enhance efficiency in finding and accessing relevant knowledge.

10. A management agenda

Ard-Pieter de Man

INTRODUCTION

Knowledge management within organizations is a challenging task. Few organizations succeed in ensuring the effective transfer, sharing and creation of knowledge. To extend knowledge management beyond company boundaries involves even more challenges.

The case studies have shown that knowledge management in networks is possible, but that there is a limit to it. Coincidence will continue to play a role in networks. The cases have revealed no grand design for knowledge management, but they also show that such a conscious design is not always necessary to get knowledge flowing. Trying to control all knowledge is not possible and is probably also counterproductive. It would require so many rules and regulations that the cost would be prohibitive. Still, there is much companies can do to improve knowledge management.

The flip-side of the limits to knowledge management is that limiting knowledge flows is also only possible to some extent. Knowledge will flow from one company to the next in the normal encounters people have or via formal communication (websites, trade journals etc.). No company is an island and as long as organizations exist, knowledge will flow in and out. Even when companies try to limit the flow of knowledge consciously, they may not succeed. The Glare case has shown that knowledge exchange continued despite official discouragement by management.

This chapter defines the guidelines for organizations. It starts by defining the steps required to develop an effective knowledge-sharing network. Next, it digs deeper into customization of knowledge management, by looking at the context of knowledge management. The next section looks at knowledge management from the opposite perspective: how to obstruct knowledge flows in networks. Knowledge flows are not always desirable and as a consequence, techniques for limiting the flow of knowledge should be part of management's tool-kit as well. Finally, some guidelines are defined for policy-makers, especially with respect to the many programmes governments have set up that require networking.

STEPS IN DEVELOPING AN EFFECTIVE KNOWLEDGE-SHARING NETWORK

In order to define implications for companies, it is effective to ask the question what a network would look like if it could be designed from scratch. In that case, a company would have to go through steps one to eight as in Table 10.1. Of course this table depicts an ideal situation. In reality, not all networks run through these steps consecutively. Even in such cases, however, the issues mentioned in the table need to be dealt with.

The first step involves defining the aims and objectives of future collaboration. Objectives may be open ended in that learning is supposed to be valuable for an indefinite period of time (Glare, horticulture) or they may be more concrete and related to project objectives (Future Store). In essence, the first step defines the scope of the network: what area will the network be active in, for how long and why? To be effective, network aims should be clear, valuable to partners and generate enthusiasm. The METRO Future Store Initiative meets these tests: building a store is a clear aim, creating technology standards is valuable to partners and the idea generated enthusiasm among the partners at all organizational levels.

Next stock must be taken of the knowledge that is required for achieving the objectives. The primary issue here is to identify the core knowledge fields that need to be connected. However, this is not a sufficient condition for success. The case studies have shown that non-core knowledge plays an important supporting role in networks. The exchange of managerial knowledge, for example, ensures that the entire network is strengthened. For example, when all companies in horticulture have better management, there are more learning opportunities for all partners. Or, as in the ASML network, the more knowledge about lead-time reduction and project management the partners possess, the better the performance of the network as a whole. Therefore this type of management knowledge should be identified as well.

Table 10.1 Steps in setting up an effective knowledge-sharing network

1. Define aims and objectives of future collaboration
2. Define the knowledge needed
3. Define the network needed
4. Select partners
5. Decide which knowledge flows are necessary
6. Identify the core problems in realizing those knowledge flows
7. Implement solution concepts to overcome these problems
8. Manage network evolution

The third step is to define the type of network needed given the objectives of the collaboration. Is a social capital network necessary, with many knowledge connections between partners? Is a structural hole network better, with one company acting as the bridge between the others? Or is modularization the optimal strategy? The cases show the power of social capital, but they also show that modularization can be applied in social capital networks as well. Both the METRO Future Store Initiative and the horticulture network use modularization effectively.

Partner selection is the fourth step in creating an effective knowledge-sharing network. The cases give some pointers on how to handle this step effectively:

- If possible use existing relationships with key individuals and organizations. It is easier to get knowledge sharing going with known partners, because a relation of trust and commitment already exists.
- Assess the relevance of partners for core activities. It is important to have partners in the network who are able to contribute valuable knowledge. Therefore partners need to be selected that are willing to share knowledge around core activities.
- Select partners in such a way as to minimize the required knowledge flows. If each partner has a clearly identifiable specialty ('knowledge module') that they can contribute to the network, fewer knowledge flows are required than when partners are only able to contribute parts of knowledge modules.

The fifth step involves deciding about which knowledge flows are necessary to enhance the core competences of the network partners and the network as a whole. A clear view on which knowledge needs to flow to which partners requires an understanding of the value that knowledge will create. The aim of this step should not be to arrive at an overall blueprint of desired knowledge flows, because in reality much more knowledge will (and usually should) get exchanged than a blueprint can capture. This step should therefore only pinpoint the main knowledge areas, in order to focus the network and in order to clarify to partners what the main value is they can derive from network participation. In the pig-breeding sector, it is clear that innovation improves the competitiveness of all partners. In the horticulture network, growers' associations are used that focus the network on specific knowledge issues.

After this, the core problems in realizing those knowledge flows should be identified. The four core problems of motivation, free-riding, crossing boundaries, and efficiency of knowledge transfer must be looked at. Depending on knowledge and network type, these problems may have a higher or lower relevance, as shown in Chapter 9.

Table 10.2 Guidelines for managing knowledge in networks

Strategize: connect the aspirations and overall goals of the companies in the network and connect those goals with the motivation of the individuals
Pressurize: create a sense of urgency in the network. Often the sense of urgency is external, for example a competitive threat, but a sense of urgency can also be created
Localize: reduce boundaries in time and location as much as possible in order to stimulate knowledge sharing
Customize: the right combination of solution concepts differs per network
Overshoot: apply many solution concepts simultaneously; dedicate much time and effort to knowledge management. There is not one golden bullet that solves all challenges
Specialize: work towards a situation in which specialization/modularization exists, because this diminishes the need for coordination

Implementing multiple, overlapping solution concepts to overcome these problems is the next step. There is no single solution concept that is effective by itself. In all cases, multiple solution concepts were applied. In the horticulture case, the case with the most effective knowledge-sharing, all concepts were applied. Of course such extensive use of solution concepts comes at a cost. The value of knowledge sharing must be weighed against the time spent in managing knowledge. Although diminishing returns were not found in the case studies, it seems very likely that they do exist. Table 10.2 summarizes some of our main conclusions on applying solution concepts, which are valid for all networks studied.[1]

The eighth and final step is managing network evolution. Continuous investment to maintain knowledge flows is necessary. It would be a mistake to assume that once knowledge is flowing, it will continue to do so. Knowledge management in networks is a permanent undertaking without a foreseeable end. New knowledge areas may become relevant, whereas others may decrease in importance. In the horticulture network, new growers' associations are set up to deal with new knowledge areas, as in the case of Plantform which aims to develop an ERP system for horticulture. Also networks may evolve. For example, in the course of time relationships may get closer, making it easier to exchange knowledge. This may mean that fewer formal means to manage knowledge are necessary or it may imply that supporting systems need to become more elaborate. Another important aspect of network evolution is entry of new members. In the Glare network, new partners enter the network in different phases of the development of the material. The better the mechanisms that integrate newcomers into the network, the sooner the network can profit from new members. Knowledge management needs to match the evolution of networks. Continuous management attention is necessary to ensure the implementation of new knowledge management techniques that match the development of the network.

The previous eight steps assume that a network can be built from scratch. In reality, companies will have partners in place and will be involved in knowledge exchange already. Even then, it remains valuable to look at these steps. This will force companies to ask the right questions about their existing knowledge management processes. Because many networks have emerged spontaneously and gradually without a conscious focus on knowledge management, it may be possible to raise their effectiveness.

Another assumption behind these eight steps is that design is possible to a considerable extent. Even though the cases have shown that management can do much to improve knowledge management, it is not possible to exclude all elements of chance and coincidence. In particular, the fact that success is rooted in historically developed personal relationships, norms and values limits the room for managerial intervention in the absence of these historical assets.

The eight steps are easier to apply in centralized networks than in decentralized networks. Nonetheless, they are not irrelevant to decentralized networks, but it does take more effort to design knowledge management processes in them. The way of working in the Dutch horticulture case provides some lessons for starting knowledge exchange in decentralized networks. The first challenge in decentralized networks is to bring companies together. To get the attention of other firms, it may be possible to engineer coincidence by bringing key individuals from different companies together in informal, low-risk meetings around a certain topic. A lead group of companies may next be set up, consisting of partners with the most enthusiasm. A small lead group of believers with a long-term view appears to be essential to get things started, as the Glare case shows. Once the benefits of membership of a group become known and business opportunities become more concrete, other companies may want to join and jump on the bandwagon. The horticulture case shows this mechanism works around growers' associations.

TACTICS FOR OBSTRUCTING KNOWLEDGE MANAGEMENT IN ALLIANCE NETWORKS[2]

Knowledge exchange and development in networks is a highly sensitive process. Some companies may knowingly try to undermine knowledge management in networks. They may fear loss of their competitive advantage, they may fear creating a competitor or they may feel they have little to learn from others. Most of these companies will not allow their knowledge workers to enter a network. However, sometimes such companies do end up in networks. There may be three reasons for this:

- Because all other players in the industry are in the network and it therefore delivers an opportunity to remain up to date with competitors' plans. The company may not be willing to actively contribute to the network, but for defensive purposes it is smart to join;
- Membership may offer an opportunity to obstruct the network. If the network benefits a competitor more than it benefits the company itself, obstruction is a good course of action. By joining the network, a company can deploy tactics that slow down the network and prevent it from making substantial progress;
- A company joins the network with the intent to share knowledge, but a change of strategy in the company has occurred and the network has become less valuable or even competitive with the new strategy. In this case the company may either leave the network or try to obstruct it.

So how can companies obstruct knowledge management in networks? In the case studies, some examples of obstructing tactics were found. Additionally, the solution concepts imply that actions taken to undermine their efficacy harm knowledge flows in networks too. Below, a number of mechanisms, partly taken from the case studies, partly the mirror-image of the solution concepts, are described.

There are three ways of obstructing knowledge management. The tactics described below can be used by companies aiming to obstruct knowledge management. They also help other companies to become aware of knowledge-obstructing tactics by other companies. As directly disruptive tactics may be discovered too easily, it may be more effective to signal commitment, while in fact undermining the network. Most tactics therefore do not aim to undermine the network directly and openly. Instead, they are stealth methods that at first sight may signal a cooperative attitude, but under closer scrutiny reveal their true, destructive nature.

The three ways of obstructing knowledge management are (see Table 10.3):

- Disrupt: directly preventing knowledge sharing from occurring;
- Delay: slowing down the network;
- Distract: ensuring the network is busy with something other than sharing knowledge.

Table 10.3 Tactics for obstructing knowledge flows in networks

Disrupt Directly hamper knowledge sharing	Delay Slow down knowledge sharing	Distract Address topics other than knowledge sharing
• Not sharing knowledge	• Cost–benefit analysis	• Internal discussions
• Disrupting communication	• Enlarging the network	• External events
• Undermining meetings	• Elaborate governance structures	
• Misalign incentives		

Disruption

Not sharing knowledge is of course the most visible type of disruption. There are, however, more subtle ways of achieving the same goal. A first group of tactics relates to communication. The use of jargon and irrelevant details, for example, exploits the crossing-boundaries problem. Instead of trying to bridge the knowledge gaps between firms, individuals do not attempt to make their own expertise intelligible to others. They do, however, contribute their expertise to the network, so at first sight this signals commitment. A similar effect is achieved by answering questions in as narrow a sense as possible (tell the truth, but not the whole truth) or by defining minimum standards of communication (which in practice always turn out to be the maximum level of communication). Communication may also be limited to a small in-crowd, preventing network members outside the core group from accessing relevant information.

As knowledge management always involves meetings, the standard tactics for undermining meetings are effective for disrupting knowledge transfer as well:

- Formal behaviour. Adhering to a strict agenda is an example of this.
- Attending but not contributing to meetings. Showing up but not contributing signals commitment (after all you took the time to come), while not stimulating the flow of knowledge.
- Sending different (or even the wrong) persons to meetings each time ensures no relationships are built.
- Meetings at inconvenient times and locations. The location problem may be exploited by nominating persons for the network who work in remote locations. Reducing travel budgets is another effective mechanism to ensure that attendance at meetings is less than adequate.

- Limiting personal contact by only using videoconferencing or leaving no time for an informal get-together before or after meetings.

A final subgroup of disruptive tactics lies inside the firm: internal procedures can be created that undermine knowledge sharing. By misaligning incentives (making someone responsible for knowledge sharing, but not rewarding them for it) and making extensive internal rules, knowledge sharing is undermined.

Delay

A more subtle approach than direct disruption of knowledge flows is trying to delay them. As time is usually essential for attaining a competitive advantage, delaying the progress of a network is very effective in making the network ineffective. An important delaying tactic is asking for a cost–benefit analysis of knowledge management in the network. This is sure to delay progress, especially because so many of the benefits of networks are hard to quantify.

Another tactic is continually enlarging the network. As networks are as fast as the slowest partner, this tactic is highly recommended when delaying knowledge sharing is your goal. It takes each new partner time to get up to speed with the network. Moreover, enlarging the network disrupts trust building. This tactic is especially treacherous because it is often hard for existing partners to say no to the new partner, because new partners bring in new competences and new knowledge. And when the aim of the network is to share knowledge, who can object to that?

Further delay can be created by implementing elaborate governance structures. Complex decision-making procedures are very successful in ensuring the network does not meet its goals on time. The United Nations and the European Union are best practices in this regard, which should serve to inspire managers in their knowledge-destroying strategies.

Distraction

The third way to disrupt knowledge management is by distracting the network. Focusing the attention of the network on other issues, instead of actually exchanging knowledge, prevents networks from achieving their goals. A network can be distracted by internal operations and by external events. As the former are easier to control, managers should first attempt to create internal distractions. An effective tactic is to start discussions about the conditions under which the network should operate, rather than getting down to business. Because clarity about the conditions is important for effective collaboration, it is hard to object to clarifying them. At the same time, such discussions can go on indefinitely. Similarly, a network may discuss solutions to solving the problems of knowledge exchange. As long as people do this, they are not actually sharing knowledge. A very good tactic is to suggest building an IT system to support knowledge sharing. Designing the IT system will take up so much time that by the time the system is operational, the original purpose of knowledge sharing is probably lost. In addition, this diverts attention from other solution concepts, so the likelihood that sufficient solution concepts are implemented diminishes considerably.

External events may distract attention away from knowledge sharing as well. Managers, however, should not rely on them exclusively, because it is always uncertain whether they will occur or not. But once they do occur, external incidents can be used for distraction. External incidents may come in many forms: a new law of which the impact on the network must be researched; a new product by a competitor that may come to market, supposedly making the network superfluous; and so on. By discussing the event and its implications for the network, the network is distracted from doing what it is supposed to do.

By applying the tactics of disruption, delay and distraction, destruction of knowledge flows is certain.

IMPLICATIONS FOR POLICY-MAKERS

Implications for policy-makers relate specifically to the many programmes aimed at innovation that governments have started, such as the European Union's Framework Programme. These programmes often require different partners to work together, because collaboration is believed to stimulate innovation. The effect of publicly funded collaboration projects is often limited (de Man and Duysters, 2005). Based on our findings it is possible to point to some mistakes in these programmes that may explain their inadequate performance:

- Partnering is often obligatory. Governments require certain different partners to be present in a network in order for it to be able to obtain a grant or subsidy. These partners may be a university or an SME or a company from a specific region. As partner selection is a key solution concept and the use of known partners is also found to increase knowledge sharing, obligatory partnering reduces the efficiency of knowledge sharing in the network. It forces companies to collaborate that do not want to collaborate.

- Partly as a consequence of the previous point, individuals from widely divergent backgrounds need to collaborate, enhancing the problem of boundary crossing. Different levels of knowledge and different cultures need to come together and again this reduces the opportunity for effective knowledge management.
- The projects mostly aim at knowledge exploration, but are managed as exploitative projects. Often extensive application, review and control procedures are put in place, which do not fit an explorative context. Our research suggests that informal solution concepts should be applied in exploratory contexts, not formal ones.
- The clarity of the goal and value created are preconditions for successful knowledge sharing, but absent from government-sponsored projects. Government-sponsored projects often have multiple goals besides the stated goal of the project. The goal of the project may be to develop new knowledge in the area of microelectronics, but simultaneously the government may want to develop a region, country or a group of companies. Or else the government wants to realize other political, social, economic or environmental aims. This builds tension into the network from the start and leads to lack of clarity over goals. This enhances the motivation problem.

The current set-up of national and international public projects aiming to develop innovations through knowledge sharing in networks therefore often does not meet the basic requirements of effective network knowledge management.

SUMMARY

Defining and implementing the correct knowledge management processes involves numerous steps and decisions. Knowledge management in networks needs to be tailored to specific situations and consequently general guidelines are hard to give. However, the key problems and solution concepts have been defined. These building blocks provide the manager with the tools to build knowledge management processes that fit the needs of a specific network. Perfection should not be strived for: networks are too complex to assume knowledge can be managed perfectly. Finally, it must be realized that it is a legitimate goal for companies to restrict knowledge flows to other companies. Tactics on how to achieve this have been defined.

NOTES

1. For details see Chapter 9.
2. Thanks to all contributors to this book for delivering examples of tactics for obstructing knowledge management.

REFERENCES

de Man, A.P. and G.M. Duysters (2005), 'Collaboration and innovation: a review of the effects of mergers, acquisitions and alliances on innovation', *Technovation*, **25** (12), 1377–87.

Index